MW00903247

ULTIMATE FRONTIER

Meeting the Challenge of Islamic Dawa (With Special Focus on Africa)

Christo Heiberg

One Printers Way
Altona, MB R0G 0B0
Canada

www.friesenpress.com

Copyright © 2023 by Christo Heiberg
First Edition — 2023

With thanks to Antony Trivet for the stunning cover-picture offered free on www.pexels.com

All rights reserved.

No part of this publication may be reproduced in any form, or by any means, electronic or mechanical, including photocopying, recording, or any information browsing, storage, or retrieval system, without permission in writing from FriesenPress.

ISBN
978-1-03-916032-3 (Hardcover)
978-1-03-916031-6 (Paperback)
978-1-03-916033-0 (eBook)

1. RELIGION, ISLAM, HISTORY

Distributed to the trade by The Ingram Book Company

To my father (b. 1930), who taught me how to think
And my mother (b. 1935), who showed me how to love

I Cor. 16:13-14

ENDORSEMENTS

Christo Heiberg presents a critical analysis of Islamic *dawa* and how the church must respond to it. Unlike other authors, so heavily influenced and compromised by political correctness, the author delivers a straightforward and fearless treatment of the subject matter, in the confidence that the truth will set us free (John 8:32). *Ultimate Frontier* is a wake-up call and a must-read for all Christians who take their faith seriously and who sincerely seek to win their Muslim neighbours with the gospel.

Tony Costa, Ph.D.
Instructor, University of Toronto.

Naiveté provides fertile ground for Islamic conquest. The *Ultimate Frontier* effectively educates Christians about the historical and current tactics employed by Islamic supremacists and jihadists in their quest for global dominion. It is a timely wake-up call to the church, which—despite the enormity of Christian persecution worldwide—still remains largely oblivious to Islamism's ominous threats. Central to Heiberg's clarion call is the Christian message of love, grace and forgiveness. His book is a must-read for churches everywhere.

Christine Douglass-Williams, International award-winning journalist
Former Canadian government appointee
Author of *The Challenge of Modern Islam*

I thank God for brother Christopher and for the book he has written. It has touched my heart. It will be an excellent tool to conquer Islamism in Africa. I am well aware of how Islam uses violence and threats to win new territory and prevent anyone from converting to Christianity. *Ultimate Frontier* will show all leaders in Africa how real the Islamic strategy is to conquer the world. It will teach our Christians how to avoid converting to

Islam, and that Allah is not the same as our God, as some might think. This book will help the church win many more converts for Christ, by speaking the truth to them in love.

Rev. Johnckson Murabyo.
MBB Ministry Coordinator, South Rwenzori Diocese, Uganda.

The *Ultimate Frontier* is a most timely and helpful book on Islamic *dawa* and invaluable in its focus on Africa as the epicenter of political Islam. The author unveils many secrets behind Islamic *dawa* in ways hardly noticed before. The book should leave no freedom-loving person untouched or un-alarmed. *Ultimate Frontier* is not only Biblically focused and intellectually careful but also bold and fearless, serving as a loud wake-up call about the hidden global strategy of political Islam. I strongly recommend it to my African brothers and anyone desiring to minister among Muslims.

Pastor Eric Ngala Mutumbi.
Principal of the Reformed Theological Seminary (RTS) Bumala, Kenya.

"People think of dawa as simple Islamic proselytizing, on par with Christian evangelization, and to be encouraged by any nation that values religious freedom and the liberty of conscience involved in choosing which religion to follow. Yet as Christo Heiberg demonstrates in this thoughtful and carefully researched book, there is much more involved in Islamic dawa, and Christians and all free people must be aware of its frankly ominous aspects. *Ultimate Frontier* is not only an indispensable guide for Christians seeking to counter the challenge of Islamic dawa and to bring the gospel message to Muslims, but for everyone concerned about the spreading of a religious ideology that is aggressive, supremacist, expansionist, violent, authoritarian, and oppressive."

Robert Spencer, David Horowitz Freedom Centre, Sherman Oaks, CA.
Author of *The History of Jihad* and *The Critical Qur'an.*

A Dawa Sign in South Africa
(Photo: Nerinus van der Ryst)

FOREWORD

I was born into a humble Muslim family in the remote western highlands of Uganda. Though I was among the top three children memorizing the Quran in Arabic, I hardly understood a word I was learning. My family rejoiced to see my progress in the Islamic faith and gave me the name Shamsuddiin, which means "son of the faith." However, by the grace of God, I received Jesus as my Lord and Savior in December 2014, and became a true son of the living God.

My father, realizing I had converted to Christianity, told me I was no longer his child. He stopped providing for me to the point of withholding food and shelter. The animals I had reared at home were all killed, my clothes were burnt, and I can't remember how many canes I got.

Since my father knew I wished to go to church, he ordered me to feed his cows on Sundays from morning till evening. I continued doing so for a month until I realized what was happening. Later, when my father discovered I was going to church again, he ordered me to cultivate a large field under the supervision of a Muslim man, who was supposed to prevent me from attending church. When even that did not work, my father made plans to have me killed. He told a relative to take me deep into the Queen Elizabeth National Park so that the wild animals could kill me. The dense forest was filled with elephants, lions, snakes, and other animals that could harm me, but God protected me. I escaped from the forest unharmed, though my feet were badly swollen because of the briers and thorns. As I came out of the woods, terribly scared late one day, not knowing what to do, I saw a car coming. I recognized the driver as the man who preached the gospel to me in church. I waved and stopped him and explained what had happened to me. He noticed how badly swollen my legs were, had compassion on me, and took me to his home, where he treated me like his own son. I have been under his care ever since. I thank God for sending Rev. Johnckson Murabyo across my path since he stood with me through everything. Through him, I came to know the author of this book personally.

I thank God for the *Ultimate Frontier*. It made me understand for the first time how real and comprehensive Islamism is. I do not doubt that it would use anything at its disposal, including terrorism, to conquer new territories, just like Mecca was first conquered long ago in the seventh century. No one reading this book will be left untouched by how serious Islamic *dawa* is, not only in its aim to conquer the world but also in eliminating its greatest foe, Christianity. May the Lord Jesus open the eyes of many and fill his people with great courage, wisdom, and love.

Shamsuddiin Jacques
Uganda
September 2022

WHAT THIS BOOK IS ABOUT

This book is first of all for Christians, not only in Africa but also in the West, as it is high time for all of us to wake from our sleep. And it is for anyone looking for hope and guidance amid very dark and troubling times. Lastly, but most importantly, it is also for our Muslim friends. Though we focus on *Islamism* and its centuries-old dream of world domination, we in no way want to alienate millions of peace-loving Muslims worldwide. It would be a fatal mistake and injustice to paint all Muslims with the same brush. I pray that this book may touch many Muslim hearts and encourage them, at the very least, to become more familiar with what both *dawa* and Christianity *are* all about, and that we are not their enemies. Moreover, may it also reach the hearts of those Muslims still vehemently hostile to the Son of God and his people, who are bent on the program of bringing *sharia* to the whole world.

I pray that this humble effort will do for countless hearts what a 2019 conference in Nairobi did for mine: to wake us up to the sheer gravity, magnitude, and reality of the global strategy of Islamism, or Islamic *dawa*. All that happened over the last few years, in terms of the pandemic, mass-protests, a looming recession, and the war in Ukraine, was only a diversion from *that* challenge that may soon engulf them all.

In the first part, we will look at where *dawa* came from, how it is being promoted, what its aims are, and why and how both individuals and societies convert to Islam. We will then look at the methods used today to subtly transform our communities, and lastly, how *dawa* advances through fear, violence, and threats. In all of this, we will focus on Sub-Saharan Africa in particular and on Europe to a lesser extent, since that is where *dawa*'s main focus lies at the moment.

In the second part, we will seek to discover how the church of Jesus Christ should respond to it all, taking the sobering words of Sun Tzu, the Chinese military strategist and author of *The Art of War* of 2500 years ago, as our cue:

> If you know the enemy and yourself,
> you need not to fear the result of a hundred battles.
> If you know yourself but not the enemy,
> for every victory gained you will also suffer defeat.
> If you know neither the enemy nor yourself,
> you will succumb in every battle.

These words of Sun Tzu, which I first came across in the works of Dr. Patrick Sookhdeo, will prove crucial for this mammoth spiritual battle that is upon us. First, we must familiarize ourselves with four political strategies that have failed us spectacularly, and how Christians in Africa suffer because of them. Then we must face our biggest foe, *fear*, praying that the ancient noble virtue of Christian valour will be rekindled in our midst. Following that, we shall marvel at the superior beauty of Christianity compared with Islam. And then finally we will look at those unique ideas of Christianity that will defeat Islamism and the entire world. We will look at the amazing love of God embodied in his people, and how it is proclaimed in the gospel of his Son. Then we will look at God's self-revelation as eternally triune, and finally at the rock-solid reliability of the Biblical canon.

In writing this book, I am greatly indebted to Dr. Sookhdeo's work.[1] He was the instrument God used to stir my heart and open my eyes in Nairobi back in 2019. Other authors, speakers and YouTubers who have made an impact on me, and without whom I could not finish this work, were (first and foremost) Ayaan Hirsi Ali, but also Mark Durie, Al Fadi, Robert

---

1 The structure of Part One mainly follows the outline of Sookhdeo's book *Dawa*.

Frankling, Tom Holland, Soeren Kern, the late Bernard Lewis, Vishal Mangalwadi, Hussein Aboubakr Mansour, Yasmine Mohammed, Robert R. Reilly, Jay Smith, Robert Spencer, Mohammed Tawhidi, Bill Warner, David Wood, and the like. I am also deeply grateful to several friends who assisted me in proofreading and editing the manuscript, and especially to Robert Brooker, Jake Sinke, and Richard van Seters, for getting me across the finishing line, as well as to Friesen Press for their invaluable guidance in mentoring this "rookie" author all the way. Lastly, I want to thank my dear wife and children for their loving patience over these past three years, as well as my congregation and friends for their ongoing prayers and support. To God be the glory.

Christo Heiberg
Good Friday, 2023

Postscript

During my most recent visit to South Africa in March 2023, yet another independent source confirmed something to me which I found truly astonishing. This lady, a committed Christian herself, who visited Saudi Arabia in recent months, confirmed what I have heard from a Christian friend living near Frankfurt, Germany (whose friends also visited Saudi Arabia recently), and from a Coptic Christian who is currently living in Canada, having been born and raised in Egypt. Each one of them—independently of each other—spoke of the very same thing: "Saudi Arabia is opening up and there is an intense hunger for the truth!" I can hardly think of anything more positive happening in the world since the fall of the Berlin Wall in 1989. Obviously, these amazingly positive developments are not reflected in the pages that follow. Please keep that in mind as you read. May the living God abundantly bless the nation and leaders of Saudi Arabia.

TABLE OF CONTENTS

PART I

DAWA: THE ISLAMIC STRATEGY FOR WORLD-DOMINATION

CHAPTER 1

AN AFRICAN WAKE-UP CALL

In 2019 I visited Kenya for the first time, attending a conference for African Christian leaders on the outskirts of Nairobi. I happened to be in East Africa for leadership training and couldn't miss the opportunity to meet brothers and sisters from all over the continent, coming together to learn more about a topic most of us in the West would rather avoid. That topic was Islamic *dawa*, the Muslim strategy for world domination. Our speaker was a former Muslim and is currently an acclaimed authority on Islam, a consultant to many governments, and an advocate for persecuted Christians. Before this unforgettable week in Nairobi I thought I was reasonably well versed in Islam; when it was over, I not only realized how little I knew but also how all the dots of what we hear and see in the world are interconnected. The impact was immense on all who attended.

After listening to Dr. Patrick Sookhdeo for four days, I knew I had a new responsibility. Around me were over a hundred brothers and a few sisters from all over Africa, many of whom had experienced Islamic extremism in their own countries, and some even in their neighborhoods. Several of them stood up to tell their stories or shared them with us during the tea breaks under the lush foliage of African trees. I recall listening in awe to a dear brother from Burkina Faso, standing tall and slender in his colorful shirt, speaking boldly about all they were experiencing in his country. Whenever I hear another horrifying report from the Sahel,[1] I cannot but see his humble, courageous figure before my eyes. Islamist attacks have risen sharply in the Sahel over the last decade, especially since strongman Moammar Ghaddafi of Libya was removed by NATO powers in 2011. The Arab Spring has turned into a bitter winter for Africa. Since then, jihadis and weapons have poured into the Sahel, mainly eliminating our African brothers and sisters in the faith. Even as I am writing, a report came in saying that "[a]rmed men have killed at least 160 in an attack on a village in northern Burkina Faso, the country's worst attack in recent years."[2] But as we have come to expect by now, it's only "armed men." The BBC article doesn't call the attackers Islamists, nor the victims as predominantly Christian. For that information we have to go elsewhere.

One night during our conference dinner, I had the privilege of meeting a lady who is reaching deep into Somalia with the gospel to encourage fellow believers who dare not meet in public. As I listened and prayed with her, I felt I stood on holy ground—as if our Lord's crown of thorns was scratching her tender brow. I struggled to hold back my tears as we prayed together, and I will never forget her incredible courage as long as I live. Many other attendees spoke of their love for Christ despite growing threats of militant Islam. When I asked a brother from Nigeria how he could still be so positive after seeing Islamists wreaking havoc in his village, he quoted Bonhoeffer: "When Christ calls a man to follow him, he calls him to come and die." Indeed, the grace they knew and embraced so passionately was not cheap but very costly.[3] Their humble faith and sincere love stirred me deeply, so that I kept asking myself, "Why are these folks so blessed? And why are we in the West often so spiritually poor and weak?" Then I recalled how Alexander Solzhenitsyn hinted at the answer in his famous Harvard

1 The Sahel is the semi-arid belt stretching from coast to coast across Africa, where the Sahara meets the savannah.

2 "Burkina Faso attack: At least 160 killed in village raid" *BBC News* website. June 6, 2021.

3 See Dietrich Bonhoeffer's "Costly Grace" in *The Cost of Discipleship* (London: SCM Press, 1975), 35-47.

speech of 1978, for which he was not too popular at the time.[4] Solzhenitsyn only echoed what St. Peter wrote about long ago in his first epistle, i.e., that gold would only be refined by fire (I Pet. 1:7), or what Samuel Rutherford (1600 – 1661) wrote from his dark Scottish dungeon in Aberdeen, that grace grows best in winter.[5]

As I sat there, wondering how these African folks must feel in light of all that our seasoned Anglican scholar of Islam was showing and telling us, I realized how serious the situation had become in only two decades. Islamic terror is spreading like wildfire throughout Africa, while we in the West must hear from super-scholars[6] that the world has become a much better place to live in during the last century. That may be true for many, but not for millions living in the Sahel and further south in the continent. For them, there is no more time for slumbering since Africa has become the critical theater of that "clash of civilizations" that Samuel Huntington and others predicted at the end of the Cold War.[7] Ever since 9/11, the Second Gulf War, the so-called Arab Spring, the Syrian War, and the elimination of Moammar Ghaddafi, the problem has spiraled out of control. It is no longer limited to the Sahel and the horn of Africa but is quickly spreading south. To say it bluntly, the so-called *War on Terror* and our attempts to impose "democracy" on other countries, have unleashed truckloads of terror *hostile* to fledgling democracies in a very vulnerable continent: Africa.

What They Won't Tell Us in the West

But there is a twist to this story: here in the West, where I live, we are being shielded from most of it, and not by accident. There is a reason why

4 For a summary of his timeless speech, see "A World Split Apart (1978 / 2018)" on soberminds.ca.

5 Faith Cook, *Grace in Winter* (Edinburgh: Banner of Truth, 1989), 64.

6 The name of Harvard psychologist Steven Pinker comes to mind. See for instance the optimistic picture of the world painted by Ronald Bailey and Marian Tupy in *Ten Global Trends Every Smart Person Should Know* (Washington DC: Cato Institute, 2021). Most Christians in Africa would not recognize this picture of the world, based on very selected data.

7 Samuel P. Huntington, *The Clash of Civilizations and the Remaking of World Order* (New York: Simon and Schuster, 2011), first published in 1996.

so much of the bloodletting and chaos in Africa does not reach the front pages of the ABC, BBC, CBC, or whatever mainline news outlet one may think of. They cannot afford to tell us. Neither can they afford to tell us about the aggressive Wahhabi campaign, sponsored from the Arabian Peninsula with our petrol dollars, reaching deep into the global south. Why? It doesn't fit their agenda, for we have been told since 9/11 that Islam is a peaceful religion. Yes, it is that simple,

Almost every day of their tenures Presidents Bush and Obama, and Britain's Tony Blair, told us that while they kept bombing the Middle East, going after extremists. We were told that what happened on that infamous day in 2001 was the work of nineteen Islamic radicals. It had nothing to do with the Quran's noble ideals and was spurred on by their hatred of our Western values of freedom and democracy. We were told that the Muslim world wants nothing to do with these extremists either. But then we came to learn that it is not so simple. The truth is somewhat different. Militant Islam was all part of Mohammed's original strategy from day one, and *that* strategy has always been a determined plan for world domination. That is what *dawa* is all about. Muslims who dare to oppose it will soon discover that they are no real Muslims in the eyes of the others at all.

Upon arrival back home in Canada in August 2019, I got a taste of this strategy once again. The BBC ran a story on its front page about an attack on the Al-Noor Islamic Centre near Oslo in Norway.[8] Thankfully, no Muslim was killed, yet the story stayed on the BBC front page for the day. I marveled at the disparity, the dissonance, the evident partiality, and even the racial discrimination. Do black lives really matter as we would like to boast here in North America? Western news outlets know well enough what is going on in Africa. So why do they keep the gruesome stories away from us, where hundreds are being killed, maimed, raped, or kidnapped month after month? Recently the U.S. State Department did the bizarre thing of removing Nigeria from its list of "Countries of Particular Concern." That while 2000 of the 4200 Christians killed for their faith worldwide in 2020 were from Nigeria, according to Raymond Ibrahim at

8 "Norway mosque shooting probed as a terror act," *BBC News* website, August 11, 2019.

the David Horowitz Freedom Center.[9] Why raise all this awareness about a solitary attack killing no one in Norway, if Burkina Faso, Nigeria, Mali, Cameroon, the DRC, and Mozambique are of little concern? The reason is straightforward: Norway is more important, and the bad news from Africa might not be so good for all our propaganda about the "religion of peace."

But it goes even beyond that. Dr. Bill Warner, host of the YouTube channel *Political Islam*, made a chilling video titled "Why we are afraid. A 1400-year-old secret."[10] He argues that classical civilization was not destroyed by barbaric German hordes but by sword-wielding Muslim armies. The so-called dark ages of Europe resulted from relentless attacks stretching from Spain to Crimea, from India to Morocco, killing tens of millions of Christians, Hindus, Zoroastrians, and others. In Andalusia (the Muslim name for Spain) a pile of skulls of defeated knights was so high that someone on horseback could not see over it, says Warner. The attacks were relentless. They kept on coming for centuries during the so-called Islamic golden age. Eventually, the Islamic conquest was only stopped by superior military power, for instance, at Tours in 732 and Vienna in 1683. If the famed political scientist Hans Morgenthau could once say that positions of power do not listen to any arguments, whether moral, legal, or logical, but *only to superior power*, then it is especially true of Islamic positions of power. Sultans simply do not negotiate with *kufar*,[11] for what can an infidel tell Allah after all?

And yet most of this history has been withheld from us. Seminary students don't hear about it, and catechism teachers don't know about it, while some Christian history books paint the Islamic golden age in such a soft light that we could almost long to have it back.[12] We are constantly reminded how sorry we should be for the Crusades. At the same time, history shows that there is no moral or military equivalence between the

9 "A Dutch Interview with Shillman Fellow Raymond Ibrahim," frontpagemag.com viewed on July 14, 2022.

10 "Why We Are Afraid, A 1400 Year Secret, by Dr. Bill Warner" *The Ship Productions – YouTube.*

11 *Kufar* is the Arabic plural for *kafir*, meaning infidel or unbeliever.

12 See as an example Jean-Pierre Isbouts, *The Story of Christianity* (Washington DC: National Geographic, 2014), 124-130.

hundreds of unprovoked Islamic assaults on Christendom on the one hand, and Catholic Europe's response since the days of Pope Urban II on the other.[13] And yet, having said so, no faithful Christian would dare to defend the grim legacy of the Crusades, nor the kind of theology that inspired many knights to ride on horseback to the holy land for Christ. Yet the question remains, why?

Why have we been in this state of denial for so long? The question becomes more poignant when one learns how Muslim youth in Egypt grow up learning *nothing* about six centuries of Christianity before Islam's arrival to the land of the Nile Delta. At the same time, the battles of Mohammed and his successors, including the elimination of Jews from Arabia, are being taught with glee, writes Egyptian-American Hussein Mansour, looking back on his childhood.[14]

The reason for this eclipse of Muslim origins and consequent Christian suffering in our circles, says Warner, is simple: *fear*. We have been so traumatized that we would rather not talk about it. All we can do now is hope it won't come to a neighborhood near us.

As I packed my bags back in Kenya after the conference, I knew I could not be silent, not only for Africa's sake but also for the sake of the church in the West. Proverbs 24:10-12 kept ringing in my ears:

> If you falter in times of trouble, how small is your strength! Rescue those being led away to death; hold back those staggering toward slaughter. If you

---

13 Without sanctioning the savagery committed in the name of Christ during some of the Crusades, we do, however, have to take issue with the popular notion that "Christendom" for no good reason brutalized, looted, and colonized a tolerant, cultured and peaceful Islam in those days. It is not so simple. Such a view disregards the events of the preceding five centuries. The Crusades' response was precipitated by unprovoked Islamic hostility for centuries, eradicating large swaths of Christendom. Islam made many bloody attempts to colonize Europe and launched frequent sudden attacks on Christian pilgrims and holy places in the Middle East, carrying off thousands of enslaved Christians. See Rodney A. Stark, *God's Battalions: The Case for the Crusades* (New York: HarperOne, 2010).

14 Hussein Aboubakr Mansour, *Minority of One* (Self-published in the USA: 2020), 38. He writes: "Stories of the bounties, concubines and slaughtering the infidel enemies of Allah were explained as a legitimate spreading of Islam to all men. They are not called conquests but *futwhat* (openings)."

> say: "But we knew nothing about this," does not he who weighs the heart perceive it? Doesn't he who guards your life know it? Will he not repay everyone according to what they have done?

To be spiritually prepared and ready for the full impact of *dawa,* is, in a genuine sense, to be prepared for the trauma that will precede our Lord's return. Through two millennia, our main adversaries as Christians were (in terms of persecution): the Jewish Sanhedrin, Romans, Persians, misguided Christian heretics and fanatics, Mongols, Buddhists and Hindus, Marxist-Leninists, Animists, Nazis and other fascists, Maoists, and today the radical Left and other angry atheists. But according to Patrick Johnston in *The Future of the Global Church,* one adversary towers above them all: Islam.[15] No adversary has slaughtered more followers of Jesus than Islam. History does not lie. By the mid-fifteenth century, Islam (helped by the Black Plague) had wiped out two-thirds of Christendom in seven centuries. No one could stop Mohammed's warriors, or so it seemed. Jerusalem had fallen, Damascus had fallen, Antioch had fallen, Edessa had fallen, Baghdad had fallen, Alexandria had fallen, Carthage had fallen, even Constantinople had fallen. Spain was only just rescued out of the dragon's jaws, while many Christians surviving apostasy or slaughter were living as humble *dhimmis* under Muslim rule. By the mid-1400s Christianity was, for all practical purposes, "on the ropes," bound to be knocked out, with Islam the uncontested super-power controlling the major trade routes, *and the slave trade!* But then came the Reformation in Europe, followed by the Enlightenment and the age of world missions.

Amazingly, polls tell us today that Christianity (in the broadest sense) still has by far the most adherents of any faith, while some Muslim clerics warn that had it not been for their apostasy laws, Islam would even cease to exist. Christianity is even making a steady comeback where it was least expected—in the traditional Caucasian northern hemisphere, sparked by the mass reaction to Marxism in eastern Europe and Russia and by an influx of Christian immigrants from the poorer global south into western

---

15 Patrick Johnstone, *The Future of the Global Church* (Downers Grove, IL: IVP, 2011), 35-51.

Europe.[16] In China, Mao's Communism arrived in 1949, expelling all foreign missionaries, hoping to stamp out Chinese Christianity finally. All that happened was that the number of Jesus-followers increased from one million to a hundred million today. There are many other miracle stories from Iran, Nepal, India, Myanmar, many parts of Africa, and the southern Levant, among others. In Turkey and Saudi Arabia thousands can't wait to lay their hands on a Bible. For, what *Yahweh* promised King David long ago, he is promising to all who love the Son of David who suffered for us and rose again:

> All the ends of the earth will remember and turn to the Lord
> and all the families of the nations will bow down before him
> for dominion belongs to the Lord
> and he rules over the nations.
>
> — Psalm 22:27

16 See "A New Christendom? The Revival of Christianity in Europe" in Steve R. Turley, *The Return of Christendom* (Turley Talks, 2019), 25-32.

CHAPTER 2

WHAT IS *DAWA*?

In the year 670, terrifying reports reached Carthage of a raid on North Africa that carried thousands of Christians into slavery. Carthage was no mean city. It had a long and illustrious history, first as a Phoenician port and then as a major trade center of the Roman Empire's western Mediterranean. Since the second century, it became one of the centers for spreading a whole new revolutionary idea and way of life: Christianity. It was here in Carthage—the hometown of church fathers Tertullian and Cyprian—where the brave young mother Perpetua laid down her life so heroically for her Saviour Jesus, suffering excruciating torture at the hands of the local Roman prefect.[1] And she was by no means the only one to have suffered such a fate in that port city for her Christian faith.

It was here in Carthage, defending his Christian faith against the empty propaganda of the Roman State, where Tertullian first coined a phrase that would be quoted ever since by the church: "the blood of the martyrs

1 *A Pinch of Incense, AD 70 to 250*, edited by Ted Byfield (Christian History Project, 2005), 187-193.

is seed".[2] It was here where the very concept of *God being one in essence but three in person* was first formulated by the same church father. Much like Alexandria to the east and Hippo to the West, Carthage was a hub of Christian activity, thought, and worship for quite a few centuries when those terrifying reports reached her in 670.

Over the succeeding decades, more incursions followed. Fortresses, towns, and entire swaths of provinces fell into permanent occupation. "Finally, in the autumn of 695, sentries on the walls of Carthage spotted a smudge of dust on the horizon—and that it was growing larger," wrote historian Tom Holland. "Then the glint of weapons was catching the sun. Then emerging from the dust, men, horses, siege engines. The Saracens had arrived."[3] Eventually, only two engines were required to wrest Carthage from Christian rule.

It always happened this way. A smudge of dust on the horizon. A glint of weapons catching the sun. Then, a couple of hours later, Arab messengers would arrive, to deliver an invitation to whoever was in charge of the city or kingdom, along the following lines.

> We were sent to you by Allah the most gracious, the most merciful. We call upon you to submit to him, to his messenger Mohammed and all his *umma,*[4] and you will have peace. But if you refuse, and prefer to continue in your disbelief, then be ready to face Allah's displeasure.

And remember: "He who obeys the messenger, obeys God" (Surah 4:80). But if you choose to fight, know for sure that we fight for the cause of God and that he "is stronger in might and stronger in inflicting punishment" (Surah 4:84). This was *dawa* in classical Islam.

It always began with a friendly invitation. But the snorting of camels and the shimmering of swords in the setting sun would have left you in no doubt as to how serious this invitation was. This was the religion of peace,

2 Tertullian, *Apologia* (chapter 50), newadvent.org. Tertullian's exact words were, "The oftener we are mowed down by you, the more in number we grow; the blood of Christians is seed."

3 Tom Holland, *Dominion* (New York: Basic Books, 2019), 187.

4 The *umma* is the worldwide community of the Muslim faithful.

but only if you completely surrendered. And you had to make up your mind pretty quickly, for on the horizon the Saracen fires were burning.

This is how Mohammed eventually conquered Mecca, after first being expelled from there by his own tribe. By the time he died in 632 all the tribes of Arabia had submitted to him in one form or another. After his death, the "rightly guided caliphs" who led the Arab Muslim community continued to seize large swaths of territory. They began with the Christian Byzantine Empire. In 635, the Arab Muslim armies took Damascus; in 636, the rest of Christian Syria; in 638, it was the turn of the *holy city* Jerusalem; in 642, Alexandria fell—the largest center of Christianity in the eastern Mediterranean; and with it all of Egypt, which was 90 percent Christian then. Listen to this report coming from Jerusalem in 636:

> Sophronius [Bishop of Jerusalem], in his sermon on Epiphany 636, bewailed the destruction of churches and monasteries, the sacked towns, the fields laid waste, and the villages burned down by the nomads who were overrunning the country. In a letter the same year to Sergius, patriarch of Constantinople, he mentions the ravages wrought by the Arabs. Thousands of people perished in 639, victims of the famine and plague that resulted from these destructions. [5]

Here is an account from the Egyptian town of Nikiou, written years later:

> Then the Muslims arrived in Nikiou. There was not a single soldier to resist them. They seized the town and slaughtered everyone they met in the street and in the churches – men, women and children – sparing nobody. Then they went to other places, pillaged and killed all the inhabitants they found... But let us say no more, for it is impossible to describe the horrors the Muslims committed when they occupied the island of Nikiou.[6]

In the year that Egypt fell, Muslims also launched an offensive against the Persian Empire. By 652 it was conquered. By 711, Muslim armies had

5 As quoted from Bat Ye'or, *The Decline of Eastern Christianity under Islam*, 1996, by Robert Spencer, *Muslim Persecution of Christians* (Sherman Oaks, CA: David Horowitz Freedom Center, 2011), 13.

6 Spencer, *Muslim Persecution*, 14.

conquered all of north Africa and were ready to cross over to Spain from Morocco, by the rock called Gibraltar. From Spain, the "Saracens," as they were called in Christian Europe, advanced northwards into France.

Meanwhile, another Muslim army moved counter-clockwise around the Mediterranean and began besieging Constantinople, the Byzantine capital in 717. Christendom was in grave danger of being wholly encircled and overrun by Islam. The Saracen advance was stopped by two crucial military victories in God's merciful providence. Byzantine Emperor Leo III stood firm, so Mohammed's warriors had to abandon the siege of Constantinople. Fighting continued until the Taurus Mountains in Asia Minor were established as the boundary between Byzantium and the Islamic Empire, *at least for then*. And in 732, only a century after Mohammed died, Charles, ruler of the Franks, defeated the Arabs in a battle between Tours and Poitiers in France, eventually driving them back beyond the Pyrenees, earning himself the name Charles Martel, Charles the hammer.[7]

Fast forward to today and consider that Europe's ruling class and public square are entirely secular and even anti-Christian, so that an influential British rabbi could ask in 2011 whether "Europe has lost its soul?"[8] Meanwhile, Islam only grew increasingly confident ever since the two world wars, until at least the first decade of the twenty-first century. We are at a moment in history now where the old ruling class of the free world, for the most part, has very little understanding of how to handle the Muslim folk who have arrived at our gates. No, there are no glinting swords this time, nor camels sniffing the air, but ultimately the strategy and goals of *dawa* are the same, though many ordinary Muslims may be unaware of it. Without even always knowing it, these newcomers to our gates and shores have arrived with a long-term mission that is no different from the aspirations of those Saracens on camelback arriving at Carthage centuries ago. *Dawa*'s fundamental strategy involves much more than "religion", since Islam, by definition, is much more than a religion. Islam is an ideology at

7 Patrick Sookhdeo, *Hated without Reason* (McLean, VA: Isaac Publishing, 2019), 71.

8 Henk Kamsteeg, "Lord Sacks: 'Has Europe Lost its Soul?'", *Israel and Christianity Today*, April 2012, 2-3.

heart—alien to any idea of the "separation of church and state". It took our governments in the West twenty years since 9/11 to begin figuring that out.

Dawa means "call' or "invitation. "Islamic theology teaches that all Muslims must engage in this outreach or *dawa*. This is, however, an outreach of an entirely different kind than Christians are used to. In *dawa*, non-Muslims are called or invited to accept Islam as the final religion since that is what Mohammed did centuries ago. He invited the surrounding pagan tribes, as well as Jewish and Christian clans, to accept his message as the final word from Allah to humanity. It is *dawa* that makes Islam a profoundly missional religion since the Quran obligates all Muslims to teach their beliefs to others. Every single Muslim is supposed to be a *da'ee*, an evangelist.

But as we have noted, this is a different kind of evangelism altogether. It is wholly different from the *Good News*, which seeks to convict and convince an individual freely to follow the Good Shepherd, who gave his life for his sheep. Mohammed was essentially a *warner*, telling us that hellfire awaits us unless we accept him as Allah's final prophet to humanity. He also warned that Allah has no son, or associate, for whoever believes such a thing commits *shirk*,[9] the unpardonable sin in Islam, which for radical Muslims, is punishable by death. Therefore, the invitation of the *da'ee* implies that one must say farewell to the gospel and to everything Jesus did for us. From now on, he is merely Mary's son, and never again Immanuel, *God with us*. Nor did he die on the cross for our sins, let alone rise from the dead.

Evangelism of a Different Kind

So how do you become a Muslim? Simply by saying with conviction, "*La ilaha illa Allah, Muhammadur Rasool Allah*", which means "there is no God but Allah, and Mohammed is his messenger".[10] This is called the *shahada*.

---

9 Meaning "association", the term refers to the pagan association of other deities with Allah. See Patrick Sookhdeo, *Understanding Islamic Theology* (McLean, VA: Isaac Publishing, 2013), 85-87.

10 I. H. Ibrahim, *A Brief Illustrated Guide to Understanding Islam* (2nd Edition), 52. Canada's current Prime Minister, Justin Trudeau, said the *shahada* in a mosque in British Columbia, seeking to win votes when he was leader of the opposition in 2013. To serious

Then one has to study the Quran and seek to live by the five pillars of Islam.[11] No heart conversion is needed, as in Christianity. Concepts like conviction of sin, a personal relationship with God, assurance of one's salvation, and a delight in doing good out of love for mankind, are essentially foreign to Islam. Allah never reveals himself to his people; he reveals only his will. That accounts for the fact that he is so distant from his followers, as all Muslims who have come to Jesus can testify.

It speaks for itself why so many nominal Christians and disillusioned Westerners are often such soft targets for Islam. They have never experienced true conversion to Christ and may even have had bad experiences in the church. In the words of Psalm 34, they have not *tasted* and *seen* that the Lord is good. Their Christianity was nominal or based on weak foundations and short-lived emotions, not on rock-solid faith and evidence. This should tell us why robust Christian evangelism and discipleship are now more crucial than ever.

Muslims prefer to call conversions to Islam "reversions", since they believe that every human being was originally born a worshipper of Allah, who then went astray. That is why the *da'ee* must call them back. There are two differences[12] between Islam and other missionary religions and sects: (1) Islam does not tolerate the mission efforts of others, (2) *dawa* is about far more than converting individuals. It is about changing societies and their structures, and establishing a Muslim state. Muslim-minority-states must become Muslim-majority-states, and Muslim-majority-states must become Islamic states under *sharia* until the whole global *umma* is under *sharia.*[13] Moreover, *dawa* not only concerns itself with non-Muslims but

---

Muslims, Trudeau is now a Muslim, according to *sharia*. See "Fess up Mr. Dressup: Shahada-reciting Trudeau all for show, but questions still should have been asked" *Toronto Sun* website. August 19, 2013.

11 The five pillars are: reciting the Islamic creed (*shahada*); ritual prayer five times a day (*salat*); giving support for the needy (*zakat*); fasting during the month of Ramadan; and making the pilgrimage to Mecca (*hajj*), at least once a lifetime. See I.A. Ibrahim, *A Brief Illustrated Guide*, 65-68.

12 Patrick Sookhdeo, *Dawa* (McLean, VA: Isaac Publishing, 2014), 1-2.

13 Islamic law.

also with *non-traditional* Muslims or moderate Muslims, as we would say, who do not favor *sharia* and are therefore not involved in real *dawa.*

Dawa as a Divine Command with a Worldwide Scope

Dawa is a divine command based on the teachings of the Quran and the *hadith.* It was the main activity of Mohammed, who supposedly[14] lived from 570 until 632 in Arabia. It was also followed by the first four caliphs: Abu Bakr, Umar, Uthman, and Ali, and was *the* secret behind the phenomenal spread of Islam during its golden age that lasted for six centuries from Mohammed's *hijra*[15] to Medina in 622, until 1258. Muslims all around the world are called by Allah in the Quran and the *hadith* to model their behaviour on the prophet's example as the first four caliphs did. Surah 33:21 says: "You have indeed in the Prophet of God a good example for those of you who look to God and the Last Day."

Thus, all Muslims *must* engage in *dawa*, for *dawa* is the fulfillment of Islam. The crucial importance of *dawa* for Muslim identity and expansion has been rediscovered in recent decades. *Dawa* is an all-encompassing program since it uses everything from literature, education, and television to building mosques, finance, the democratic process, social media, and even *jihad* to further its agenda. Its resurgence since the seventies is already resulting in tremendous success. For that very reason, the openly stated strategies of *dawa* are not so readily available in print for a Western audience, so as not to awaken sleeping dogs. A key source in English, produced by the *Muslim World League* (MWL) in Mecca back in 1975, was one such book that has disappeared from the public eye.[16]

An excellent instrument for the promotion of *dawa* since the second half of the twentieth century is the very influential Muslim Brotherhood,

---

14 Scholarly research in the West is increasingly heaping doubt on the origins of Mohammed and Islam. See Dr. Jay Smith's many videos on *PfanderFilms*, as well as the documentaries by Dan Gibson: *The Sacred City* (2016) and Tom Holland: *Islam, the Untold Story* (2012).

15 Mohammed's flight from Mecca to Medina in 622 and the start of the Islamic calendar.

16 Sookhdeo, *Dawa*, 3.

founded in Egypt in 1928.[17] The organization's strategic goal is to "re-establish the caliphate, a totalitarian theocratic imperial regime," to maintain political power and expand it worldwide. The [Brotherhood's] ultimate objective is to lead the caliphate to place the entire world under Islamic totalitarian rule."[18] However, since the Brotherhood does not openly promote violence, it has been accepted in the West as a peaceful and democratic partner in the political process.

17 The founding members of the Brotherhood, Hasan al-Banna and Sayyid Qutb, resurrected the vision of a worldwide caliphate in the wake of the abolition of the Ottoman Caliphate in 1924 by the secular Turkish leader Kamal Ataturk, soon after the Ottoman Empire's collapse during World War I.

18 J. Michael Waller, "The Muslim Brotherhood: Doctrine, Strategy, Operations and Vulnerabilities" in *Meeting the Ideological Challenge* (McLean, VA: Isaac Publishing, 2015), 67.

CHAPTER 3

THE HISTORY AND AGENTS OF *DAWA*

Now that we have a good idea of what *dawa* is all about, we need to ask: How does *dawa* fit into the big scheme of things for Muslims? And who, if any, is responsible for doing *dawa* in today's world? We hope to find the answers to these questions by looking at the historical roots of *dawa,* and then by asking how it is being promoted throughout the world today.

The History of *Dawa*

The Quran is the holy book of Islam. Muslims believe that it is eternal, and that no human hand had any part in its composition. They believe it was revealed to Mohammed through the mediation of the angel Gabriel in a cave near Mecca for twenty-two years between 610 and 632, *and* that it has been perfectly preserved ever since. It is in the Quran that Muslims find the call to *dawa* first of all, since the term *dawa* appears more than a dozen times in the Muslim holy book. In Surah 16:125, we read:

> Call to the way of your Lord with wisdom and fair exhortation and reason with them in a way that is best. Your Lord knows best those who have strayed away from His path and He knows best those who are rightly guided.

And in Surah 3:104, we read:

> Let there be a group among you who call others to good, and enjoin what is right, and forbid what is wrong: those who do this shall be successful.

We see here the most essential elements of *dawa*: (1) issue an invitation, (2) do so with good arguments, (3) enjoin what is good (*halal*) and forbid what is wrong (*haram*).

Dawa is not only taught by the Quran. The second most authoritative source of the Muslim faith, the *hadith,* is equally clear about it, as is Mohammed's *sira* (biography).[1] The *hadith* is purported to be a collection of traditions about Mohammed's life and sayings (his *sunna*). A good example of *dawa* is when Mohammed sent out one of his followers to Yemen with an invitation to submit to Islam:

> The prophet sent Muadh to Yemen and said: "Invite the people to testify that none has the right to be worshiped but Allah, and I am Allah's Apostle, and if they obey you to do so, then teach them that Allah has enjoined on them five prayers in every day and night... and if they obey you to do so, then teach them that Allah has made it obligatory for them to pay the zakat from their property and it is to be taken from the wealthy among them and given to the poor" (as narrated by Ibn Abbas in Sahih Al-Bukhari, Vol. 2, Book 23, No. 478).[2]

The earliest record of an invitation issued to the Jews of Medina was recorded by Sahih Muslim 3:17, 4363:

> ... the Messenger of Allah... came to us and said: "(Let us) go to the Jews ... The Messenger of Allah ... stood up and called out to them (saying): "Oh ye assembly of Jews, accept Islam (and) you will be safe [aslim taslam].

1 While referring to the *hadith* and Mohammed's *sira*, let us keep in mind that there are no literary sources on Mohammed's life until two centuries after his death in 632. The existing sources are from the ninth century and later. Many scholars have raised serious concerns about the historicity and reliability of these sources. See Mark Durie, *The Third Choice* (Deror Books, 2010), 82.

2 Sookhdeo, *Dawa*, 8-9.

> [And after repeating these another two times, he said]: "You should know that the earth belongs to Allah and His Apostle..." warning them to oblige.[3]

According to Australian scholar Mark Durie, this is the earliest record of the invitation *aslim taslam* (accept Islam and you will be safe). Mohammed's followers later used this formula for declaring war on Christian nations.

The *hadith* also records that Mohammed sent letters to neighbouring kingdoms inviting their rulers to embrace Islam. According to al-Tabari, in his *History of the Prophets and Kings* of the tenth century, Mohammed decided in 628 to send letters to many world rulers inviting them to Islam.[4] These kingdoms included the king of Persia, the emperor of Rome, the king of Abyssinia (Ethiopia), and others. When the Byzantine and Persian rulers eventually declined the invitation, Muslim forces invaded their lands after Mohammed's death.

Other *hadith* speak of the rewards that Allah will give to any who are instrumental in converting "unbelievers" to Islam. Even before the final judgment, every Muslim will be questioned in his grave whether they invited their neighbours to worship Allah or not.

Dawa, therefore, had genuine implications for history and Christianity in particular. The Byzantine Empire was enemy number one to the seventh-century Arabs and to medieval Islam. In his bestseller *The Lost History of Christianity* [5] historian Philip Jenkins tells the grim tale of how Islam largely wiped Christianity off the map from Algeria to Afghanistan many centuries ago, leaving only a remnant of *dhimmis* behind.[6]

According to Muslim tradition, the first four caliphs (Abu Bakr, Umar, Uthman, and Ali), who reigned from 632 to 661, simply followed the prophet's example after his death. That means that the Islamic state would

---

3 See Durie, *The Third Choice*, 111.

4 "Mohammed's letters to the heads of state", *Wikipedia* (viewed on September 3, 2021), wikipedia.org.

5 Published by HarperOne in 2008. Chapter 4 entitled "The Great Tribulation" deals with this horrifying but rather unknown epoch in the life of the Christian church.

6 Christians and Jews who refused to convert were classified as *dhimmis* under Islamic law. They could continue following their faith, but only under severe discriminating conditions, which included paying the *jizya*, a poll tax for "People of the Book" who did not convert. Polytheists had no such option. They were killed on the spot.

issue a call to its non-Muslim neighbours to embrace Islam. The recipients could either convert or accept dhimmitude.[7] If they refused both, *holy war* ensued, i.e., *jihad.* This means in practical terms, *you either submit to Allah, or Allah's people will make you submit to them.* This practice was followed intermittently right up to the mid-thirteenth century, which saw the spectacular spread of Islam throughout the world in all four directions from Arabia.[8] This period is nostalgically called "the golden age" by Muslims, when Islam was unstoppable and subdued every imaginable foe by the edge of its sword, and when Islamic science and culture reached its zenith. Even as Islam was divided into splinter groups, the concept of *dawa* was carried forth by each group.

Following the great conquests, Islam was often spread further by Sufis (followers of mystical Islam) and Muslim traders.[9] South-east Asians for instance were often won over by such traders and Sufis who engaged in *dawa.* Sufis were also influential in converting Mongol tribes coming from the East. As these Mongol conquerors from the East converted to Islam on the central Asian steppes, it led to further mass conversions of many peoples in the wake of widespread massacres committed by the Mongol invaders. The most notorious and bloodthirsty of all Mongol-Muslim rulers was Timberlane. The Ottomans—a Turkish clan who established a principality in Anatolia (today's Turkey) around 1300—later conquered Byzantium and the Balkans by military conquest.

Thus, *dawa* and *jihad* always went hand in hand. That's how Mohammed conquered Mecca when he lived in Medina. It all began with an invitation, for the caliphate spreads by submitting to Allah's invitation: *aslim taslam.* If you accept the invitation, there is peace. If you refuse, there is war, meaning you will either become a third-class citizen under *sharia* or die. Yes, classical Islam is indeed a religion of peace, but "peace" on Allah's terms.

7 For the meaning of dhimmitude see the previous footnote.

8 Somewhere around 2007 I met a young Syrian Christian in Grand Rapids who hailed from Aleppo. He told me that most Syrian Muslims knew deep in their hearts that their forebears were Christians who were forcibly converted to Islam and that they never embraced Islam voluntarily.

9 See Sookhdeo, *Dawa*, 11.

In Sub-Saharan Africa, Islam spread in two ways: from North Africa down into the West African Sahel and from East African beachheads on the coastline—in what is today Somalia, Kenya, and Tanzania—westwards. It sometimes spread through military conquest, from Morocco to West Africa, Egypt to Sudan, or Oman to Zanzibar. Islam was also spread by traders, either by traveling on camelback down the Saharan caravan routes, by sailing down the Nile, or by coming down the Indian Ocean.

India suffered five traumatic Muslim invasions between the eleventh and the sixteenth centuries. The fourth invasion by the Turkic Mongol ruler Timberlane (1336 - 1405) was simply ruthless. After crossing the Indus River in 1398, Timberlane left a trail of blood and destruction behind him. His brutal atrocities left deep traumatic scars on the Indian psyche that remain to this day.

Modern-day *dawa* was pioneered and updated by the founder of the Muslim Brotherhood, Hasan al-Banna (1906-1949) and by Sayyid Abul A'la Mawdudi (1903 – 1979).[10] They aimed to reverse Islam's decline after the colonial period and the loss of the Ottoman caliphate in particular. The colonial period ended with the French and the British carving up the Ottoman Empire after World War One, and with the secular Turkish leader Kemal Ataturk abolishing the caliphate in 1924.[11]

The Brotherhood's aim was twofold: to bring Muslim countries back to *sharia* and to establish the "house of Islam" —*Dar al-Islam*—in non-Muslim countries. Once the "house of Islam" is established in a country, it can begin to sprawl until it conquers, making such a country part of the *Dar al-Salaam* ("house of peace") where all conflict has ceased. That was the vision and program of Mohammed. Convert the *Dar al-Harb* (the "house of war" where infidels still rule) into the *Dar al-Salaam*, where Allah rules. Or to put it differently, establish the *umma* (the faithful Muslim community) anywhere and expand it from there.

10 Ibid., 12.

11 Christopher Catherwood, *Christians, Muslims and Islamic Rage* (Grand Rapids: Zondervan, 2003), 48.

Dr. Susanne Schröter, director of the Frankfurter Research Centre for Global Islam, mentioned on *Deutsche Welle* how the race for Islamic global dominance was spurred on by the Iranian Revolution of 1979. [12] The Arab Sunnis realized they had to step up their efforts to expand Sunni Islam so as not to fall behind the Persian Shias, rejuvenated by their 1979 revolution. Buoyed by revenues from rising crude oil prices since the seventies, the Saudis began, among other things, to build mosques everywhere in the majority world, even where very few Muslims lived.

The Agents of *Dawa* [13]

Since the 1970's many conferences were held to revive the concept of *dawa*. The Muslim World League (MWL) launched the reorganization of international *dawa* activities in Mecca in 1975. Islamic missionary efforts have grown significantly since then. Today there is an extensive network of *dawa* organizations globally (notably in Sub-Saharan Africa and the West) with funding coming mainly from oil-rich Arab countries. The ultimate goal is the creation of Islamic states all over the world, with the various Islamic movements working across sectarian divides to achieve this goal. The Saudi-funded MWL and the Organization for Islamic Cooperation (OIC) play crucial roles internationally in this regard. Organizations like the IIIT (International Institute for Islamic Thought) and CAIR (Council on American Islamic Relations) fulfill a similar role in the United States of America.

The OIC is a coalition of 57 Muslim-majority member states, stressing the need to bolster and streamline the work of *dawa* worldwide. Tremendous emphasis is placed on educational and cultural centers to promote Arabic as language and Islamic culture. In 1981 the OIC pledged: "We are determined to cooperate and to provide... the means to achieve these ends". This pledge was repeated at an OIC meeting in Dakar, Senegal in 1991.

---

12 "Saudi Arabia exports extremism to many countries – including Germany, study says". *Deutsche Welle* website, August 9, 2017.

13 See Sookhdeo, *Dawa*, 15 ff.

The propagation of *dawa* is also the duty of national governments and the media. Consider that Christian mission work is typically done by churches and individuals, who often struggle to raise the funds needed to start or maintain a mission somewhere. Muslims usually don't deal with this problem. The Saudis in particular have prioritized printing and disseminating the Quran wherever it wishes throughout Africa and the world. I experienced this contrasting reality personally when a brother in East Africa requested Bibles for many hundreds of Muslim-background believers. We could only provide a few hundred. When I went to a mosque asking for free Qurans, I could have as many as I wanted.

Dawa is also promoted and sponsored by Muslim states. Many Muslim countries see it as part of their foreign policies, which means it is an item on their national budget. The Saudis, for instance, have contributed at least 76 billion Euros (US $86 billion) over the last forty years toward promoting Wahhabism, Sunni Islam's most austere version of the faith.[14] This includes printing the Quran in massive quantities and building mosques where hardly any Muslims are yet to be found, as many African Christians can testify. These new mosques then serve as beehives, drawing new worshippers.

All fifty-seven member-states of the OIC are, to a greater or lesser extent, involved in doing *dawa*. Compare this fact with what retired Roman Catholic Cardinal Robert Sarah called "an orphaned church", when he referred to the church in Africa—left behind alone—after the vast majority of mission-sending churches from the West lost interest in their spiritual offspring, due to liberal theological trends and/or a major decline in funds. In addition to that, many evangelicals in the West nowadays espouse the notion that it is no longer necessary to be involved in overseas missions since "they are now coming to us", or because it looks too much like colonialism, "if we go over there telling them what to do."[15]

---

14 See "Saudi Arabia exports extremism…." *Deutsche Welle* website, August 9, 2017.

15 Uninformed Christians in the West don't realize that immigration from the majority world represents a mere fraction of the majority world's population and that Christian folks "over there" still very much covet and appreciate our concern, assistance and guidance, as long as we deal with them as equals.

But what about individual Moslems? Are they also supposed to be involved in *dawa*? Sheikh Abdul Azeez, the grand mufti of Saudi Arabia, said it is the duty of both the Muslim community and of every individual believer to engage in *dawa*.[16] We already saw that every Muslim would be questioned in the grave whether they invited their neighbours to Islam. A former leader of the Muslim Brotherhood, Mustafa Mashhour, went so far as to say:

> It is well known that Islamic Law has made it our responsibility to invite others to Allah and to permit the good and forbid the wrong. Every one of us will be questioned by Allah as to whether he did invite his family, neighbours, friends, and acquaintances to Allah, to adopt the Book of Allah and the Sunnah of the Messenger of Allah… As for inviting people to Islam, a Muslim will be rewarded for it and penalized for the negligence of this aspect.[17]

The Ongoing Promotion of *Dawa*

The role of the media, especially television and the internet, is very important in promoting and doing *dawa*. East Africa for example has up to five Muslim channels, as far as I could observe on my travels. These channels are constantly disseminating Islamic teaching. A friend told me in Tanzania that *Al Jazeera*, broadcasting from Qatar, and sponsored by the Muslim Brotherhood, has one message for the "free world" and another for an Arabic audience. This double-speak is an old habit of revolutionary movements, to have a benign message for the outsiders and a more militant one for the insiders.[18] Meanwhile, the few Christian channels in Africa mainly promote the misery of the "Prosperity Gospel", doing the cause of Christ no favour.

16 Sookhdeo, *Dawa*, 15.

17 Ibid.,16.

18 The *African National Congress* (ANC) used this strategy very effectively during "the struggle" of the seventies and eighties in South Africa, showing one face to the West, while having another one internally. See Anthea Jeffrey *Peoples War* (Jeppestown, RSA: Jonathan Ball, 2019).

Dawa is also being propagated through education and training. *Da'ees* are trained in all branches of non-Muslim cultures to improve their mission and communicative skills. They are encouraged to study Western beliefs, likes, dislikes, strengths, weaknesses, and vulnerabilities. They are also encouraged to make ample use of inter-faith dialogue. An eight-step manual for *da'ees* was published in Malaysia in 2003. The faithful are coached to understand the various types of people they may be reaching out to. *Da'ees* are trained to be flexible and to modify their approach at all times for maximum results. The Malaysian manual provided eight steps for the *da'ee* to follow:[19]

1. Court the individual by showing great concern for his welfare. Build a friendly relationship without pushing Islam.
2. Awaken the individual from his apathy by drawing his attention to the wonders of God's creation and its purpose, while sharing neutral activities such as conversations, outings, and meals.
3. Start the process of indoctrination with Islamic doctrine and practice, providing books and guidance on the Islamic faith, while encouraging them to seek company with Muslims and to avoid sinful practices.
4. Move on to detailed instruction on Islamic worship and practice, emphasizing that Islam demands everything to be done to please God.
5. Explain that Islam is more than a religion. It is a social and political system, a civilization, and a whole way of life. Explain that individual faith is not enough and that one must be part of an Islamic community obedient to *sharia.*
6. Convince the new convert of the necessity of establishing a "full-fledged Islamic state" with coercive power to enforce full compliance to Islamic Law, following the example of Mohammed in Medina.
7. Move on from the Islamic State to the necessity of continual *jihad* to ensure the survival of Islam.
8. Mold the convert into a "walking Quran" who can witness to Islam in every place and situation.

19 Sookhdeo, *Dawa*, 20-21.

Many of us must have experienced at least some of these steps in our dealings with Muslims. A prevalent tactic is to start a conversation by saying that we are all brothers and sisters serving the same God, that Muslims also love Jesus, and that they are even more concerned about the blasphemy of Jesus in the West, than we are. It doesn't take long for the Muslim friend to state that the Quran was perfectly preserved, but that the Bible has been corrupted, a claim the Quran never makes.[20] Nonetheless, these are the sorts of arguments that set the table for the Muslim *da'ee* to begin his offensive of converting the unsuspecting listener.

Another effective method is to push for interfaith dialogue with Christians. Christians accept such invitations in the hope that the Muslims will be interested in learning more about Christianity, while *they* have the exact opposite intention. Their main goal is to make us familiar with Islam to convert us to Islam eventually. Muslims believe Christians have an inferior religion and will easily convert once they know more about Islam. The second objective of interfaith gatherings is to prove to the world that they are well-disposed towards their host country. A serious mistake liberal Christians make is to engage in mutual worship with Muslims or to invite Muslims to use their churches for prayer.[21]

---

20 See chapter 19.

21 When St. Martha's Lutheran Church in Berlin opened its doors to Muslim worshippers every Friday during Ramadan in 2020, due to Covid restrictions, a report on *Deutsche Welle* sought to portray it as a demonstration of kindness. While every effort should be made to foster better relations, this kind of gesture should not be one of them. Traditional Muslims will view it as a sign of weakness. The Muslim call to prayer says it repeatedly: "Allah is Greater... there is no God but Allah". In terms of *dawa*, *that* church building must soon be claimed for Islam. See "Berlin church offers Muslims space to pray" *Deutsche Welle* website, May 20, 2020.

CHAPTER 4

THE AIMS OF *DAWA*

Having looked at the meaning, history, and agents of *dawa*, we now want to focus on its goal. What is *dawa* aiming for? What is its endgame? It is crucial to realize that *dawa* does not merely seek the conversion of individuals (which it certainly does), but also the transformation of every society until it has conquered the whole world. Let us, however, first look at the conversion of the individual.

The Conversion of the Individual

Religious mobility differs a lot from one religion to the other. Conversion in Islam is quite different from what it is, for example, in Judaism or classical Christianity. While it is easy to become a Muslim, it is quite a different story in traditional Judaism. The threshold for joining the synagogue is high. And yet, though it may be high, exiting Judaism is not hard. It might be uncomfortable, but hardly any would risk their lives for doing so. In Biblical Christianity joining is not so simple either. But once again, it is relatively easy to leave. No one would threaten you with death or seek to harm you if you choose to renounce your faith.

When we come to Islam, it's a different story. There is no need for heart conversion like in Christianity. That's one reason why prison inmates turn to Islam relatively easily. Formerly, they might have felt angry and resentful, but now they receive divine sanction for feeling that way and they have a new cause to fight for. Instead of feeling guilty for what they may have done, they now believe they might have been right all along.

But here is the catch. Few new converts realize that it is virtually impossible to leave Islam. There is no exit door. While checking in might be easy, checking out is near impossible. Former Shiite and author of *Iran's Great Awakening*, Hormoz Shariat, says: "It is easy to become a Muslim—simply recite a phrase in Arabic—but it might cost your life to leave Islam."[1] That is certainly true in Muslim-majority countries and regions, and might also become true in the West. One thing is certain, once you have joined the *umma*, formally quitting is very hard. Unfortunately, most naïve converts to Islam realize this too late. It is not shared with unsuspecting readers of popular *dawa* flyers here in the West.

We say it is near impossible, yet thousands *are* leaving, more than ever in 1400 years. Why? Because, in many cases, they have found something, or rather Someone, worth living and dying for, and worth risking everything for. Pastor Shariat tells the story in *Iran's Great Awakening* of going to Turkey some time ago to train Iranian church leadership. The young underground house-church leaders were so hungry that they regularly met for prayer and singing until late at night, even after twelve hours of teaching. Shariat decided to visit them on the last night when they were still singing, for he was wondering, "Do they know that tomorrow, at the airport, they might be arrested, jailed, and tortured? I should prepare them for what may come." They stopped singing, and he instructed them once more about the reality of persecution. He said, "Some of you may be called to give the ultimate price—your life—for your faith." They listened attentively and respectfully. When Shariat finished, a few of them spoke up:

> Pastor Hormoz, please do not worry about us. We know what we have gotten into. When we were Muslims, we were willing to die for Allah, who

1 Hormoz Shariat, *Iran's Great Awakening* (Melissa, TX: Iran Alive Ministries, 2020), 192.

is distant and cruel. How much more are we ready to die for Jehovah, an intimate and loving God? So please don't worry about us.[2]

Why Do People Convert to Islam?

Pastor Shariat also tells the story of his conversion to Christianity and how the Lord has been using his television channel to bring about amazing things in Iran. His story began before the Iranian Revolution when a brave young American girl from Oregon converted to Islam so that she could marry him. Donnell was a nominal Christian, disillusioned with the lukewarm Christianity of her upbringing, and deeply impressed with the Muslim devotion she saw in Tehran while working there. And so, when she met the man of her dreams, abandoning Christianity and becoming a Shiite was a matter of simple logic. Her story is unfortunately all too familiar.[3] That is why we must ask ourselves, "Why do people convert to Islam in Africa and the West?" Patrick Sookhdeo provides a list of reasons, [4] to which I have added a couple.

1. For *material reasons.* In Africa and elsewhere, ordinary folks are often poor. Converts can be bought with almost anything, like candy (in the case of children), water, food, free education, and houses. In Cambodia, new converts once each received $1000 to join the mosque. In Sabah, Malaysia, Christian children were tricked into converting with candy, causing a massive outcry in the Christian community. I was personally told by South Africans how many of their fellow Africans had been offered money to join Islam in KwaZulu Natal.
2. For *free education*: In Africa, a *madrassa* is often the closest and cheapest school where a child can receive at least some form of education. That education however revolves around one thing: reading and reciting the Quran in Arabic. Yet, because there is no other nearby option, Christian parents, not grounded in their faith, sometimes find it hard to resist the pressure of sending their children to a local *madrassa.*

2 Ibid., 197-198.

3 Ibid., 5.

4 See "Dawa Through Individual conversion" in Sookhdeo, *Dawa*, 28-32.

3. For *free healthcare.* A third way to lure at least nominal Christians and other Africans is through free or relatively cheap healthcare. Primary healthcare in Africa is expensive (except maybe in South Africa). The African context allows for many forms of exploitation of the needy. *Deutsche Welle* reported how fake medicine and drugs flooding the continent were killing "hundreds of thousands in Africa,"[5] making many ordinary Africans suspicious of the healthcare they are receiving. This offers a considerable opportunity to Muslim charities like the *Red Crescent* to offer trusted medicine for free.
4. For *humanitarian aid.* Typically, Muslim humanitarian assistance is only meant for Muslims. There are exceptions, like in the case of the heroic work of *Gift of the Givers* helping to secure the release of a South African undercover Christian missionary couple from Al Qaeda captivity in Yemen.[6] The Quran, however, simply does not teach an indiscriminate love for all, let alone for your enemy, as Christianity does.

   Thus, when disaster strikes—as in the Boxing Day tsunami that hit Aceh, Indonesia in 2004—whoever is not a Muslim is last in line for anything, even though American planes may have dropped down most of the aid. That may cause desperate nominal Christians to turn to Islam during a disaster.[7]
5. For *political and historical reasons.* Weak or nominal African Christians may turn to Islam because they are told that Christianity is a white man's religion and Islam is for Africa. Even the world-famous Cassius Clay once changed his name to Mohammed Ali believing this lie, according to Dr. David Wood on his *Acts17 Apologetics* YouTube channel.[8] Wood proved

5 "Fake medicine kills hundreds of thousands in Africa" *Deutsche Welle* website, December 4, 2019.

6 See the moving account of Yolande Korkie, *558 Days… A True Story* (Vereeniging, RSA: Christian Art Publishers, 2016). Yolande was first set free. Her husband Pierre died when U.S. marines tried to liberate him and an American hostage.

7 A Kenyan Christian lady, who formerly lived as a Muslim in Zanzibar, told me this story: When a Christian boy got lost in that port city, Christians went to the local mosque asking for help by using the mosque's megaphone to notify the public. They were turned down since the child was a Christian!

8 "How Mohammed Ali was deceived by Islam. And why Cassius Clay was his greatest name" David Wood on *Acts17Apologetics-YouTube,* viewed on December 4, 2021.

from Islamic sources that Mohammed was fair-skinned and enslaved black people, and we all know that Jesus and his apostles were not Europeans.

6. For reasons related to *marriage and sex*. While Muslims can have up to four wives, Christians may only have one. Africa was polygamist before Christianity arrived, so some Africans may choose Islam for this reason. In the Democratic Republic of the Congo, African Christians often needlessly delay marriage because of expensive dowries and wedding ceremonies. Marrying a Muslim on the other hand, poses no such problems at all, yet all the children from a mixed marriage will be Muslim according to *sharia*.

   This is not where it ends though. In some African countries, Muslim boys are rewarded for impregnating Christian girls. A colleague in Uganda mentioned that Muslim men have impregnated up to three hundred Christian girls in their Anglican diocese in recent years. Many reports have reached the West from countries like Pakistan, Nigeria, and Egypt telling how Christian girls were kidnapped, raped, and then forcibly married, a practice that is not limited to those countries.

   Then there are Islam's gender roles, which may appeal to some men since it promotes misogyny and demands unqualified submission from their women. And there is also the enticing Muslim hereafter, filled with the sensual delights of pure wine, lush palm trees, and bashful voluptuous virgins, covered only in silk. In paradise, a Muslim's wife must look passively on while her husband is enjoying himself with the *hoooris* (perpetual virgins), of which every man gets at least two, or as many as seventy-two if he died in *jihad*.

7. For *social reasons*. Young people may feel disenfranchised from their communities. This has become a disturbing phenomenon in the secular West. When children have suffered from parental neglect or abuse, or when they have been exposed to too much corruption and hypocrisy, they become the low-hanging fruit for Islamic *dawa*. Islam presents itself to them as a religion offering everything from a new identity to social acceptance, security, and stability.

8. For having *a proper funeral*. Unrooted Christians may convert to Islam in Africa to have a burial place. In the Sahel, on the fault line between the Christian-Animist south and the Muslim north, Africans are often not

> allowed a burial place in Muslim-dominated areas. This is such a dreadful prospect to many that they turn to Islam when death approaches.

It should be clear to all that genuine Christian believers should not be at risk here, for these empty arguments will not even persuade the unregenerate, well-schooled in a Biblical worldview. That is why robust Biblical evangelism, and radical discipling of new Christians, will be critically important throughout the upcoming generations.

On the flip side of conversions to Islam is the ongoing steady flow of Muslims to Christianity worldwide, despite apostasy laws, something I personally witnessed in East Africa.[9] So why do they continue to come despite all the threats? Because of the "expulsive power of a greater affection," to use a famous line coined by the great Scottish preacher Thomas Chalmers.[10] The Father's love, the Son's selfless suffering for us, and the new life of the Holy Spirit, are too overwhelming to resist, when a thirsty soul begins to yearn for glory, honour, and immortality.

The conversion of society and culture

Islamic *dawa* seeks to win over individuals and address society's structures, and institutions. This goal is derived from the Islamic doctrines of the oneness *(tawhid)* and sovereignty (*hakimiyya*) of Allah.[11] If there is only one God, then there can only be one law for all: *sharia*. It all stems from the time when Mohammed was both prophet, lawgiver, and ruler in Medina.

Therefore, in our terms today, Muslims who place a major emphasis on the *political* aspirations of Islam, who are referred to as Islamists. They consider themselves the only true Muslims, following in the path of Mohammed's *sunna*. The others are unfaithful. This has markedly changed the Muslim landscape over the last few decades. During many of the previous centuries, the familiar face of Islam (even in many Muslim-majority countries) was one of Muslims keeping their faith relatively private and seeking to live in harmony with their neighbours. This was true from

---

9 See "At the Foot of the Ruwenzoris" on soberminds.ca.

10 Iain Murray, *A Scottish Christian Heritage* (Edinburgh: Banner of Truth, 2006), 73.

11 Sookhdeo, *Dawa*, 29.

Indonesia to Morocco and in places like Britain, Holland or Germany since the 1960s. But things began to change since the latter part of the twentieth century.

In Egypt, for instance, Islamization took up speed since the assassination of President Anwar Sadat (who signed a peace accord with Israel), and then really accelerated since the nineties. Saudi Salafist Wahhabism began seeping into the country. More and more men were seen dressed in white and women in black. Burqas became more numerous, beards grew longer, and the message from the mosque got louder. Weddings became much more conservative, with belly dancers making way for speakers blasting Islamic songs. Shopkeepers began to display more religious symbols.[12] So, what changed, and why?

The colonial era—of "infidels" or the "kufar" ruling over Muslim lands—had passed. The Cold War—of two superpowers keeping the rest of the world in check—had also passed. Furthermore, the West began to unravel politically, morally, and culturally, after two world wars helped destroy Christianity's credibility. Then came the sexual revolution of the decadent sixties, followed by the internet revolution of the nineties, and everything went downhill so rapidly that Lord Jonathan Sacks, Chief Rabbi of the British Commonwealth, could ask, "Has Europe lost its soul?" From what he said that night, and from what we know since then, one sadly has to conclude, "Undeniably, it did!"[13] And that applies not only to Europe, but to the rest of the West as well.

All of this helped spur on a great revival of Islam during the twentieth century, driven by the burning desire to address Western cultural and political dominance. We know from science that nature abhors a vacuum. That is even more true in the world of culture and politics, and above all in the spiritual realm. Listen to Dr. Mona Abul-Fadl (1945-2008) of the International Institute for Islamic Thought (IIIT). She said that her organization is,

---

12 See Mansour, *Minority of One*, 62-64.

13 This incredible speech was delivered after the financial crisis at Rome's Gregorian University, see "Lord Sacks: 'Has Europe Lost its Soul?'", by Henk Kamsteeg, in *Israel and Christians Today*, April 2012, 2-3.

> dedicated to the revival and reform of Islamic thought... in order to enable the Ummah to deal effectively with present challenges, and to contribute to the progress of human civilization in ways that will give it meaning and direction derived from divine guidance. The realization of such a position will help the Ummah regain its intellectual and cultural identity and re-affirm its presence as a dynamic civilization. [14]

Nothing less than the Islamization of civilization is the goal. We should note that such a civilization, brought about by "divine guidance" through *sharia* is for Abul-Fadl a "dynamic civilization." Western culture is considered beyond its shelf life. It is dying, decadent, divisive, and disintegrating. It needs a total overhaul, and only Islam can do the job and fill the vacuum. In so doing, Islamists want to restore Islam to its golden age, which will change their shame to honour. That golden age lasted from Mohammed's migration (*hijra*) from Mecca to Medina to the end of Abbasid rule in 1258, over six hundred years. Islamization is so much buoyed by the obvious spiritual and cultural decline of the West that Dr. Abul-Fadl could write in an IIIT publication,

> The exultant optimism [in the Western world] which had marked the onset of the [20th] century had to all intents and purposes, become extinguished. There was an impoverishment in philosophy, the cornerstone of the Western intellectual tradition, and theology, periodically resuscitated from recurrent bouts of exhaustion, could hardly shoulder the burdens of a new transitional epoch unfolding in the guise of a "postmodernity". Confusion and skepticism became pervasive.[15]

Indeed, Western civilization is unable to cope with postmodernism. It is too weak. Confusion, apathy, relativism, and pessimism rule the day. Abul-Fadl offers an answer: "An Islamic reading of the West can contribute to the sanctification of (its) culture."[16] A famous Muslim Brotherhood slogan states, "Islam is the Solution!"[17] The Canadian Islamic Congress went so far

---

14 As quoted in Sookhdeo, *Dawa*, 30.

15 Ibid.,31.

16 Ibid.

17 Mansour, *Minority of One*, 57.

in a popular pamphlet to say that "when Muslims faithfully followed the true teachings of Islam, they and the rest of the world prospered. Whenever Muslims did not follow the teachings of Islam, they, along with the rest of the world, suffered greatly."[18]

Islamic *dawa* wants to convert whole societies and their structures. Back in Mohammed's day, Arabia was in a state of ignorance (*jahiliyyah*). Full surrender to Allah saved Arabia. *Tawhid* (God's oneness) destroyed all *jahili* (ignorant) powers. That should happen again today, according to political Islam.

During the colonial period, Islam was passive, as it endured a period of shame. But the time has now come to move to a more revolutionary role, seeking to completely transform society, working very subtly where the *umma* is still a minority (like in Europe), but very openly, forcefully and even brutally where it is gaining the upper hand (like in Nigeria and other parts of Africa). As such, Islam resembles totalitarian systems like Fascism and Communism.

All of this was accomplished in the golden age through *dawa* and *jihad*, and this is how it must now happen again. For true educated Muslims, the memory of centuries ago, when they were a persecuted and despised minority in Mecca, is still a fearful memory. The possibility that Islam might have been squashed was real. That is why being a minority anywhere today makes them fearful and why outsiders or infidels are not to be trusted. Their sources also teach them that it is normal to have contempt for non-Muslims and to discriminate against them. Many ex-Muslims can testify how they were brainwashed from early childhood that Christians and Jews are dirty and despicable, and that befriending them is *haram* and against the will of Allah.[19] Former Egyptian Muslim Hussein Mansour and former Palestinian-Egyptian Muslim Yasmine Mohammed (living in the U.S. and Canada respectively) convey in great detail how deep the prejudice against "infidels" runs in traditional Muslim homes, often leading to

18 Gillian Cosgrove "How the Muslims won the election — Islamic Congress takes credit for helping Liberals fend off Tories" in *National Post*, August 7, 2004, A8.

19 See Catharine Porter, "Mosque warns against saying Merry Christmas", in *Toronto Star/ News*, December 28, 2002, A6; See also Mansour, *Minority of One*, 26, 51, 94; and Yasmine Mohammed, *Unveiled* (Victoria, BC: Free Hearts Free Minds, 2019).

severe parental abuse and domestic conflicts when taboos are ignored. In fact, non-Muslims should count themselves fortunate if Muslims allow them to exist peacefully among them at all.

The *umma* concept has recently undergone a significant revival. It is the driver of Islamization. The *umma* is a community with shared values. It expresses group consciousness (felt unity) that transcends differences and distance among Muslims. As the community of Allah and his prophet, the *umma* lives under *tawhid*, i.e., Allah's oneness, and is the political and social embodiment of *tawhid*. Times of crisis only serve to deepen one's primary loyalty to the *umma*.

CHAPTER 5

METHODS OF ISLAMIZATION

Islamic *dawa* has both the individual and the community in its scope. That much was made abundantly clear in chapter four. The conversion of a community is what is commonly called Islamization. In this chapter, we want to take a closer look at some of the many effective *peaceful* methods of Islamization.[1] These methods help bring about Islamization in Muslim-minority contexts, like in Europe and Sub-Saharan Africa, as well as in secular Muslim states.

Migration and Demographics[2]

Like so many others, Dr. Yusuf al-Qaradawi (main spiritual advisor to the Muslim Brotherhood and *Al Jazeera TV*, based in Qatar) saw a divine cause behind Muslim migration to the West, when he said, "Thanks to Allah, Islamic presence in [the] West existed through divine predestinations

1 See Sookhdeo, *Dawa,* chapters 6 and 7.

2 Ibid., 39-44.

and natural causes that facilitated its existence, through no planning or arrangement on the part of us as Muslims."[3]

The late Libyan leader Muammar Qadhafi was well-known for saying Islam would take Europe over without firing a single shot… through immigration and procreation. That seems to be happening now, which is why this issue is driving European politics for the last number of years. It inspired someone like British journalist Douglas Murray to publish *The Strange Death of Europe: Immigration, Identity, Islam* in 2017.[4] Ironically the same Colonel Qadhafi had the foresight to warn Europe that, should he be taken out, Europe would be flooded by migrants pouring through Libya into Europe, turning the Mediterranean into "a sea of chaos."[5] Sadly, this is what happened after NATO powers, under the inspiration of President Obama's Secretary of State, Hilary Clinton, plotted Qadhafi's liquidation during the so-called Arab Spring in 2011. Qadhafi's predictions came true when almost two million refugees and economic migrants walked into Europe from its Mediterranean shores, almost causing the demise of German Chancellor Angela Merkel—who invited the refugees to come to her country in 2015. The sudden influx of such large numbers of immigrants was blamed as the leading cause of rising crime and violent clashes between opposing parties in cities as far north as Malmö and Oslo in a once peaceful Scandinavia, so that in February 2023, *The Telegraph* could report that Sweden has become "a gangster's paradise."[6] The refugee crisis caused an outcry across Europe's political spectrum, fueling the rise of right-wing parties and fascism.

In his book, *African Exodus*, German-Ethiopian entrepreneur and scholar, Dr. Asfa-Wossen Asserate, made a compelling case that mass migration from Africa into Europe will come to haunt not only Europe but the entire world very soon. Worldwide there were 65 million refugees by 2017, while 4.4 million Africans were on the run that same year, 20 percent

---

3 Ibid, 40.

4 Bloomsbury Publishing: London, 2017.

5 "Gaddafi's Grim Prophecy Comes True. Countless Refugees Swarm Europe", *Sputnik International*, September 17, 2015, on sputniknews.com.

6 Fraser Nelson, "Sweden has become a gangster's paradise—and a case study in how not to integrate immigrants", The Telegraph – Comment. 2 Feb. 2023, telegraph.co.uk.

more than in the previous year. At the center of the refugee crisis lies what Asserate calls "the arch of instability stretching from Mali to Afghanistan."[7] Thankfully some refugees coming to Europe bring with them the gospel of our Saviour, and many other refugees embrace the gospel upon arriving there. And yet, the flood of migrants, legal or illegal, is steadily causing Europe's Muslim population to rise, placing the entire fabric of its fragile civilization under huge pressure, as most Europeans feel that political Islam is incompatible with European values.

We should remember that *dawa* through migration is based on the example of Mohammed's migration from Mecca to Medina in 622, the *hijra*. The *hijra* saved Islam from extinction in its first hour and has become the paradigm for future conquests and success. Migration is seen as the essential link to establish the *umma* in non-Muslim territory, as a beachhead of sorts from which to expand and transform the *Dar al-Harb* into the *Dar al-Islam*.

Meanwhile, the population explosion of many Muslim-majority countries, coupled with rising Muslim emigration and the demographic growth of new Muslim communities in their host countries, are all seen by traditional Muslims as the fulfillment of Allah's divine will. The largest Muslim presence in Europe today is in France, where the Muslim minority is already 10 percent, enforcing no-go zones in the country's major cities. In the Lowlands in 2014, Muslims already made-up 26 percent of the population in Brussels, 25 percent in Rotterdam, 24 percent in Amsterdam, 17 percent in Antwerp, 14 percent in The Hague, and 13 percent in Utrecht, according to Soeren Kern of the Gatestone Institute.[8] Rotterdam is the most Islamized city in Europe. Many of its neighborhoods look like they have been lifted from the Middle East.[9] Little wonder Dutch politician Geert Wilders came to the US telling his audience in a packed auditorium:

---

7 Asfa-Wossen Asserate, *African Exodus: Migration and the Future of Europe* (London: Haus Publishing, 2018). See Chapter One, "On the Run," 1-25.

8 "The Islamization of Belgium and the Netherlands in 2013" by Soeren Kern, *The Gatestone Institute*, January 13, 2014, on gatestoneinstitute.org.

9 Harry Antonides, "Rotterdam, Capital of Eurabia", *Christian Renewal*, September 23, 2009.

> "I come to America with a mission. All is not well in the old world. A tremendous danger looms, and it is tough to be optimistic. We might be in the final stages of the Islamization of Europe."[10]

Meanwhile, in a talk to the *UK Islamic Mission*, prominent Muslim Ismail al-Faruqi stated:

> "We are here to stay, we are here to plant Islam in this part of the world, and we must utilize everything in our power to make the word of Allah supreme... Allah has carved out a mission for you... and this mission is to save the West, to save the humanity of the West by converting that humanity to Islam." [11]

Note that Al-Faruqi did not say their goal is to save humanity *from the West* but to save the humanity *of the West.* That is a very bold statement. Not only do they see our culture as inherently lost and void of meaning, they see us as lost and needing *their* help. Islam is our only hope! It *is* the solution, says the Muslim Brotherhood. Al-Qaradawi of the Muslim Brotherhood mentioned four *dawa*-related activities that Muslim minorities anywhere should engage in:

- Invite non-Muslims to Islam through preaching, dialogue, and a good example.
- Care for new converts to Islam, teaching them how to live.
- Care for newly arrived Muslim immigrants, showing them how to practice Islam.
- Defend the umma, and defend Islamic lands in the face of hostile powers and trends. [12]

Muslim-majority countries see their populations in minority countries as a political weapon to effect change. The late doyen of Middle Eastern studies, Dr. Bernard Lewis of Princeton University, predicted in 2006 that

10 Geert Wilders is the Leader of the Party for Freedom in the Netherlands. He delivered this speech at the Four Seasons in New York City in January 2012.

11 Sookhdeo, *Dawa*, 41.

12 Ibid., 40.

Muslims would be a majority in Europe by the end of the twenty-first century. Moreover, a researcher at the Centre for the Study of Political Islam, Nikoletta Incze, told Hungarian public television in June 2018 (citing a Harvard Study) that the Islamization of a country cannot be stopped once its Muslim population has reached 16 percent.[13] Continued demographic growth in the West, Africa, and elsewhere offers Muslims the political leverage they need to bring about the changes that are in line with their political ideals. In some places, Islamization has accelerated so dramatically over the last few decades that it is now almost complete. Nigeria, Africa's most populous Christian nation, is a prime example.[14]

Islamization will always aim to protect Islam from criticism in its host nation, to increase Islamic education, and to introduce *sharia* family law where possible. Eventually, it will strive to change society into a full-blown Muslim state. Islamization is all about bringing everything under Allah's rule.

Does this mean that the battle is almost lost for Western Europe? Oxford demographics professor David Coleman warns about jumping to conclusions prematurely, pointing to the declining birth rate among British Muslims.[15] Moreover, many voices in Islam are raising the alarm about a growing number of young people defecting from the faith without making it publicly known, due to the stigma and risk associated with apostatizing. Islam's honour-and-shame culture, coupled with its strict apostasy laws, is preventing millions of Muslim youths worldwide from going to their parents or imams to talk about their nagging concerns.

The battle is not over yet. Strong resistance to *political* Islam is building in places like Germany, Italy, Hungary, France, and Austria, to name but a few. *The Gatestone Institute* reported in 2021 that Germany's ruling party, the Christian Democratic Union, and its coalition partner

13 Nem Mutat ellenállást az Iszlamizációval szemben Europa? *Hiradu.hu.*, June 22, 2018, on hiradu.hu.

14 Johnnie Moore and Abraham Cooper, *The Next Jihad* (Nashville, TN: W Publishing, 2020), 6.

15 Sookhdeo, *Dawa*, 41.

in the Bundestag, adopted a far-reaching policy-paper called *Preserving Free Society, Promoting Social Cohesion, Fighting Political Islamism.*[16] While whole-heartedly commending law-abiding Muslims who respect Germany's democratic order, it warns against limiting the debate about Islamism in Germany to issues of violence and terror. That should change. It is necessary to focus more on the underlying ideology. The paper's proposals include improving research and analysis of political Islam in Europe and the methods by which it is spreading, calling for the banning of the foreign-funding of mosques, and the reduction of foreign-funded imams operating in Germany. Similar measures have recently been approved in Austria under the leadership of its former leader Sebastian Kurz. Italy's new Prime Minister Giorgia Meloni's outspoken views on immigration are no secret either, nor are those of Hungary's Victor Orbán, both of whom are not ashamed to promote Christianity and its values. It is clear the time of focusing merely on terror threats is over. Political Islam promoted by *dawa* has come under the microscope of some significant European leaders and political parties.

In France, the capitulation to political Islam caused a major political earthquake in the spring of 2021, when a group of retired generals warned in an open letter that France would slide into civil war if the government failed to control mass migration and creeping Islamism in the country.[17] A public survey found that more than 70 percent of the French public supported the letter, which was followed up by a second one from anonymous *acting* generals and other military staff.

It is thus not so simple to conclude that the outcome of this clash between two rival civilizations has already been decided. Immigration and birth rates may taper off, and no one really knows how much the impact of secularism coupled with a deep dissatisfaction vis-a-vis Muslim extremism might affect future generations of Muslims. Iran, and parts of Africa, are good examples of how extremism turned millions of Muslims

---

16 "Germany: New Strategy to Combat 'Political Islam'" by Soeren Kern, *Gatestone Institute*, May 27, 2021, on gatestoneinstitute.org.

17 "France: Generals Warn of Civil War Due to Creeping Islamism", by Soeren Kern, *JewishPress.com*, May 9, 2021, on jewishpress.com

against Islam, at least secretly for now. It is believed that only 40 percent of Iranians attend the mosque regularly, with Saudi Arabia also facing struggles. Meanwhile, the hunger for the Bible in these same countries, is insatiable. The harsh rule of Shia clerics caused an exodus from Islam in Iran while simultaneously sparking a revival of Christianity despite severe threats and penalties. The advocacy group *Open Doors* has noted that there is often far greater openness to the gospel among Muslim refugees in Germany (who have suffered under harsh Islamic extremism) than among Germany's more settled Muslims who have enjoyed freedom and prosperity for decades.[18]

There is another, until recently unknown, factor that is having a significant impact on Islam, not only in the West but deep in the Muslim-majority world too. A steady rise of fearless polemicists, exposing Islam's porous historical foundations, is beginning to shake the *umma* like never before during fourteen centuries. The list of these Christian and secular warriors is only growing by the day, causing more than a proverbial splash in the pond.[19]

They are all striving to show the Muslim faithful what has been hidden from them by their clerics for many centuries. All of this is causing no small consternation, with thousands of Muslims saying on the internet that they are leaving the faith, many turning to the Messiah, the Son of God. It is often claimed that more Muslims have come to Christ in the last fourteen years than in the previous fourteen hundred years.

And yet, notwithstanding all of the above, it is no secret that migration is an ancient tool of *dawa* to expand the reign of Allah around the globe. It

---

18 This fact was personally conveyed to me by a German friend and was confirmed by two other individuals involved in ministry in that country.

19 In whose wake many others have risen, a leading voice was the Coptic priest, Father Zakaria Botros, once named by *World Magazine* as its "Daniel of the Year" in 2008. Other online apologists followed, like Dr. Jay Smith of *PfanderFilms*, former Saudi radical Al Fadi of *CIRA International*, Hatun Tash, Sam Shamoun, Christian Prince, and a Somali couple presenting *Somali Christian TV*. Above them all, in terms of impact, was Dr. David Wood, whose *Acts17Apologetics* YouTube channel got almost 200 million views before Wood decided to leave the platform due to its debilitating censorship. Wood was the spiritual father of another influential apologist, Dr. Nabeel Qureshi, who recently died of cancer.

is particularly effective in parts of Africa, Western Europe, and Southeast Asia, where Muslims seek to boost their population sizes to gain the upper hand politically. We have seen that in recent times in parts of Indonesia, Malaysia, Sudan, West Africa, East Africa, and even further down south on that continent, that a deliberately orchestrated shift in demographics radically changed the face of the land in a matter of a decade or two.[20] It seeks to tilt the balance of power away from the cross or a secular state to the crescent, in a given region. In the majority world where government surveillance and protections are weaker, Muslim migration may sometimes be accompanied by ruthless bouts of ethnic cleansing, as we now see happening in the Sahel, central Nigeria, the remote eastern parts of the Democratic Republic of the Congo, and in northern Mozambique.

All of this underscores how crucial political leadership and the church's vitality will be, if the West and the Rest hope to escape Islam's goal of world domination over the next few decades.

Exploiting "Democratic" Vulnerabilities

Political Islam is keenly aware of how it may exploit the political vulnerability of the West and Sub-Saharan Africa by (among other things) making ample use of the democratic process. They are not alone in doing so. Marxist revolutionary movements have never been stooges in how to exploit not only the democratic process but Western naiveté for revolutionary purposes. The difference between the two ideologies is that political Islam believes it is divinely inspired, with fourteen centuries of Allah's favour behind it. At the end of the day, or so they believe, the messenger of Allah and the *umma* will be victorious, when finally, Isa (Jesus) will return from heaven to break the cross and destroy all the pigs (Jews and Christians).[21]

As we have said before, the biggest mistake that unsuspecting Christians (and Westerners) can make is to think that most Muslims think as we do. So many of us are living in this credulity all the time. We will see later how Swedish journalist Paulina Neuding mentioned this as the primary

20 See Sookhdeo, *Dawa*, 42-43.

21 Patrick Sookhdeo, *Understanding Islam* (McLean, VA: Isaac Publishing, 2013), 256-258.

reason why the Swedes were caught fast asleep, underestimating creeping Islamization in their country.[22] Only when we begin to understand how classical Islam thinks and views history, will the tide begin to turn in this long battle of ideas. Remarks made by a Bangladeshi Islamic activist, Motiur Rahman Nizami, reveal the centuries-old Islamist vision not only for his own country but for the entire world: "We are not in a hurry. We don't expect anything to happen overnight but pursue a slow but steady policy towards total Islamization of the country."[23]

Islamists are adept at exploiting Western vulnerabilities to strengthen their position. They know well how to use Western obsession with racism, discrimination, political correctness, and, in recent times, critical race theory to their favour. A sad illustration of this fact was the horrific grooming-gang scandal in Britain, in which possibly thousands of poorer white British girls were systematically groomed and then raped by predominantly Pakistani gangs. One such sorrowful story was published under the title *Please let me go – The horrific true story of a girl's life in the hands of sex traffickers* by Caitlin Spencer. The pseudonymous author states on the back-cover that she had been "raped so many times, abused by hundreds, if not thousands" that she can't even recall how much, as she was passed on from one gang to another.[24]

The reason why something so dreadfully evil could go unnoticed for so long was because the police and the press in the UK did not want to touch the issue, since they were all terrified by the backlash it might provoke, that they are stirring up racism.[25] In other words, Britain's great nation sold out its children in deference to political correctness.

22 See chapter 12 on the "Four Failed Strategies of the Worldly Powers".

23 Sookhdeo, *Dawa*, 45.

24 Caitlin Spencer (pseudonym), *Please Let Me Go* (London: John Blake: 2017).

25 In Pakistan – a country known for its countless sexual assaults on Christian women and girls – the Human Rights Commission expressed its deep dismay that former Prime Minister Imran Kahn could link the incidence of rape to so-called "obscenity", making it hard for men to control their urges. The problem, he said, was an import from the West and India. See "HCRP 'appalled' by Imran Kahn's remarks linking incidents of rape with obscenity, demands apology," *Dawn*, April 6, 2021, on dawn.com

Another typical example of how Islam exploits Western vulnerabilities comes from Germany. Though polygamy is officially banned in that country, the German television news channel *RTL Extra* aired a program showing how German taxpayers funded Muslim polygamists.[26] The report showed how Muslim men residing in Germany are taking advantage of the social welfare system by bringing two, three or four women from across the Muslim world into Germany and then marrying them in the presence of an imam. This practice is so common that an estimated one-third of Muslim men living in Neukölln (near Berlin) is considered to have two or more wives. This is not the end of the story. Once in Germany, these women request social welfare benefits, including the cost of a separate home for themselves and their children, on the claim of being a "single parent with children."[27] The *RTL Extra* report says that even though this welfare fraud is an "open secret" costing German taxpayers millions each year, government agencies are reluctant to take action due to political sensitivities.

There is yet another way in which Muslims exploit Western vulnerabilities, namely by pointing out real or perceived human rights violations or by expressing solidarity with whoever may feel themselves to be the underdog. The sheer hypocrisy of such acts will only escape those ignorant of the status quo in most Muslim countries, and of what is written in their holy books. A good example of an Islamist exploiting Western vulnerabilities occurred when Turkish leader Tayyip Erdogan told German Interior Minister Hans-Peter Friedrich that Berlin was guilty of "a human rights violation" for insisting that Turkish immigrants should seek to integrate into German society and learn its language.[28] Such comments may sound pious to the superficial observer until you realize that Christians in Turkey can hardly stick their necks out of the door, as the imprisonment

26 "'Different and Threatening': Most Germans See Islam as a Threat" by Soeren Kern, *Perspectives on Europe and America*, May 3, 2013, on soerenkern.com.
See "Germany Polygamy: Minister says migrants must abide by the Law" *BBC* website, June 15, 2016.

27 We will see in chapter 14 how the same thing is happening in Canada.

28 "Erdogan Criticizes German Attitude to Turks", *The Local*, November 2, 2011, on thelocal.de

of American missionary Andrew Brunson has illustrated in recent years.[29] Turkey is a country where Christians have been systematically eliminated since the early twentieth century.[30]

Also keep in mind that Mr. Erdogan wants to take his country back to the glory days of the pre-secular Ottoman Empire and that Turkey never apologized for the Armenian genocide, while Germans have been walking in proverbial sackcloth about the holocaust for eighty years now. One can hardly imagine Turkey inviting Westerners, let alone Christians, to come and settle over there, if only they are willing to learn Turkish and integrate into their society. And yet Erdogan feels confident to lecture Germany on human rights, with so many ill-informed Westerners loving every bit of it.

Another example comes from Canada, a country recently reeling under "revelations" of hundreds of unmarked graves near Catholic and Anglican residential schools—which was later proved to be a hoax. In the wake of these "discoveries", and the untold sadness it evoked from the country's First Nation peoples, seventy-five imams expressed their solidarity with Canada's indigenous peoples. The Canadian imams extended their condolences "at this time of immeasurable trauma and grief."[31] While the Holy Spirit exhorts us in Scripture to weep with those who weep, and to share in the grief of others, one can only wonder if this outpouring of condolences on the part of Muslim imams will also lead them to delete from the Quran and the *hadith* those many passages calling for the summary killing of all pagans who refuse to surrender to Allah. Knowing how Islam views "pagan-worshippers," one wonders how long this "solidarity" will last if *sharia* comes into full effect.

---

29 An interview with Pastor Brunson was published by *Open Doors* on its website opendoorsusa.org on September 7, 2021, "Why Andrew Brunson never heard from God in prison".

30 Sookhdeo, *Hated Without a Reason,* 140-146. Between 1877 and 1922, entire Armenian, Assyrian, and Greek Christian communities were annihilated, reducing Turkey's Christian population from 32% in 1900 to 1.8% in 1927 and further down to 0.2% today.

31 "Imams in Canada express solidarity with Indigenous people," by Hilary Beaumont, *Al Jazeera* website, July 9, 2021.

Canada's vulnerability was also shown in a September 2020 issue of *The Trumpet.* It reported that Canadian politicians are unfazed by the rise of radical Islam, stating that "one thing unites the right and the left", namely its "tacit acceptance of Islamic fundamentalism".[32] Both the Liberal and Conservative parties in Canada are known to have key party members with close ties to the Muslim Brotherhood, while the said organization has now been banned from countries such as Morocco, Tunisia, Sudan, Jordan, and Egypt because of its radical views. The Conservatives in Canada were not shy to silence and even cancel members of their party who warned against the dangers of radical Islam and the Muslim Brotherhood in particular.[33]

Why do so many in the West still not get it? Columnist Ayaan Hirsi Ali explains how it all works in a piece called *Why Islamism became woke.*[34] She explains how extremists are using progressive rhetoric to fool the West:

> It is very simple. It is all meant to deceive and is part of *dawa.* Al Qaeda, for instance, can upload English-language documentaries on transgender rights on its social media channel while simultaneously broadcasting sermons on its Arabic station, suggesting how Muslim men may beat their wives.

Hirsi Ali's interview, posted on *UnHerd*, featured a photo of a Muslim woman, fully clad in a black burka, holding a *Black Lives Matter* poster!

Moreover, while many Christians surrender politics to "the world" as either too dirty or too dangerous, praying that God will "build and protect his church", Muslims are stepping up their participation in the political process all over the world, Canada serving as a good example. Back in 2004, Gillian Cosgrove wrote for the *National Post* how Canada's Muslims won the federal election for the Liberal Party, fending off the Tories and

---

32 "Canadian Politicians Team Up with Radical Islam", by Daniel Di Santo, *The Trumpet,* September 3, 2020, on thetrumpet.com.

33 Ibid. Two such unfortunate individuals were Mrs. Ghada Malek, PC candidate for Mississauga (a Coptic Christian), and Dr. Salim Mansur, an outspoken Muslim critic of political Islam, who said the Conservative Party is in "full mode of appeasing the Brotherhood."

34 "Why Islamism became woke" by Ayaan Hirsi Ali, *UnHerd*, July 13, 2021, on unherd.com

saving the country from a Conservative government.[35] A decade later, the Canadian Broadcasting Corporation reported that during the 2015 federal election, Muslims stepped up their "usually below-par turnouts" to new record levels since, as one Muslim activist observed, "there was so much at stake." The article reported that the Muslim "segment of the population [is] expected to grow so rapidly" and that Muslims are estimated to make up 7.2 percent of the Canadian population by 2036.[36]

What a contrast to the attitudes of so many Christians who argue for withdrawal from the public sphere. Perhaps Christians in the West should listen to arguably Europe's foremost philosopher of the last generation, Jürgen Habermas, when he pleads for the return of "religion" to the public square, no doubt having Christianity in mind.[37] Habermas knows democracy can't survive without (this) "religion" taking its rightful place in the political debate. Many Christians don't understand that. They dream of survival while abandoning their God-given calling to help shape public opinion.

All these trends of exploiting vulnerabilities are also apparent in Sub-Saharan Africa, even though Islamists are less likely to hide their militant side in that part of the world. In a country like South Africa, Islamists are gaining positions of influence despite a relatively small Muslim share of the population. Many African countries have disproportionately high numbers of Muslims in senior political positions.[38]

---

35 Gillian Cosgrove, "How the Muslims won the election", *National Post: Commentary*, August 7, 2004. She wrote, "[t]o put it bluntly, Muslims now hold the balance of power in at least 100 ridings". More than 80 percent of Canada's 700 000 Muslims at the time voted in the election, with the Liberal Party their overwhelming favourite, and hardly 3 percent voting Conservative.

36 "Muslim Canadian federal election turnout driven by fact 'so much was at stake", by Shanifa Nasser on *CBC News* website, November 20, 2015.

37 Eduardo Mendieta and Jonathan Vanantwerpen (editors), *The Power of Religion in the Public Sphere* (West Sussex: Columbia University Press: 2011), 4-5.

38 Sookhdeo provides more examples from Kenya, Tanzania, and the Ivory Coast, in *Dawa*, 85-87.

The Spread of *Sharia*[39]

Another very effective method of promoting *dawa* is by spreading *sharia* zones. Somewhere near London in the United Kingdom, one is greeted by a not-so-uncommon sign these days,[40]

You are Entering a Sharia-Controlled Zone
Islamic Rules Enforced
No alcohol
No pornography and prostitution
No music and concerts
No gambling
No drugs and smoking

For a Better Society

These are only some of the more benign rules of *sharia. Sharia* fully implemented involves much more. How much more? One way to know is to compare *sharia* with the *United Nations Universal Declaration of Human Rights*, which states that all humans are equal before the law in Article 7:

> All are equal before the law and are entitled, without any discrimination, to equal protection of the law. All are entitled to equal protection against any discrimination in violation of this Declaration and any incitement to such discrimination.[41]

Moreover, the same UDHR seeks to guarantee worldwide the freedom of conscience, expression, obtaining or imparting information, movement, etc. In America, these values have been enshrined in the *American Declaration of Independence* of 1776, which famously states:

---

39 Ibid., 46-51.

40 "As Islamic extremists declare Britain's first Sharia law zone, the worrying social and moral implications" DailyMail.com, July 29, 2011.

41 Sookhdeo, *Dawa*, 47.

> We hold these truths to be self-evident, that all men are created equal, that they are endowed by their Creator with certain unalienable rights, that among these are Life, Liberty and the pursuit of Happiness. [42]

Immanuel Kant (1724 – 1804) wrote from Königsberg in the eighteenth century: "There is only one Innate Right, the Birthright of Freedom" and that the essence of such freedom implies our independence from "the compulsory will of another".[43] That is why these ideas and values became inseparable from the freedom-loving societies of the West. During the years of the Second World War, the patriotic American painter from New York State, Norman Rockwell, became famous for his four paintings enshrining these rights and freedoms. The paintings were entitled "Freedom of Speech," "Freedom of Worship," "Freedom from Want," and "Freedom from Fear." Less than eight decades later freedom-loving people are desperately fighting to save these freedoms from extinction.

This makes it all the more impressive that an increasing number of renowned secular scholars—among whom are British historian Tom Holland and Canadian psychologist Jordan Peterson—have noted that these values stem from a uniquely Judeo-Christian cradle, and from Jesus of Nazareth in particular. It is hard to imagine that any other ideology or movement will have the spiritual stamina and fortitude to fight for and uphold these incredible values once Christianity has been relegated to the fringes of society as a persecuted minority.

Islamic *sharia* stands in direct opposition to these values. Traditional Muslims view *sharia* as a divine code of law that defines their faith and practice in every aspect of life. While Westerners traditionally see themselves as freedom-loving people, Islam views itself as a people in submission to Allah and *sharia* rather than a people of liberty. While not denying that far more emphasis should have been placed on our duties and responsibilities in the West (for at least the last century), it needs to be stressed that traditional Muslims place virtually *all* emphasis on duties and taboos

---

42 *Charters of Freedom – Founding Documents of American Independence* (Old Saybrook: Konecky & Konecky), 56.

43 Immanuel Kant, *The Science of Right*, in Vol. 42 of *Great Books of the Western World* (Chicago: Encyclopedia Britannica: Chicago, 1952), 401.

according to *sharia*, instead of on any supposed rights and freedoms. These Islamic duties and taboos range from proper personal hygiene, religious devotions, and marriage, to transportation, public decency, apostasy, business, slavery, and war. Nothing in life is excluded.

Sharia literally means "the path to the water". It seeks to distinguish between *halal* and *haram*, i.e., what is good and permissible from what is bad and forbidden. It does not address the heart or conscience but only outward acts. *Sharia* also defines all the punishments for forbidden acts. Physical penalties under *sharia* may include beheading, crucifixion, amputation, stoning, and public lashing in some countries and regions. "It is a remarkable fact," writes Ayaan Hirsi Ali in *Heretic*, "that after Friday prayers in Saudi Arabia, many men flock to the central squares to watch the implementation of Islamic justice."[44] Can anyone imagine Catholics, Baptists, Copts, or Jews doing the same after they have been to the church, the chapel, or synagogue, she asks? One of the Saudi kingdom's leading executioners told *Arab News* that he had executed as many as ten people in a single day. His children help him keeping his razor-sharp sword clean for severing the next unfortunate head.[45] Meanwhile, the Quran also forbids sympathy for those about to be punished, since they were disobedient to Allah (Surah 24:2).

Sharia keeps the Muslim world shackled to the seventh century, and yet astonishingly, an overwhelming majority of the world's five largest Muslim populations—Indonesia, Pakistan, Bangladesh, Egypt, and Nigeria—support *sharia*, according to a Pew Research Report of 2013.[46] It is essential to realize that *sharia remained the same* since the early Abbasid period (750-950) when it reached its full development.[47] *Sharia* reflects the social, religious, political, and economic conditions of the Islamic society of those times. Thus, whoever wishes to live under *sharia* today desires to live under Arab Muslim law of a millennium ago. Let us list just a few of the discriminatory laws under *sharia*:

---

44 See Ayaan Hirsi Ali, *Heretic* (New York: HarperCollins, 2015), 137.

45 Ibid., 141.

46 Ibid., 139-140.

47 Sookhdeo, *Dawa*, 46.

- A woman shall be compensated less than a man if she was inflicted with an injury.
- A Muslim shall only change his religion at the pain of death.
- Women may not appear in public without a *hijab*.
- Mohammed, the Quran, and Islam must at all times be safeguarded from all criticism.
- It is forbidden to deceive a fellow Muslim but perfectly fine to deceive an infidel.
- Anyone charged with committing an act of homosexuality should be killed

As we have said before, the problem with us Westerners is that we think everyone else thinks like us. The traditional Western worldview, values, and thought have all been shaped by our Judeo-Christian heritage and then by modernity. The UNDHR mentioned above is mainly based on that heritage, as were Rockwell's celebrated paintings.

The Muslim-majority-world grew out of altogether different soil. Despite some shared stories and beliefs, it has very little in common with the heritage and thought-world of the Judeo-Christian tradition. African Christians by and large know this well. Still, the ruling elites of the Anglosphere and Europe are only very reluctantly waking up to this fact, often preferring to live in denial.

The moral of the story is that *sharia* has little sympathy for our freedoms. The *Cairo Declaration of Human Rights in Islam,* adopted by the OIC on August 5, 1990, states as follows, (1) "all the rights and freedoms stipulated in this Declaration are subject to the Islamic Shariah" (Art. 24), and (2) "the Islamic Shariah is the only source of reference for the explanation or clarification of any of the articles in this Declaration (Art. 25)."[48]

There is thus an apparent clash of values between the UNDHR and the CDHRI. In no way can the two be reconciled or coexist in peace. The Strasbourg-based European Court of Human Rights ruled in 2003 that Islamic Sharia is "incompatible with the fundamental principles of democracy." An *Economist* poll published in 2015[49] reported that over 50 percent

48 Ibid., 48.

49 "Islam in Europe," *The Economist*, January 7, 2015, on economist.com.

of respondents in countries like Germany, Spain, France, and Switzerland felt Islam was incompatible with the West, with Britain and Sweden not far behind. Similarly, German Islam scholar Susanne Schröter wrote in *Die Tagespost* that "Islamists are not interested in democracy. On the contrary, they reject democracy because they only consider politics legitimate if it follows regulations that adhere to the politics of Muhammed in the seventh century."[50]

But that is also why Muslim communities in these countries often clamour for changes, not only to protect Islam but also to adopt its faith and worldview. Yet, little or no protection will be offered to non-Muslim communities once *sharia* is fully adopted. This has already been proven in *sharia* no-go zones in European cities like Paris, Malmö, London, Rotterdam, Brussels, and elsewhere.

To be plain and simple, demands that began with the need for prayer rooms at airports, *halal* foods, and the *hijab* will end with the elimination of democracy, the subjugation of Christianity and other religions, and the rule of *sharia*. There is no stopping halfway. The current battle for Africa's largest nation, Nigeria, is a salient reminder of this fact.[51] Moore and Cooper report in *The Last Jihad* that twelve of Nigeria's northern states were already governed by *sharia* by 2020. Changes made to the Constitution in 1999 enshrined Islam to such an extent that it feels as if the entire nation is Muslim, even though only half of its two hundred million citizens are. Or, as one military general told the two authors:

> The Constitution mentions Islam dozens of times in some form, but despite this country being half Christian—and a kind of democracy—there is not a single reference or inference related to Christianity.[52]

Such is the price to be paid for abandoning politics, or for being involved perhaps, and corrupt at the same time.

---

50 "Susanne Schröter: 'Der politische Islam schafft massive Probleme'", *Die Tagespost*, October 18, 2019, on die-tagespost.de.

51 See Sookhdeo, *Dawa*, 51.

52 Moore and Cooper, *The Next Jihad*, 6.

Islamic Finance and the *Halal* Industry[53]

The last two decades saw a spectacular rise in Islamic finance and banking. Islamic finance helps to strengthen the Islamic identity of Muslims. Western governments often support the introduction of Islamic finance by supporting its banks and institutions. London has become the global center for Islamic finance, and the UK is the most favoured location for *sharia* investors. Though less than two percent of South Africans are Muslim, it has one of the strongest Islamic finance sectors outside the Muslim world. According to Patrick Sookhdeo, this fact only empowers Islamists while weakening Muslim moderates, for Islamic finance is widely used to further *dawa*.[54]

Halal food-laws are very effective means by which *sharia* gains a foothold in Muslim-minority contexts. The *halal/haram* (good/evil) distinction and teaching are central in the Quran and *hadith*. Several criteria must be met for food to qualify as *halal* since *halal* food marks the boundary between the *umma* and the infidels, not unlike Jewish *kosher* laws. The difference with *kosher* products is that *halal* food is being marketed for us all, since all of us are Muslims (without knowing it) according to Islam, and Allah knows best what is good for us. Moreover, there is even a growing perception among the general public in the West and elsewhere that *halal* food is safer. The *halal* food market is currently estimated at $685 billion worldwide. Some African countries like Zimbabwe and Botswana, which have virtually zero Muslims, have a meat trade that is almost 100 percent *halal*. By buying and eating *halal*, we are all financing *dawa*, as we are doing with our high demand for Middle Eastern oil, flying Qatar and Turkey Airlines or signing up for *Al Jazeera Television*. An online video that went viral in South Africa claimed that it is almost impossible today to buy any food from a supermarket in the Western Cape, without buying *halal* and thereby supporting *dawa*.

The Islamization of Knowledge[55]

Ever since the late seventies and early eighties, the idea of the Islamization of knowledge has been pushed by Islamic scholars. It involves the

53 See Sookhdeo, Dawa, 51-57.

54 Ibid., 51-53.

55 See Sookhdeo, *Dawa*, 73-77.

transformation of every academic discipline in the light of Islam. All ideas and concepts opposed to the spirit of Islam must eventually be purged from textbooks and libraries in the Muslim-minority world. Mona Abul-Fadl explained it in these words: "The West is ripe for an Islamic transformation, and Islam is the civilizing agent and force of renewal and regeneration that the West needs."[56]

All systems of knowledge must be based on Allah's revelation. *Tawhid* is the central principle of unity and must control all human knowledge. The bottom line is one God, faith, law, and knowledge. Islamists view the disintegration of Western secular knowledge as the logical result of rejecting *tawhid*. The Islamization of knowledge includes: (1) the funding of academic chairs, (2) encouraging Muslims to take up positions in non-Muslim universities, (3) mass publication, and (4) the establishment of Islamic universities to promote and cultivate Islamic culture.

Islamic institutions tend to maintain a moderate face to Western academia and Christian institutions cooperating with them. Dr. Abul Fadl holds that the fate of civilization lies in the balance of culture, not in power. Transforming culture should be the goal of Islamization. Rather than making a direct bid for power, Muslims must first Islamize knowledge, says Abul Fadl.

The Islamization of knowledge logically leads to something else, the sanitizing of Islam. To make Islam look as good as possible to the ignorant Western mind and any potential convert, all traces of its dark side must be purged. Islamists, therefore, have launched a large-scale project at sanitizing Islam. One essential part of this project is to control the narrative about Islam. This is nothing new or strange. As much as the Soviet-era rulers sought to control the narrative about the USSR or the Communist Party of China is doing today, Islam is doing its best to make sure the free world does not get all the facts. One clear example is how every flyer explaining Islam has a chapter on "Women in Islam." The objective is to allay any fears that women may be oppressed in Islam or be discriminated against in any way.

---

56 Ibid., 73.

In fact, any oppressive system—whether one ruling a home, a cult, or a state—will seek at all costs to prevent the truth from leaking out, portraying itself in the best possible light by "controlling the narrative". Otherwise, it must disintegrate. Unfortunately, Western mainstream media are increasingly exhibiting these features as well, protecting the interests of a small powerful globalist elite, while betraying the interests of the people at large. An oppressive system only reveals its true face when it has gained enough confidence to intimidate opponents into submission. That is what happened during the Bolshevist Revolution in 1917-18, or during the rise of National Socialism in Germany in the 1930s. It is also what happened during the vast expansion of Islam through its golden age. Fear works, but it only works when the opposition is relatively weak and, above all, morally and spiritually compromised.

Therefore, Christians must forever be ready to support those who dare to break the silence and stand up for the truth against whatever form of tyranny, for this is what it means to follow the Lamb. We must also be on the lookout to avoid a very common opposite error, namely to lend credibility to counter-propaganda, painting a distorted image of the "adversary".

Muslim history nowadays is being sanitized on many levels, like clearing from universities textbooks that are deemed unfriendly, or by closing post-graduate programs in Islamic studies that are deemed too revealing, or by erasing Muslim atrocities from history that are too damaging. Meanwhile, Western atrocities (like those during the Crusades) are being emphasized and exaggerated all along. Unpleasant features of Muslim history are left out, while those who dare to point it out run the risk of being labeled Islamophobic. Dr. John Azuma, a former Muslim from West Africa and currently associate professor at Columbia Theological Seminary, states it as follows:

> Hence, in the study of Islam in the West, the dominant convention is that a critical approach is reserved for the Christian past but forbidden for the Muslim past… The net result is a romantic picture of the history of Islam avoiding and sometimes denying such issues as the jihadists' slaughter and massive enslavement of traditional African believers.[57]

57 "The Legacy of Arab-Islam in Africa – Author Interview", *Samuel Green – YouTube*. See John A. Azumah, *The Legacy of Arab-Islam in Africa* (London: Oneworld Publications, 2021).

Another example is the effort by Turkey to squash all references to the Armenian genocide of 1915, while responding in anger to Western countries who don't do the same. Another example (according to Lutheran author Alvin J. Schmidt) is how Dante of Alighieri's *Divine Comedy* of the fourteenth century has been eliminated from many libraries.[58]

Other examples of the sanitizing of Islam are found in pamphlets promoting Islam to contemporary uninformed people. In *You Deserve to Know About Islam*, the reader is completely left in the dark about Islam's real ideological and militant side; only good and beautiful things about the religion are mentioned, to which few will object.[59] In *A Brief Illustrated Guide to Islam*, we read,

> The Prophet Mohammed (pbuh) was a perfect example of an honest, just, merciful, compassionate, truthful and brave human being. Though he was a man, he was removed from all evil characteristics, and strove solely for the sake of God and His reward in the Hereafter. Moreover, in all his actions and dealings he was ever mindful and fearful of God.[60]

We will later see how Muslim brochures like *You Deserve to Know About Islam* or *A Brief Illustrated Guide* and countless others, succeed in pulling the wool over countless ignorant eyes.

Islamization through Education and Islamic Centers[61]

Educational centers around the world are also promoting *dawa*. A good illustration is the Muslim Council of Britain. It required state-run primary schools in Britain to (1) make changes in attire, allowing for the *hijab*, (2) create Muslim prayer rooms, (3) allow for alternative sports activities that would avoid cross-gender contact, and (4) introduce Islamic worship

58 Alvin J. Schmidt, *The Great Divide* (Boston: Regina Orthodox Press, 2004), 19. Because Dante has Islam's prophet weeping in the lowest circle of hell in Canto 28, this Western classic is on the blacklist of shunned textbooks for students in many Western universities, all due to Muslim pressure.

59 *You Deserve to Know About Islam* (Niagara Falls, ON: Masjid al-Noor Islamic Society).

60 I.H. Ibrahim, *A Brief Illustrated Guide to Understanding Islam*, 2nd Edition, (Houston, 1997).

61 Sookhdeo, *Dawa*, 81-84.

where any number of Muslims attend.[62] Sookhdeo writes how an unsuspecting high school of a thousand students in South Africa was radically changed by sixty Muslims flooding its membership meeting and voting for a Muslim chairperson. A week later, Christian prayers, banners, and Bibles were forbidden. Within a year, the principal and most Christian teachers were replaced.

Moreover, some Western universities that used to be hotbeds for Marxism have been turned into havens for Islamic radicalism. Several Islamic terrorists in Britain had links to British universities. Two of the seven 2005 London bombers studied at British universities, while Muslim societies at universities tend to be dominated by Islamists.

What is more, these centers at many Western universities are usually funded by rich Arab states. Several peace-loving Muslim academics in Britain have warned in the past that these institutions represent the views of those who fund them, and that such funding always comes with strings attached. A report from 2009 stated that the largest amount of foreign funding to British Universities came from Arab and Islamic sources. Between 1995 and 2008, eight universities (including Cambridge and Oxford) accepted a combined sum of 233.5 million pounds from Muslim rulers. 23 percent of all foreign gifts and grants to American universities between 1996 to 2012 came from Middle Eastern countries, amounting to $294 billion. The top donors were Saudi Arabia, Qatar, the United Arab Emirates, and Kuwait. Saudi donor Prince Alwaleed Bin Talal donated $20 million each to Georgetown University and Harvard in 2005, to be spent on their Islamic Centers.

Mosque building[63]

The Muslim World League highlighted the importance of mosques as the focal point of *dawa* in 1975. In Muslim-minority countries, the campaign began by simply asking for prayer rooms. Today Britain and France each have at least two thousand mosques. In Sub-Saharan Africa mosques are sometimes built at intervals of a few kilometers along main roads and railroads.

62 Ibid., 81-82.

63 See Sookhdeo, *Dawa*, 89-91.

The belief is that Allah claims everything as far as the call to prayer (*adhan*) is heard. It was mentioned to me that there is currently a plan to build a mosque at five-kilometer intervals along the railway from Lusaka (Zambia) to Beira (Mozambique), running through Zimbabwe. At the same time, hardly one percent of the immediate population is Muslim. This proliferation of mosque building is seen as a sign of growing Muslim confidence. The mosque's role in *dawa* is essential. Islam teaches that there is a special blessing living within the reach of the call to prayer. By the same token *sharia* declares the sound of church bells as *haram*; the very work of the devil.

The saying goes: build a hive, and the bees will come. Mosque-building has been a very successful *dawa* strategy. In Tanzania, where many road-side mosques were built in areas where initially no Muslims lived in 1990, most of them were filled by 2013, often with former (nominal) Christians. Visiting a coastal city in South Africa in recent years, I was personally informed how Muslims began laying the foundation for a mosque in a neighborhood with hardly any Muslims in sight, and without any building permits, to the dismay of the residents. Construction was only put on hold after significant community opposition.

Beyond South Africa and Namibia, Christian church buildings in Africa often look shabby and shaky compared to mosques. That is meant to send a message to the everyone about who is the strongest. Oversized structures dominating the landscape intend to make a statement, like the spectacular newly inaugurated mosque in Cologne, Germany.

The explosion of mosques is meant to sink deep into the consciousness: the landscape is changing! And it is often not only changing in one direction but in two. Mr. Edouard de la Maze, president of the Observatory of Religious Heritage in France, informed the French media how that is happening in his country. While every two weeks, a new mosque is being built somewhere in France, one catholic church building or monument is being destroyed.[64] He spoke to the media in April 2021 after another "accidental fire" destroyed a church in Normandy. This fire occurred two years after an "accidental fire" destroyed the famous Notre Dame in Paris. Two-thirds of the fires destroying church buildings in France are due to arson. In

64 Either by demolition, destruction, transformation, collapse or fire.

2018 alone, there were 877 attacks on catholic places of worship, a fivefold increase in ten years.[65]

Not only does the visible landscape change by mosques springing up like mushrooms, the same holds true for the audible landscape. When a Turkish mosque in Eschweiler, thirty miles west of Cologne, began for the first time to issue the *adhan*, calling Muslims to prayer, it was dubbed an "historical event" and attended by dignitaries, including the Turkish consul.[66] The local imam expressed his hopes that "the public call to prayer will be a symbol of a tolerant, intercultural and interreligious common coexistence." The local mayor echoed similar sentiments. However long such tolerance and coexistence will last is an open question, considering that the sonorous *adhan*—five times a day, seven days a week—can be heard loud and clear from great distances. Hearing the cry "Allahu Akbar!" ("Allah is greater!") every day will undoubtedly remind all of Europe that it is fast becoming Eurabia, a part of the Middle East.

In fact, on New Year's Eve of 2015, Cologne's ladies found out with shock what such "tolerance and coexistence" might mean for the future. Many of them were unexpectedly groped and sexually harassed by some of the million-plus refugees Chancellor Angela Merkel invited into Germany the previous summer, when these women joyfully welcomed the New Year on the city square on *Silvesternacht*. The event left an even deeper scar on the European consciousness than terror attacks of recent decades did. Even more shocking was the response of the German police who told the women that night: "You should have known. Make sure you celebrate elsewhere in the future."[67]

Interreligious Dialogue[68]

I mentioned earlier how attending a conference in Kenya inspired me to raise awareness about Islamic *dawa*. Three-quarters through that

65 "One Mosque Built, One Church Destroyed, Every Two Weeks in France" by Catharine Salgado, in *The National Pulse Podcast*, May 9, 2021, on thenationalpulse.com.

66 "The Islamization of Germany in 2013" by Soeren Kern, *Perspectives on Europe and America*, January 15, 2014, on soerenkern.com.

67 See Ayaan Hirsi Ali, "Silvesternacht" in *Prey* (New York: Harper Collins, 2021), 64-67.

68 See Sookhdeo, *Dawa*, 91-93.

conference, having heard in detail from our speaker how Islam and militant Islamic movements are sprawling deep into Sub-Saharan Africa, and after hearing several African pastors share their stories of Islamist persecution, a prominent white clergyman of the Dutch Reformed Church in South Africa stood up to share his thoughts. He suggested that religious dialogue, including "pulpit exchange," could help stem the tide. He explained how—as a gesture of good-will after the horrific attack on two mosques in New Zealand in 2019 (killing over fifty Muslims)—Cape Town's most historic Dutch Reformed Church invited a local imam to come and tell her faithful more about the Muslim religion. The imam spoke from the pulpit where Dr. Andrew Murray and other faithful Christian pastors preached for well over a century.

The African pastors were confused, still somewhat hesitant perhaps to oppose a white man in a public setting. You could hear a pin drop as our speaker, Dr. Sookhdeo, patiently tried to convince the Afrikaner churchman in several exchanges that his idea was not so bright. What in the world could cause such naiveté, one may ask? This is a good example of what was mentioned before: believing that they think like us, and that we share similar agendas. Because we want peace, they also want peace, at least the kind of peace we have in mind. Thus, if we are nice to them, they will be nice to us, so let us have dialogue, common prayer, and even "pulpit exchanges." The problem with these assumptions is that they are rooted in a typical liberal worldview, underestimating man's fallen nature, our adversary's deceptive strategies, and the nature of the battle between good and evil.

Dialogue will work with some. But what about the rest? Just as true Christians want to follow Jesus, most Muslims want to follow Mohammed (see Surah 33:21). Jesus taught his followers to love their enemies. Mohammed and the Quran taught the opposite. These two views are mutually exclusive, which should not surprise us, since the two monotheist deities behind them are polar opposites of each other.

Why did this former DRC General Synod moderator not get it, after hearing everything we were told about Islamism that week? His liberal views blinded him from a reality that was encroaching upon his very own country. For as the former Somali Muslim Ayaan Hirsi Ali stated:

> Islamists achieve far more through *dawa* than when they confine themselves to blowing things up and stabbing people to death. The threat is not as obvious. Jihad and the use of violence tend to provoke an immediate response. With *dawa*, on the other hand, it is possible to talk about charity, spirituality, and religion—and then compare it to regular religious proselytizing missions. In a free society, what reasonable person would take issue with that?[69]

Islamists love to engage in interreligious dialogue with Christians to promote Islam because they know they enter such a conversation with a clear advantage. Hasan al-Turbani, former leader of the National Islamic Front in Sudan, said interreligious dialogue belongs to the duties of *dawa*.[70] The late Ahmed Deedat from Durban, South Africa, once said interreligious dialogue aims to weaken and divide Christian churches and hinder Christian mission to Muslims. In fact, Friday prayers in the mosque often call for division among Christians.

So, what are some very likely consequences of such dialogue? It could very well be that Christians begin to tamper with their doctrine, even with Bible translations, to find a *via media* that would not offend, believing the popular unfounded notion that "all three Abrahamic religions" are basically the same. With time it might lead them to try and avoid terms that would offend Muslims—like calling Jesus the Son of God or believing the living God is triune—while affirming that Mohammed is a prophet of God. That may then cause them to turn on each other, for some may love these compromises, while others won't. And so, the mosque's prayer for division will be answered. Finally, they may also refrain from speaking up for persecuted brothers and sisters in Muslim lands, fearing to harm "good relations" and hoping in vain that they will get an opportunity to speak about it later. And, of course, they will refrain from challenging Muslims about *their* beliefs and their critique of Christianity, something these Christians typically won't be afraid of doing when meeting with Mormons, Hindus,

69 "Why Islamism became woke" by Ayaan Hirsi Ali, *UnHerd*, July 13, 2021, on unherd.com.

70 Sookhdeo, *Dawa*, 91.

or atheists, for that matter. The underlying reason for all of this is fear. And that again points to the absence of the Holy Spirit's power and presence among his people.

A good case in point is the *Yale Statement* of November 2007.[71] Three hundred evangelical leaders signed the *Yale Statement* in response to a Muslim open letter called *A Common Word Between Us and You*. The *Yale Statement* came close to accepting Islam as a legitimate way to God, Mohammed as a prophet of God, and the Quran as the revelation of God. Though the three hundred Christian signatories would probably not agree with such an understanding of their views, they have unwittingly given the impression that they did. They neither affirmed the deity of Christ nor his exalted person and office. Seemingly unwittingly they succumbed to the Quran's view that Mohammed is superior to Jesus.

Interfaith dialogue is being funded widely, even by Western governments, since it creates the impression of peaceful coexistence. While Westerners might cherish such meetings for their "common interests and partnership," political Islam's aim with these dialogues is quite different: to advance through *dawa* by subtly weakening the church's *spiritual immune system*.

Just how vulnerable well-meaning Westerners can be and how easily their spiritual immune system can be compromised, was shown in the immediate aftermath of 9/11. These were days in which Lance Morrow could write in *Time Magazine* that "healing is inappropriate now, and dangerous. There will be time later for the tears and the sorrow. A day cannot live in infamy without the nourishment of rage. Let's have rage." He even called for "a ruthless indignation that doesn't leak away in a week or two."[72]

Yet a few days later, Barbara Amiel, writing for Canada's *Maclean's*, mentioned how "our leaders seem to be hugging every available member of the Islamic community in sight."[73] They did so believing that 99.9 percent of Muslims "are not terrorists." And so it was in these days, on a Saturday

71 Ibid., 91-92.

72 Lance Morrow "The Case for Rage and Retribution", *Time Magazine*, September 11, 2001.

73 Barbara Amiel, "Terrorism's real 'root cause'", *Maclean's*, October 8, 2001, 21.

in September 2001, that Trinity Episcopalian Church at Copley Square in Boston held an interfaith event with Muslims. The following Sunday morning, the Reverend Samuel T. Lloyd spoke about the participation of Dr. Walid Fitaihi of the Harvard Medical School, representing the Islamic Society of Boston, as follows:

> Many of us experienced a remarkable moment of hope at the service yesterday when Dr. Walid Fataihi (sic), a doctor at Harvard Medical School and member of the Islamic Society of Boston, spoke words of healing and support. His gentle, holy manner touched everyone in the church. And it seemed an enormously hopeful sign of a divided world looking for ways to draw closer together.[74]

For the Reverend, this interfaith event was an affirmation of a common humanity, indeed of reconciliation and hope. But what of Dr. Fitaihi? What was his perspective? That became clear not in Boston but far away in Egypt four days later when the weekly *Al-Ahram Al-Arabi* placed a letter from the Harvard doctor on one of its pages:

> On Saturday, September 15, I went with my wife and children to the biggest church in Boston ... to represent Islam by special invitation ... I sat with my wife and children in the front row, next to the mayor's wife. In his sermon, the priest defended Islam as a monotheistic religion, telling the audience that I represented the Islamic Society of Boston.
>
> After the sermon was over, he stood at my side as I read an official statement issued by the leading Muslim clerics condemning the incident [i.e., the attacks]. The statement explained Islam's stance and principles, and its sublime precepts. Afterwards, I read Koran verses... These were moments that I will never forget, because the entire church burst into tears upon hearing the passages of the words of Allah!!
>
> Emotion swept over us. One said to me "I do not understand the Arabic language, but there is no doubt that the things you said are the words of Allah". As she left the church weeping, a woman put a piece of paper in my hand; on the paper was written: "Forgive us for our past and for our

74 Durie, *The Third Choice*, 226-227.

> present. Keep proselytizing to us." Another man stood at the entrance of the church, his eyes teary, and said: "You are just like us; no, you are better than us."

It is incredible what ignorance and fear can do to a people without deep convictions and faith. And that even after the statement from the esteemed Muslim clerics, read in that Boston church, which called the Manhattan cataclysm of 9/11 an "incident"! Forgotten already is all the rage *Time Magazine* spoke about, for fear was now in overdrive. Dr. Mark Durie, from whose book I got this remarkable story, commented: "Fitaihi's report of American Christians crying on hearing the Quran evokes for Muslim readers the story of the conversion of the first group of Christians to come to Islam. On hearing the recitation from the Quran, their eyes flowed with tears, and they entered Islam."[75]

The only type of dialogue Christians may engage with Muslims in—which would honour Christ, strengthen his church, and even reach Muslim hearts—is robust polemics in love. For this purpose, a brilliant new book has recently appeared: *Questions to ask your Muslim Friends*. It is crucial for every Christian seeking to reach out to Muslims.[76] Tools like these place us on a level playing field with our Muslim friends, where we may challenge each other's practices and beliefs by asking honest questions and giving honest answers. Such an approach will not only demand Muslim respect but will also inspire Christian bravery and faith. Anything less than that, especially when *they* have the liberty to speak freely, but *we* must always hold back, will prove not only to be futile, but downright dangerous for the entire world. The robust, friendly polemics of someone like Dr. Jay Smith at *Speakers Corner* in London for many years, is a good example of how to engage our Muslim friends fearlessly in truth and love.[77]

---

75 Ibid, 227.

76 Co-authored by Beth Peltola and Tim Dieppe (London: Wilberforce Publications, 2022).

77 See his videos on *YouTube*.

CHAPTER 6

DAWA AND DECEPTION

Inherent to *dawa* is deliberate misinformation. Even a cursory study of Islam will prove that it is, *par excellence,* a religion of deception. Allah is actually called the best of deceivers or schemers in the Quran.[1] As I am writing, I have access to half a dozen Muslim pamphlets promoting Islam to a Western audience. Reading them, one can hardly believe that you are dealing with the same ideas promoted in Islamic sources.

One of these pamphlets is called *You Deserve to Know about Islam*. It is an excellent example of how Islam is presented to the West, since it is very brief and straightforward. Reading it, one cannot but marvel at how this movement from the seventh century is being photo-brushed from beginning to end. You have to ask yourself: "Does this speak of the same Quran I have on my bookshelf? Is this the Mohammed we are told about in the *hadith* and the *sira*?"[2] Why is so much hidden behind a veil?

Why is so much detail about Islam's prophet contained in the *hadith* and *sira* hidden from the public eye and from the vast majority of Muslims?

1 Surah 3:54 and 8:30.

2 The official biography of Mohammed dating from two hundred years after he died.

Is it because it would be too much to stomach? It would indeed be hard for anyone to associate things like the following with a holy man: raiding unsuspecting caravans; having fits that feel like demon possession; marrying a six-year-old girl and consummating the marriage when she was nine; overseeing the beheading of over seven hundred Jewish captives on a single day; then taking the prettiest widow for yourself as a wife; having eleven wives plus concubines, and being sexually intimate with many of them every night; or taking revenge on a young poetess for having annoyed you, by ordering her execution. These are but "the ears of the hippo," as Africans would say. It baffles the mind that "holy books" could hold forth such a life *as most worthy of all to follow*. Why do none of these popular pamphlets share these details about Mohammed with us, or the grim punishments for apostasy that await new converts, should they later have second thoughts? Why not be honest about the position of women and "unbelievers" under *sharia*? What about forced marriages, polygamy, wife-beating, female genital mutilation, and honour killings?

Yes, we understand there will be peace for all who submit to Allah, but what about the rest? If the Quran and the *hadith* can be so blunt and bold about all these things, why hide it from our eyes? There are many quotation marks in the popular pamphlet *You Deserve to Know About Islam*, but do not think it refers the reader to any sources. Nothing can be verified. We must simply trust the author. And then, in the back, there is the usual list of glowing comments by famous individuals such as Prince Charles, George Bernard Shaw, James A Michener, Mahatma Gandhi, etc.[3] What a contrast to Christianity where every hint of deception is condemned by all the prophets, the Messiah and his apostles. Christianity never seeks endorsements from anyone, least from celebrities, for God alone is true, while all men are said to be liars *in themselves* (Rom. 3:4).

Another good example of deception concerns the well-known phrase from the Quran so often quoted in the West, that "there is no compulsion in religion" (Surah 2:256). It leaves the impression that faith is an intensely personal thing in Islam, that everyone is free to make up their own mind. The context of Surah 2:256 tells a different story. It has coercion

3 *You Deserve to Know*, 3.

and compulsion written all over it. When looking at things a bit closer, one realizes that the Quran contains peaceful and militant passages. The peaceful ones reflect the earlier Meccan period in Mohammed's life when he tried to persuade others by reason. The militant passages followed later when he moved to Medina and advanced his new religion by the sword. What is more, the later violent passages always "abrogate" the earlier peaceful ones if there should be any contradiction. Are outsiders made aware of this, when Muslim flyers quote seemingly benign sayings in the Quran?

Another example of the blatant disinformation campaign the world is being subjected to is the well-known saying promoting Islam as a "religion of peace." No one will deny that millions of Muslims worldwide want to live peaceably with those around them. But that unfortunately does not mean that *Islam* is a peaceful religion. According to its founders, Islam means *submission*, and that's the only way to achieve peace.[4] Hussein Mansour writes:

> The violence (of Islamic origins) is viewed as merely a means to achieve the final peace of messianic-like days. The beheading of the infidel is the prerequisite to settle the rivalry. The annihilation of the Jew is an (sic) necessity to end malice and all conflict. To usher in a world without enemies of Allah is to clean the world of its contradictions and its incoherencies.[5]

A Quran in my possession explains in its introduction that *jihad* is, in *most cases*, a "peaceful ideological struggle" and has nothing to do with violence. Yet that is hard to believe in light of what is so clearly written in Surahs 2, 5 and 9 of that same Quran, to name but three.[6] However, the paragraph explaining *jihad* goes even further, cleverly quoting Jesus' words from Matthew 10:34: "I have not come to bring peace on earth, but the sword." The author states that "it would not be right to conclude that the religion preached by Christ was one of war and violence, *for such utterances relate*

4 The plain sense reading of Surahs 2, 3, 4, 5, 8 and 9 among others in the Quran makes this crystal clear.

5 Mansour, *Minority of One*, 73.

6 *The Quran*, translated by Maulana Wahiduddin Khan, (New Delhi: Goodword Books, 2010), p. xiv – xvii.

purely to particular occasions" (emphasis mine). The comparison is simply astounding. This author wants to exonerate Islam by pointing to these words of Christ, as if to say, "See, they also have violent texts!" Not only did Jesus' words never refer to any call for violence whatsoever (as *all* Biblical scholars would know), but they are being used to help "prove" that the Quran is not wrong in calling us to *jihad*, at least sometimes. Ironically, Jesus' reference is not about taking up the sword but that those who follow him should prepare to face the sword for his name's sake. As Tertullian wrote, Christians were not called to slay, but, if necessary, to be slain for Christ.[7]

The battle between Christianity and Islam has first of all to do with transparency, with how radically different the two faiths view the virtue of honesty. God's apostle sets the standard in I Cor 4:1-2 and II Cor 4:1-2. There is no place for deception in the Christian mission. Paul wrote to the Corinthians saying, "we have renounced secret and shameful ways; we do not use deception, nor do we distort the word of God." In *dawa*, deception is the name of the game. Muslims are taught to use double-speak to defend Islam, "even with their mother's milk."[8]

Dawa and *Taqiyya*

It is hard for Westerners to realize how deeply rooted and pervasive Islamic deception is. It is unfathomable, to say the least. Australian imam Mohammed Tawhidi, who trained at the best Islamic institutions in Iran, Iraq, and Egypt, provides three hundred pages of evidence of lies and deception. This deception is called *taqiyya* by the insiders of Islam.[9]

Ever since the U.S. launched the so-called *War on Terror* twenty years ago, the notion that anyone questioning Islam as a religion of peace was an Islamophobe, was widely promoted. President Obama went so far as to claim that it is simply unthinkable that any world religion could perpetrate violence by virtue of its faith. We were told that our issue was with a few

7 Tertullian, *De Corona*, Chapter 1, on newadvent.org.

8 Mansour, 21.

9 See *The Tragedy of Islam - Admissions of a Muslim Imam* (Adelaide: Reason Books, 2018).

militant Muslims who hijacked their religion.[10] It was not with the real representatives of Islam.

All of this was a fantasy world of politicians. Those who know what they are talking about tell us that violent Islam is actually less of a concern. The more subtle side of *dawa* should really concern us, since it is so hard to spot. Daniel Pipes, author and expert on Islam, observed that non-violent methods are often far more effective than violent ones and pose a far greater threat to democratic societies.[11] Michael Waller, an authority on the Muslim Brotherhood, perhaps the most influential Muslim organization in the world today, lists the following points summarizing the movement's strategy:[12]

- It believes that the end generally justifies the means and that all forms of violence are permissible to achieve and maintain that end;
- It recognizes that violence must be waged when necessary and condemned, when necessary, but never be rejected outright as a tool of political warfare;
- It believes that violence is often unnecessary, undesirable, and counter-productive and that some of its best gains are made through political, economic, legal, social, and cultural means;
- It believes that everyone, Muslim and non-Muslim, who resists its doctrine or refuses to submit to its domination, is a strategic enemy.

When reading these points carefully, how can anyone possibly deny that the total submission of the whole world to Allah and *sharia* is the Brotherhood's goal? Waller says that the Brotherhood operates overtly when possible and covertly where it is banned or suffering from a negative reputation. It also uses many front organizations to perform charitable, cultural, religious, political, economic, and social work, thereby masking its real intentions from a gullible world.[13] The main difference between the Brotherhood and the Salafis is that the former believes it is legitimate to use the democratic process, while the latter doesn't.[14]

---

10 See chapter 12.

11 Sookhdeo, *Dawa*, 4.

12 Waller, "The Muslim Brotherhood", 69.

13 Ibid.,71.

14 Mansour, *Minority of One*, 52.

An example of the Brotherhood's surreptitious nature was revealed in its response to a planned attack on the U.S. Embassy in Cairo, coinciding with another catastrophic attack on the U.S. Embassy in Benghazi, Libya, on September 11, 2011. The Brotherhood leadership had just come to power in Egypt and was reluctant to condemn these attacks. Only a "backlash from Washington" caused it as an organization—and Mohammed Morsi as Egypt's new president—to soften its position. But again, deception was written all over it. In its English-language statements (included in a letter to the *New York Times*) it sounded resolutely against violence and expressed condolences, but in its Arabic statements, it remained firm. That caused a U.S. Embassy official in Cairo to thank the Brotherhood for its condolences offered, and to add: "By the way, have you checked out your own Arabic feeds? I hope you know we read those too."[15]

I was once told in a hotel in Tanzania that the same could be said of *Al Jazeera's* English and Arabic language channels. There is one message for the world and another for the insiders in Arabic. *Al Jazeera* is based in Qatar, where most of the Brotherhood's elite reside and from where much terrorism is reportedly being sponsored.[16] Qatar was also the first to recognize the Taliban as Afghanistan's new government in August of 2021.

But why is it so crucial to understand the deceptive nature of *dawa*? Because the advance of Islamification in any society will be very hard to reverse by peaceful means, says Patrick Sookhdeo.[17] Muslims may use democratic means to gain political power. Still, they will then use that power to ban further elections as un-Islamic, for how could "infidels" and "apostates" know better than Allah how to run a country? Freedom of speech is used to promote the Muslim cause, but once the political goals are achieved, free speech is shut down to prevent any criticism. As such, Islam bears the hallmarks of a totalitarian ideology aimed at drastically reshaping society and then putting a complete stop to all further change. Little wonder Bertrand Russel could write in 1920 that "Bolshevism is to

15 Waller, "The Muslim Brotherhood" 69-70.

16 "Follow the Money. Qatar Accused in London of Funding Terrorism" *The Duran*, on theduran.com.

17 Sookhdeo, *Dawa*, 4.

be reckoned with Mohammedanism, rather than with Christianity and Buddhism."[18] The courageous Shia imam Mohammed Tawhidi, wrote:

> As imams we were commanded to stay silent, to manipulate the truth and even trained to escape questions which corner us, through deception and convenient answers. These subjects are known as "Lessons in Eloquence", which revolve around literature but also taught us terminologies and phrases that would help us escape or divert certain questions that could expose the reality of Islamic extremism.[19]

This remarkable man, nominated for the "Australian of the Year Award" in 2019, quoted one of his teachers, who said about Islam's first caliphs: "We must not mention their wrongdoings, because the many virtues they have will exceed and hide their mistakes and atone them."[20]

It can safely be said, says the Australian imam, that most Muslims are extremely sensitive about this subject. Extremists are known to react violently whenever the corruption in Muslim ideology and customs is exposed. Imams are trained to hide the truth, not only from the world but even from their own people. That is why Tawhidi calls for the exposure of those many scholars who hide the violence and terrorism committed in the history of Islam. He relates, for instance, how the tragic murder of Mohammed's daughter, Fatima, with her unborn child, committed by Abu Bakr and Umar, was all covered up in Islam. This Islamic technique of deliberately hiding the truth has a particular name, *taqiyya*.[21]

Moderate Muslim Voices Failing to Get Our Attention

By far, not all Muslims are actively involved in *dawa*, even though they are supposed to be. Many Muslims want to live peacefully with their neighbours and just continue with their lives. Millions of them would hate to live under an Islamic theocracy, because they are very concerned about the

18 Stephen Ulph, "Islamism and Totalitarianism: The Challenge of Comparison" in *Fighting the Ideological War* (McLean, VA: Isaac Publishing: McLean, 2012), 45.
19 Mohammed Tawhidi, *The Tragedy of Islam*, 80.
20 Ibid., 81.
21 Ibid., 181. See also Mansour, *Minority of One*, 52.

aims and strategies of *dawa, and* long to see an Islamic reformation. But it seems they are in the minority.

We have just heard the voice of one such Muslim scholar, Mohammed Tawhidi. In an urgent message to the *Christian Broadcasting Network* (CBN), Tawhidi voiced his deep concern about the advance of radical Islam around the world, especially in Western countries. He says it is still possible to stop its advance, but Western powers lack the willpower to do so due to their paralyzing political correctness.[22] Fareed Zakaria of CNN is another moderate voice calling out radical Islam. He is alarmed about the spread of Wahhabism, the worst form of Sunni Islam.[23] Zakaria mentions that despite all the noise about Iran being the world's "main sponsor of terror," it is well-known that 90 percent of all terror attacks are Sunni-based and have connections with Saudi Arabia.[24] Tawhidi confirms this. Thankfully, some high Saudi officials are growing increasingly uneasy about Saudi links with international terrorism and its brutal application of *sharia.*

These moderating voices are by no means the only ones. In a book entitled *Reforming Islam – Progressive Voices from the Arab Muslim World,* at least a dozen or more advocates for reform speak out from within Islam.[25] In Canada, after the horrific attack of 9/11, several Muslim leaders spoke out against radicals in their own country. When a Toronto Mosque warned against saying "Merry Christmas", and against the befriending of Christians, Syed Sohail Raza of the Muslim Canadian Congress replied: "These are the kinds of bigots we don't need in our religion, and we don't need in Canada."[26]

The only problem is that such bold moderate Muslim voices are often in the minority and have Islamic sources and history against them. The story of Shaykh Mohammed Hisham Kabbani of Detroit is a good case

---

22 Muslim tells Christians, "We tried warning you, it's time to wake up," *CBN News*, February 5, 2019, on cbn.com.

23 For many such voices see also *Reforming Islam,* ed. by Stephen Ulph and Patrick Sookhdeo (McLean, VA: Almuslih Publications, 2014).

24 Terence Ward, *The Wahhabi Code* (New York: Arcade Publishing, 2018), 8.

25 Edited by Stephen Ulph and Patrick Sookhdeo (Almuslih Publications: McLean, 2014).

26 Catharine Porter, "Mosque warns against saying Merry Christmas" in *Toronto Star*, December 28, 2002, A6.

in point. He warned in the nineties that "extremism has spread to 80 percent of the Muslims in the U.S." and that most mosques in the country are run by extremist ideologies. He was silenced and vilified, even called a Zionist agent who brought the entire Muslim community in the U.S. under "unjustified suspicion." But then 9/11 happened. In the years following, federal investigations and terrorism trials proved that Kabbani was indeed correct.[27]

Former Somali Muslim, Ayaan Hirsi Ali, hopes for an Islamic reformation *along the lines* of the Protestant Reformation in her influential book *Heretic – Why Islam Needs a Reformation Now.*[28] It seems though, that Hirsi Ali is unaware of two realities:

- First, the very battle cry of the Protestant Reformation was *Ad Fontes!* — which is Latin for "back to the sources." The Reformation aimed to reclaim the Biblical message, especially its core, the gospel. However, a similar call in Islam is precisely what Hirsi Ali does not want. That is what Wahhabism is all about; going back to Mohammed and everything taught in the Quran.
- Secondly, Islam has no real equivalent for the foundational Judeo-Christian principle of man as the *Imago Dei*, the image of God. The absence of this idea in Islam lies at the root of its dire impotence to deal with systemic inequality and brutality. Though more could be said about it, the *Book of Common Prayer* defines the image of God in man as our freedom "to make choices: to love, to create, to reason, and to live in harmony with creation and with God".[29]

That is why, when Christians persecuted or mistreated others, they instinctively knew they were acting against God's purpose for humankind, against Christ's commands, and the Holy Spirit's urging. That is why such ill-informed zeal eventually always called forth condemnation from within. Whenever "Christians" abused power, which sadly happened too

27 Waller, "The Muslim Brotherhood", 89-91.

28 See Ayaan Hirsi Ali, "Why has there been no Muslim reformation?" in *Heretic*, 53-76.

29 *The Book of Common Prayer and Administration of the Sacraments and Other Rites and Ceremonies of the Church* (New York: Church Publishing Incorporated, 2016), 845.

often, there was someone in their base, or something in their conscience, reminding them: "this is not how you learned Christ." (Ephes. 4:20-21).[30]

One such example was the heroic courage of bishop Ambrose of Milan, who confronted emperor Theodosius in 390. Theodosius had committed a heinous atrocity (despite Ambrose's warnings) by letting his troops kill seven hundred Thessalonians, including women and children, to avenge an uprising that killed the city's governor. Ambrose acted swiftly against his friend, who was known to be a good man but prone to fits of anger, saying, "The emperor is within the church, not above it." The emperor was summarily excommunicated. When he nonetheless turned up at church, Ambrose personally refused him entrance. The emperor was barred from attending for eight months, and when he finally returned, he had to kneel before all the faithful and humbly asked the Lord for forgiveness.[31]

All of church history is a testimony to the fact that the people of God, especially those in power, were called to repentance by ordinary men and women of faith when the Lord's holy commands were violated. Examples run from Nathan confronting David, Elijah the wicked king Ahab, to John the Baptist condemning Herod's adultery. In church history, there are too many examples to mention. One thinks of William Wilberforce ending slavery, Rev. Beyers Naude and others speaking out against apartheid, Dietrich Bonhoeffer leading the protest against the Third Reich, or Rev. Martin Luther King protesting racial segregation in the U.S.[32] Does Islam have an equivalent tradition? Moreover, there is no such thing in Biblical Christianity that for saving the face of the *umma* and serving the purpose of *dawa*, we may gently sweep evil under the rug and commit *taqiyya*. When that is done, it is a blot on the church and Christ's name.

---

30 British historian Tom Holland made this point somewhere in an interview about his latest book *Dominion, How the Christian Revolution Remade the World* (New York: Basic Books, 2019), see 503-514.

31 Nick Needham, *2000 Years of Christ's Power,* Vol. 1, (London: Christian Focus, 2016) 187-188.

32 Having lived in South Africa from 1962 until 2001, I recall that we did not feel shame about apartheid simply because the world condemned it but because the Bible did. The National Party dismantled apartheid well before 1994, following the Dutch Reformed Church's repudiation of the policy at its General Synod of 1986.

Thus, in Protestant terms, a call for reformation in Islam would only constitute a call back to the Quran, to Mohammed, to *sharia*, and yes, to *jihad* against the infidels. And yet, amazingly enough, this is what some ill-informed Western "experts" called for after 9/11 to curb Islamic terror![33]

We should bear in mind that the combined weight and momentum of Muslim theology and history, helped on by the Muslim resurgence since the 1970's, and the millions of dollars gained from of oil-revenue, all meant that the twenty-first century was going to be Islam's golden opportunity to re-implement Mohammed's dreams for a worldwide caliphate. That is what the courageous moderate voices in Islam are up against. They will be blamed for squandering an opportunity that comes around once in a millennium.

Consider also that it is not "peaceful" members of any movement who determine the élan of that movement in the longer term, whether that be atheists, fundamentalists, fascists, humanists, communists, environmentalists, woke folk, or whoever. Those who are *actively* involved—the so-called movers and shakers—set the agenda and the goals. Those who lobby, strategize, and supply the bulk of the funds determine the élan of a movement or organization. Peaceful (including non-active) members will ultimately be swept aside and eliminated, or be intimidated into conforming, when the rubber meets the road. This has been the common strategy in all violent revolutions.[34] That is why we must urgently pray for those voices who dare to oppose Islamism from within.

33 Patrick Sookhdeo. "The Role of Religion in the Battle Space Since 9/11", in Bekele and Sookhdeo (eds), *Meeting the Challenge*, 34.

34 As we know from the Bolshevist Revolution in 1917. In South Africa, for instance, the Marxist-inspired ANC made sure that it eliminated all peaceful black political rivals since the mid-1980s, through a brutal campaign of violence and internationally funded propaganda, to secure a pole position going into the elections of 1994. See Anthea Jeffrey, *People's War.*

CHAPTER 7

DAWA AND VICTIMHOOD

Before going any further we need to look closer at the central concept of the *umma* in *dawa*. At the end of chapter three, we said that the *umma* concept has recently undergone a significant revival. It is the driver of Islamization. The *umma* is a community with shared values. It expresses a group consciousness (felt unity) that transcends sectarian differences and distance among Muslims. As the community of Allah and his prophet, the *umma* seeks to live under *tawhid*, which is Allah's oneness, and as such, is also the political and social embodiment of *tawhid*. Times of crisis in Islam only serve to heighten the *umma's* importance and one's primary loyalty to it. In this regard, another vital aspect in the process of the Islamic push for world domination needs to be highlighted: the age-old Islamic inclination to victimhood.

The *Umma* and Victimhood

Islamists often use the *umma* principle to foster a victimhood syndrome in the West and elsewhere. It portrays Muslims in Muslim-minority countries as vulnerable and besieged, that is, as victims. By doing so it calls for a "liberation struggle," seeking to gain sympathy from the political left, similar to Communist insurgencies in many countries during the twentieth century. The *umma* uses *perceived* Islamophobia and discrimination in Western countries as powerful tools to further its *dawa*-agenda.

Under colonial rule, *sharia* was dormant in most Muslim countries; only Muslim family law was retained. The end of colonialism saw a rise in nationalism, binding Muslim and non-Muslim together in favour of a secular option for a while. That situation then reversed after the Arab Spring, when Islamists came through the ranks as serious contenders for power throughout the Middle East, expressing a deep hostility to Christianity and other minorities, as well as to democratic values and the idea of a secular sphere. To camouflage their tyrannical aspirations, the Islamists portrayed themselves as the "scapegoats of the world", or the "underdogs", to shore up sympathy and support from ignorant people far away. This notion of being the "underdog" is then enforced when right-wing fanatics commit senseless attacks against Muslims somewhere, or when another random drone attack kills innocent civilians in the Middle East. Nonetheless, it is this sense of being the underdog which then motivates random counter-attacks on Christians and other non-Muslims in Muslim lands or regions. All of this explains why the Arab Spring in the Middle East morphed into an icy Islamic winter for Christians in the Levant and deep into Africa.

The resurgence of Islam since the 1970s has strongly impacted Muslim communities everywhere, with thousands of ordinary Muslims suffering the consequences, as *dawa*, *sharia*, and *jihad* gained ever greater popularity. All of this was helped on by the growing instability of major Western democracies (like France, Britain, and the U.S.). The Islamist sees this as a civilizational conflict between the *umma* and the West, in which the former is victorious. Authors like Sayyid Qutb and Mona Abul-Fadl saw the clash of civilizations coming even before Samuel Huntington did in his famous book of 1996. In Muslim minds, it is simple: the sun is rising on the *umma* in the East but is eerily setting on the once-so-powerful West.

Like Mohammed in Medina, Muslims must now regain self-confidence. While many multi-national conferences among Muslim states in the 1980s (largely unnoticed in the West) all focused on the "weak" *umma*, a new century saw a new age dawning. Islamization was introduced as the solution, and Saudi Arabia—with its strict brand of Wahhabi Islam and its vast oil wealth— was earmarked to play a critical role in the Islamic resurgence. In all of this, victimhood syndrome plays a crucial role. Without it, Islamists won't be able to justify their own agenda or count on the support it is receiving from gullible Westerners on the left or right.

What we must not overlook, however, is the fact that the victimhood syndrome was originally conceived and brilliantly used by the prophet of Islam himself. Australian scholar Mark Durie makes this abundantly clear in his book *The Third Choice* when he tells the story of the early spread of Islam in the time of Mohammed.[1] Mohammed's attitude toward his native Arabs, then toward the Jews and eventually toward the Christians, went through a metamorphosis during the twenty-three years since his first "revelations" in Mecca to his death in Medina in 632.

Mohammed—who grew up an orphan and was cared for by an uncle, Abu Talib—went through periods of self-doubt and self-rejection as he began preaching Islam, due to the opposition he encountered from his native Quaraysh people and by most of his own family. His first supporters were his first wife, Khadijah, and another uncle, Hamza. Every time he was plagued with doubts, he received comfort from them and yet another revelation from the angel Gabriel, confirming his calling and convictions, all of which became part of the Quran. And so, according to his earliest biographer Ibn Ishaq, while Muhammed was still in Mecca, he was beginning to contemplate using the sword against those rejecting him. The verses in the Quran justifying violence were in fact revealed as Muhammed escaped from Mecca by the skin of his teeth in Surah 22:39-40:

> Permission to fight is granted to those who are attacked because they have been wronged – God indeed has the power to help them – they are those who have been driven out of their homes unjustly, only because they said: "Our Lord is God."

In other words, it was out of the crucible of rejection in Mecca that the small Muslim community's resolve was born to advance through violence.

1 Durie, "Muhammed against the unbelievers", in *The Third Choice*, 81-116.

In Islamic terms, those who side with the *umma* will be the winners, and those who don't will be the losers.

It is vital to grasp the *fitna* concept in this regard as well.[2] The Arabic word for trial, persecution, or temptation is *fitna.* Every time Mohammed was opposed, questioned, mocked, or rejected, it was experienced as *fitna*, meaning that the entire truth and validity of his message was called into question, a source of great anguish and doubt to him. The whole purpose of fighting was to eliminate *fitna*, according to Ibn Kathir, one of the earliest commentators on the Quran. Thus, whoever calls the truth of Islam into question, commits a crime far worse than killing; for *fitna* was "more grievous than slaying". This is what is often meant in the Quran by the words "fighting against" Allah or the *umma.* It does not have to mean literal fighting but simply resisting or rejecting Mohammed's message, since that causes *fitna* and must be eliminated. And thus, *jihad* was revealed as the solution to end all *fitna* after the Battle of Badr, when Mohammed's men defeated an overwhelming force of pagan Meccans: "Fight them until there is no more [religious] persecution, and religion belongs wholly to God" (Surah 8:39).

What happened concerning the Meccan unbelievers is that Muhammed progressively set aside all restraints which stood in the way of total victory. First, a divine doctrine was announced lifting restrictions on fighting in certain months of the year. Then another to set aside treaties made with the Meccans. Then yet another word from Allah was revealed allowing Muslims to fight against those who did not persecute them but who only disbelieved. Then another doctrine was revealed, pronouncing eternal rewards for those dying in *jihad.* And then still another pronouncing that Muslim warriors may take the wives of slain captives as sex slaves (concubines).

When Mohammed conquered Mecca, he discouraged wholesale slaughter, saying his followers should only slay those who resisted them. However, he issued a hitlist of some to be killed under any circumstances. Three were apostates, two insulted him in Mecca, and two were mere slave girls who sang satirical songs about him. They all caused *fitna.* As Robert

2 See Durie for "Muhammed's fitna worldview" in *The Third Choice*, 96-99.

Spencer wrote: "... nothing was good except what was advantageous to Islam, and nothing evil except what hindered Islam."[3]

Mohammed's subsequent big struggle was with the Jews of Medina, who would not believe. Until now, the "People of the Book" (Jews and Christians) were hardly in Mohammed's focus. Here we notice the same progression of justifying hostility. When he found the questions of the rabbis of Medina troublesome, divine revelations were sent down to him.[4] Again and again, when they challenged him, it was turned into an opportunity for self-validation, bringing forth fresh revelations of the Quran, first in calling the Jews "monkeys and pigs" (Surah 7:166; 5:60; 2:65), then "prophet-killers" (5:70), then "losers" (for having broken their covenant with God, 2:27), then in announcing hellfire against them (2:62; 5:44), and finally that his coming had abrogated Judaism and that Abraham was, in fact, a Muslim and not a Jew (Surah 3:67). Mohammed was initially positively disposed toward the Jews. But when most rejected his claim to prophethood he turned violently against them. The same fate would later befall thousands of Christians facing the Muslim caliphs.

Finally, when the Quarayza Jews of Medina surrendered unconditionally, Mohammed besieged them based on a command from the angel Gabriel. They were all marched to the marketplace of Medina, where trenches were dug in the sand. Next, six to nine-hundred Jewish men were ordered to step up to the trenches. Then they were all beheaded in one afternoon. Afterward, their women and children, still in shock, were taken as booty, a reward for the Muslim warriors. Hence, the prophet of Islam, the erstwhile orphan, who experienced rejection at many levels from his native tribe and the Jews, had become, in Durie's words, an "orphan-maker." The self-doubter had become the ultimate rejecter, enforcing his creed by force of arms to supersede and replace all other faiths.

Once Medina was cleared of all Jews, Mohammed launched a campaign against the Jews of Khaybar. During this campaign, we first hear of *a third choice*: surrender to Allah, die or become a *dhimmi*.

---

3 As quoted in Durie, *The Third Choice*, 104.

4 See the first hundred verses or so of Surah 2.

We must realize that Mohammed, and even more so the caliphs after him, treated Jews and Christians alike as People of the Book. Since they caused *fitna* by resisting Islam, violence was justified if they refused the third option of dhimmitude. *Fitna* makes the *umma* feel inferior. That is why whoever rejected Islam was seen as fighting against Allah, and that validated terror, to deliver the *umma* from their victimhood. Sahih al-Bukhari once wrote: Islam shall be made "victorious through terror."[5] A modern illustration of this mentality is found in the astonishing claim made by a Muslim convert, Marmaduke Pickthall, in his 1927 lecture "Tolerance in Islam". Alluding to the genocide of the Armenians in Turkey, he said, "Before every massacre of Christians by Muslims, of which you read, there was a more wholesale massacre or attempted massacre of Muslims by Christians."[6] Anyone remotely familiar with the history of Turkey would know there is zero factual basis for this outrageous claim. What Pickthall had in mind is that Armenian Christians refused to become Muslims under Ottoman rule. They caused *fitna* and that justified genocide.

Facing the Victimhood Syndrome

Many Western observers, unfamiliar with the victimhood syndrome, have fallen prey to its plots and schemes. They failed to see how the *umma*'s complaining about the past has always been used to justify violence in the present and to weaken the moral resolve of their foes to respond with courage. While good parents know well enough *not* to allow their children to get their way with "moaning and groaning", we in the West—due to our ignorance of history and our suicidal post-colonial introspection[7]—are almost entirely clueless about how to deal with Islamic self-pity and victimhood.

This was especially true in the years following 9/11. Our knee-jerk reaction in the wake of those horrific attacks was illustrated in the incredible story emanating from the Boston Episcopalian Church mentioned

5 As quoted in Durie, *The Third Choice*, 115.

6 As quoted in Durie, *The Third Choice*, 113-114.

7 See “White Guilt and the Western Past” by Shelby Steele, in *The Wallstreet Journal*, May 2, 2006.

in chapter five.[8] It is also illustrated in the book *Christians, Muslims, and Islamic Rage*, published in 2003. The Christian author's vantage point was that the roots of present-day Islamic rage go back to a thousand years of Muslim grudges. He refers to Osama bin Laden's rants about the crusades, the loss of Andalusia (Spain) in 1492, the defeat of the Ottoman Empire, and to more recent events in the Gulf. The author even cites the celebrated scholar Bernard Lewis to support his thesis that Muslims hate us because of what they believe we have done to them.[9]

The same folly can be seen in German journalist Jürgen Todenhöfer's letter to the leader of ISIL, Abu Bakr al-Baghdadi, calling on the terrorist leader to forsake his reign of terror.[10] In his letter called "Warning to the West", the journalist puts virtually all the blame for Islamic terror on the shoulders of the West and Christianity and nothing on Islam, revealing a shocking ignorance and bias.[11] Todenhöfer claims to be a Christian.

These authors fail to see that all of this was and still is a very clever strategy by Islam to justify their deeds and weaken our resolve, and that it is mostly based on false propaganda. Hussein Mansour, growing up in Egypt, said they were taught by many to hate the Coptic Christians because *they* supposedly hated the Muslims first. Once he broke the taboo and met with these people, he realized how warped his mindset was and how he had been brainwashed all his life.[12] The moral of the story is that Christians mainly acted in self-defence; there simply never was any moral equivalence between "their" deeds and "ours," says Mansour.

To prove just what a helpful tool the victim-mentality has become, one only has to take a page out of the playbook of Boko Haram, a decade and more after 9/11. When a Nigerian Christian university student was abducted and shown to be on his knees in an orange jumpsuit, reminiscent

---

8 Under the sub-heading "Interreligious Dialogue".

9 "How Christians should think about the past" in Catherwood, *Christians, Muslims, and Islamic Rage*, 35-52.

10 Jürgen Todenhöfer, "An Open Letter to the Caliph of the 'Islamic State' and His Foreign Fighters" in *My Journey into the Heart of Terror* (Vancouver: Greystone Books, 2014), 227-234.

11 Todenhöfer, "A Warning to the West," in *My* Journey, 235-248.

12 Mansour, *Minority of One*, 25-27.

of ISIL executions in the Levant and Libya, an Islamist youth clad in black stood behind him with a handgun in his right hand. The terrorist began speaking,

> "We are saying to Christians, we have not forgotten what you have done to our parents and ancestors, and we are telling all Christians around the world, we have not forgotten and will not stop. We must avenge the bloodshed that has been done, like this one."[13]

He then raised his pistol, pulled the trigger, and killed the student point-blank. The student, named Ropvil, was twenty-two; the killer was only twelve. This false and unfounded victimhood syndrome had brainwashed a mere youth to justify his heinous deeds. Another example of terrorist self-pity by Boko Haram was recently seen in a dramatic video featuring a prayer by one of their leaders, weeping for Allah's help,

> "May Allah protect us from the [Nigerian Army's] evil. We forsook our parents, uncles and aunties to practice your true religion. It is because of your religion that we placed knife on... necks... Oh Allah give us victory."[14]

As in Turkey's case mentioned before, anyone knowing Nigeria's history would know that there is no moral equivalence between the horrific crimes Islamists have committed against Christians, and what a handful of Christians may sometimes have done in revenge, or what the British colonial power might have done before them.

---

13 Moore and Cooper, *The Next Jihad*, 88.

14 Ibid.,123.

CHAPTER 8

DAWA THROUGH FEAR

The more peaceful means of *dawa*—or the methods of Islamization—finally include two hugely important strategies. One is tailor-made for the West and Muslim-minority contexts, the other for the Muslim state. They are Islamophobia on the one hand and dhimmitude on the other.

Islamophobia

The growing fear of being accused, yes even to be charged with Islamophobia, is yet another fine arrow in the quiver of *dawa.* As we know by now, such fears rise sharply every time another ideologically-possessed *lone wolf* has launched a cowardly attack on innocent Muslims or any given Muslim symbol, or for that matter on politicians and parties who are deemed too friendly to immigration. Who can forget the horrific attacks on Utoya Island in Norway in 2011 or on innocent Muslims at two mosques in Christchurch, New Zealand in 2015, to name but two of the worst right-wing terror attacks in recent years? Though such attacks have been few compared with Islamic terror attacks, the *Global Terrorism Index* of 2020 gives ample reason to be concerned about the rise of extreme right-wing (or left-wing) terror worldwide.[1]

In the early summer of 2021, four members of an unsuspecting Muslim family going for an afternoon stroll in London, Ontario, were run over by a minivan, leaving a nine-year-old boy behind as the sole survivor. The police suspected a hate crime. The trial of the young man responsible for the deaths of the Afzaal family is set to take place in 2023. In the wake of the tragedy, the *National Post* and other news dailies in Canada addressed the problem of Islamophobia head-on. One such column was written by the mayor of Brampton, Mr. Patrick Brown, under the headline “Islamophobia is a scourge on Canadian society. We must erase it.”[2] Brown mentions how, after another senseless attack in Quebec in 2017, he rose in the legislature of his province, declaring: "Islamophobia is real, and we need to condemn it unreservedly."

He was mystified as to how the issue could even be a polarizing one, as it indeed was. To his dismay, he saw ninety-one hands in the legislature raised against a new bill seeking to root out the problem. Brown went on to mention how he learned from a close childhood friend how much bias and hate Muslims in Canada have to endure simply because they are Muslims. He added: "There are many reasons why bias and hate grow, but the most troubling emanate from the chamber of the extreme far-right..." That Brown thinks "Islamophobia is disgusting" comes as no surprise. He has seen crimes related to race or nationality rise 54 percent from 2018 to 2020, right where he lives near Toronto. We can agree with much of what Mayor Brown wrote, and also want to make a few observations:

- It would be a shame if peaceful Muslims in Canada generally feel afraid to go out onto the streets due to a realistic fear of hate crimes.
- The author, unfortunately, fails to define *what* Islamophobia is, which is the Achilles heel of his entire argument.

1 "The Religion of Peace" website lists over 40 000 Islamic terror attacks worldwide since 9/11; see thereligionofpeace.com.

2 “Patrick Brown: Islamophobia is a Scourge on Canadian Society. We must Erase it.” *National Post*, June 22, 2021, on nationalpost.com

- When he mentions that "there are reasons for" Islamophobia, he does not provide any but blames "the extreme far right," which may in itself give rise to other phobias in Canadian society.
- One may rightly ask if the lack of unified support to quell Islamophobia does not stem in part from the absence of an adequate working definition for the problem (at least in the press) and the vague and often unfair accusations made by politicians.

To the day, exactly six months earlier in January, the same *National Post* published an article[3] by a professor of Sociological and Anthropological Studies in Ottawa. Dr. Stuart Chambers' piece was entitled: "Islamophobia in western media is based on false premises".[4] The article argued that "specific individuals" are scapegoating Muslims to further their own agendas, making an industry out of Islamophobia. The author wrote: "Like other forms of intolerance, however, Islamophobia can be objectively assessed. Empirical studies effectively expose this prejudice, one that plagues both sides of the political spectrum."

Chambers then called several individuals guilty of scapegoating Muslims and turning Islamophobia into an industry, like Canadian conservative author Mark Steyn, Dutch politician Geert Wilders, British conservative commentator Douglas Murray, American neuroscientist Sam Harris, American comedian Bill Maher and Somali-American activist Ayaan Hirsi Ali. With each name, he added a brief quote illustrating the individual's alleged Islamophobia. For instance, "most Muslims either wish or are indifferent to the death of the societies in which they live" (Steyn); or, "the Quran is a source of inspiration for, and justification of, hatred, violence and terrorism in the world" (Wilders); or "violence is inherent in the doctrine of Islam" (Hirsi Ali); or "there is a direct link between the doctrine of Islam and Muslim terrorism" (Harris).

Chambers continues: "None of these characterizations, however, are sufficient from a scholarly viewpoint. Self-evident positions and gross

3 Which originally appeared in *The Conversation.*

4 "Islamophobia in Western Media is based on false premises", The Conversation, *National Post, January 21, 2021,* on nationalpost.com.

exaggerations tend to detract from the main issue: *whether the depiction of Muslims as violent extremists is misleading*" (emphasis mine). Chambers then shows how globally speaking, Muslims overwhelmingly reject suicide bombings and other forms of violence against civilians in defense of Islam. "Studies found that Muslims view such extremism as rarely or never justified, including 96 percent in Azerbaijan, 95 percent in Kazakhstan, 92 percent in Indonesia, and 91 percent in Iraq". He also references other studies and polls done in the U.K., finding that nine out of ten Muslims condemned violence committed in the name of Islam, as well as studies done in the other European nations and the U.S. He also mentions studies showing how few Muslims in the world ever wish to have anything to do with an organization like ISIL.

The author concludes: "The main assertion that Muslims largely support extremist violence is groundless. Because Islamophobia distorts the western image of Muslims, scientific studies serve as an important corrective in two important ways. First, they expose Islamophobic attitudes that have gripped the West since 9/11, and second, they help to decrease the spread of anti-Muslim abuse by providing a rational forum for discussion." Again, it behooves us to make some observations about this article as well:

- The professor, like the mayor, fails to provide a clear definition for Islamophobia aside from referring to it as "prejudice."
- He mentions several individuals, quoting a single line from their respective works, as an illustration of their "prejudice" without seeking to verify the credibility of their statements.
- He then says that these "gross exaggerations" detract from the main issue, namely whether "the depiction of Muslims as violent extremists is misleading." Remarkably, none of the so-called "gross exaggerations" he listed claimed any such thing, i.e., that Muslims are all violent extremists, making the professor's conclusion logically invalid.
- The author's conclusion that that there are therefore no grounds for "the main assertion that *Muslims largely support extremist violence*" (emphasis mine) is in itself a caricature of the very so-called Islamophobic quotes he listed, since none of those quotes allege that "Muslims largely support extremist violence".

- The professor's empirical approach also failed to include the possible impact of *taqiyya* (deception) in its assessment of opinion polls, as well as the fact that most of the polls he refers to were taken in countries opposed to Islamic "fundamentalism" to begin with. It would be easy to find polls and statistics painting quite a different picture. To quote just one, on June 4, 2003 the *National Post* reported that Palestinians ranked Osama bin Laden as their favourite world leader. The rest of the world picked Tony Blair.[5]

In other words, the professor's supposed "empirical" approach was not so empirical. It has not succeeded in exposing the prejudice. We are thus in urgent need of knowing *what* we are talking about when we raise the specter of Islamophobia, or else we risk fomenting the problem instead of solving it. A flyer issued by Canadian Citizens for Charter Rights and Freedoms, raising concerns about an anti-Islamophobia motion in the House of Commons in 2017, warned that Islamophobia is not defined anywhere in Motion M-103 (or in Canada's legal system) and that it could easily be used to target any criticism of Islam and to seriously limit religious freedom. How can we solve a problem that is not defined?

But, if we define Islamophobia as *the irrational fear of and prejudice against Muslims in general, regardless of whether they support extremist violence or not*, then it's hard to see how anyone could disagree that the problem needs to be rooted out, the sooner, the better. But what if the real reason for most supposed "Islamophobia" in the world *does* have a rational and empirical basis? What if it is *not* based on a blanket suspicion that all "Muslims support extremist violence"? What if it can easily be proven that it is based on premises like the following:

- that classical Islam can clearly be shown to be far more than a religion; that it is indeed an ideology with bold aspirations for global domination;
- that most Muslims worldwide (as is also clearly shown by polls) do support *sharia*, and that it is entirely incompatible with democratic values and universal human rights;

5 "Palestinians rank Osama bin Laden as their favourite world leader", *National Post*, June 4, 2003, A2.

- that Muslims by and large are reticent to take a public stand against the palpable violence committed by fellow Muslims in the name of Allah for whatever reason;
- that Muslims are generally also unwilling to take a stand against those many Muslim-majority countries known for their suppression of women and children, of ex-Muslims, and other faiths, especially Christianity;
- that Islamic terrorists have a relatively easy job justifying their cruel deeds from either the Quran, the *hadith*, or Mohammed's *sira*;
- that most of the Islamic conquests in history came through the sword's power and other forms of coercion, and not through free persuasion.
- and lastly but most importantly that deception, which is such an integral part of *dawa*, may also explain why most Muslims would not come out in favour of violence to expand or defend Islam in the world. One only has to consider how opinion polls completely underestimated the support for Mr. Donald Trump prior to two presidential elections in the U.S. to realize that many factors determine what people would reveal about their deepest convictions in opinion polls.

What if people's fear and frustration are based on these things? Could that be called "irrational fear" or "bigotry motivated by prejudice"? Do human beings anywhere have the right to be concerned about their children's future, if their concerns are based on the valid premises of empirical data, well-known documented history, and sound reason, and *not* on irrational fears and hatred? And what if the political leaders turn a blind eye to it all, blaming those who have such concerns as being guilty of "Islamophobia"? What common good will such a dereliction of duty by such leaders bring about for any civilization? And is that a responsible way of governing a country and of caring for its citizenry, after all?

Or maybe the mayor, the professor, and our ruling class may want to think about the following: Why did so many Afghans try to cling to an American military aircraft taking off from Kabul airport in the third week of August 2021, with some—among them an Afghani national football player—plunging to their death? Were they simply afraid of the Taliban because they worked for the Americans? Or is there much more to it? Were they perhaps scared to death of *sharia*, implemented to the letter? And if they were clinging to planes, willing to plunge to their death, may we not cling to the little good that remains of a dying Western civilization? Should we be called bigots, racists, and Islamophobes for doing so? And most importantly, how is it even fair to those tens of thousands of our dear Muslim brothers and sisters who have fled to our shores to escape the harsh rule of *sharia*, if we are so nonchalant about their fears?

In other words, what exactly is Islamophobia? Could we define the term before proceeding any further? This is a crucial question since an international authority calls Islamophobia a key strategy of *dawa*.[6] Muslim minorities persistently complain about Islamophobia and consequently demand laws to protect them. The result in many Western countries is often a speedy move towards a situation where Islam is immune from any criticism, while it remains open season for going after Christians. Let it be known that banning speech critical of radical Islam and Islamic terrorism is nothing less than a step towards legitimizing violence committed in the name of Islam. A good example in recent times came from France, where the French opposition leader, Marine le Pen, was criminally charged for merely *posting* images of ISIL atrocities on her Twitter page. Thankfully she was acquitted of these charges in 2021.[7]

In Muslim-minority countries, Islamic organizations often pursue litigation against anyone perceived to be critical of any aspect of Islam. One of the most active American organizations in this respect is CAIR: *Council on American-Islamic Relations*, based in Washington, DC. And in Canada, anyone critical of Islam can be dragged before the *Human Rights Tribunal*, suffering extensive financial loss.

An excellent example of the increasing paranoia and fear in the West, not to speak the truth concerning militant Islam, is clearly illustrated by the following: The FBI's *Counter-Terrorism Analytical Lexicon* of 2008 does not contain the words "Islam", "Muslim" or "Jihad" at all.[8] This is quite remarkable, given that the *Global Terrorism Index* cites Islamic terror

6 Sookhdeo, *Dawa*, 69-70.

7 "France's far-right leader Marine Le Pen acquitted of hate speech charges", *France24*, May 4, 2021, on france24.com.

8 Sookhdeo "The Role of Religion", 35

movements as the main instigators of international terrorism for decades already, according to its 2020 report.[9]

We often learn best by way of comparison. To illustrate just how much Islamic *dawa* has succeeded in the West, it is helpful to compare the flagrant double standards between Islamophobia and Russophobia. According to U.S. law, any American Muslim may object to fighting fellow Muslims in a theatre of war nowadays. But in a possible war with the Russian Federation, every Christian soldier in the U.S. must take up arms against a country that claims to be 70 percent Christian and did not seek trouble with us. To repeat what is boldly written in Muslim sources, or what is publicly committed by Islamist groups, is considered Islamophobic. To believe and spread the latest unfounded hateful rumours about Russia, its people or its leader, is considered ultimately virtuous. No evidence is needed when scapegoating them, yet asking questions about all our state-promoted propaganda is tantamount to high treason.[10] In fact, when Russians are the targets, racist criticism is in perfectly good order. Yet simply mentioning atrocities committed by those shouting *Allahu Akbar* will be suppressed by the media, and should be left unspoken by the public, out of deference to political correctness. Islamophobia is out, and Russophobia is in, ever since the turn of the century. In fact, it was the late Dr. Stephen Cohen, doyen of American-Russian studies in the U.S., who warned us for years that the greatest threat to U.S and world peace is not Russia, but Russophobia. Sadly, his voice was like one crying in the desert.[11]

---

9 *Global Terrorism Index 2020 - Measuring the Impact of Terrorism*, Institute for Economics and Peace, Sydney, 2020. Download, GTI2020Terrorism.pdf

10 There are too many examples to mention. Here is one. While Ayaan Hirsi Ali meticulously references and documents every single claim she makes about Islam in her book *Prey*, she can make an entirely unsubstantiated and unqualified claim that the Russian government was supposedly involved in "destabilizing liberal democracy" in Europe and the U.S. She knows no accountability will be required from her for making these unfounded claims. See *Prey*, xiii.

11 "American Scholars Say the Real Threat to the U.S. is Russophobia (HBO)", *VICENews* on *YouTube.*

And yet consider this: the best remedy for any irrational fear (i.e., phobia) is to become better acquainted with the object of your phobia, yes, with your supposed enemy. What, if anything, would better expel unfounded myths and irrational fears? So go visit Moscow and Mecca and compare. But that is exactly what our illiberal media and political establishment won't have us do. For they know *then* it is game over, and the willfully blind will no longer be able to lead a gullible public into the ditch.

Dhimmi Consciousness

It was often claimed that Jews, Christians, and other monotheist non-Muslims did not have it so bad under Muslim rule during the 600-year Islamic golden age, yes, that the Islamic State protected them. This notion was shown to be manifestly false by the work of Egyptian-born Jewish author Bat Ye'or in her now famous work *Islam and Dhimmitude – Where Civilizations Collide,* published in 2001. According to *Wikipedia,* Ye'or describes dhimmitude as the "specific social condition resulting from jihad" and the "state of fear and insecurity" non-Muslims experienced under *sharia.*[12]

So, what is dhimmitude, and why do Jews and Christians need protection in an Islamic state? The Quran and *hadith* make it abundantly clear that for the so-called "People of the Book" there are only one of three possible ways of responding to the invitation of *dawa*, namely: say the *shahada* and become a Muslim; pay the *jizya* and submit to the *umma*, or refuse both and face the sword.[13] In other words: conversion, subjugation, or elimination. The second option turns you into a *dhimmi*, a second-class citizen. Pagans don't even have this choice. They must simply convert or die. The status of the *dhimmis* under *sharia* was codified and expanded over centuries by the Pact of Umar, dating from the time of Mohammed's second successor.[14] *Dhimmi* status is based on two Islamic principles:[15]

---

12 "Bat Ye'Or", *Wikipedia*, viewed July 30, 2021, on wikipedia.org.

13 Michael Youssef, *Jesus, Jihad and Peace* (Franklin, TN: Worthy Publishing, 2015) 115.

14 Irshad Manji, *The Trouble with Islam Today* (Toronto: Vintage, 2005), 69.

15 Sookhdeo, *Dawa*, 93-94.

- Muslims are far superior. The Quran says to all Muslims: "Ye are the best of peoples, evolved for mankind enjoining what is right, forbidding what is wrong, and believing in God" (Surah 3:110).
- Christians and Jews should be humiliated and subjected to the payment of *jizya*: "Fight those who do not believe in God… (even if they are) People of the Book, until they pay the *jizya* with willing submission, and feel subdued" (Surah 9:29).

In other words, dhimmitude is state-sanctioned discrimination against second-class citizens. Muslim scholars defend the practice by saying it protects Jews and Christians under *sharia*. But protection from what? From wild animals or alien invaders? No, from being killed, unnecessarily hurt, or harassed by the Muslim public or state. As long as you accept your second-class status, you will be left alone most of the time, unless a brutal tyrant like caliph Al-Hakim (985 – 1021) comes along and launches unprovoked persecutions. If you are "lucky" enough, you may live under a more enlightened ruler like king Saladin (1138-1193) of Jerusalem, who treated Jews and Christians well.[16]

Whatever the case, you will be a second-class citizen in your own country, facing all sorts of discrimination and humiliation, much worse than what African people suffered under apartheid in South Africa from 1948 to 1990. First of all—let all Jews take note—you will have to wear a badge (often yellow) and other distinctive clothing to make it clear that you are a *dhimmi*. Even a modest critic of dhimmitude, Phil Jenkins, admits that the Pact of Umar, which defined the status of the *dhimmis* and the rules under which they lived, only became harsher with time.[17] What follows are some of the numerous laws restricting and humiliating the *dhimmis* in their daily lives, enforcing the notion that they are inferior to Muslims. The *dhimmis* were, for example,

- obligated to wear identifiable clothing
- to live in a specially marked house

16 For references to Saladin and Hakim see Philip Jenkins, *The Lost History of Christianity* (HarperOne: New York, 2008), 109.

17 Ibid.

- only allowed to ride mules and donkeys, and never a horse
- not allowed to bear arms
- excluded from public office
- not equal with Muslims before the law
- obligated always to yield the right of way to Muslims in traffic
- to yield their chairs to a Muslim at the marketplace
- not allowed to be a guardian of a Muslim child
- to worship within close distance of a mosque
- to not speak of their faith in public

The humiliating impact of these discriminating laws motivated Spanish Christians and Jews to throw off the yoke of Islam in the Reconquista, driving their Muslim oppressors out of the Iberian Peninsula after living for centuries as *dhimmis* under *sharia*.[18]

Dhimmi status became the formal expression and acceptance of legalized discrimination and oppression in the Muslim world. The basic rule is that the *dhimmis* cannot be proper citizens of the Islamic state. By paying *jizya*, Christians and Jews formally acknowledge their inferiority and submission to Muslims. However, this agreement with the *dhimmis* lasts only as long as they behave meekly and do not bear arms. If they fail in these areas their protection falls away.

With the rise of secular nationalism in the nineteenth century *dhimmi* distinctions in Muslim countries seemed to have phased out. Certain Muslim countries like Syria, Iraq, Iran, and Turkey gradually accepted secular constitutions and abandoned dhimmitude. This, however, enraged radical Muslims, who saw these countries as violating *sharia* regarding the *dhimmis*. And so, as secular Islam struggled and Islamization gained strength, dhimmitude returned. *Sharia* now calls for the full-scale reinstatement of dhimmitude in Muslim-majority countries.

Bath Ye'or demonstrated that living for many centuries in a dominant Muslim society, *dhimmis* could not help feeling deeply affected on a

18 Hank Hanegraaff, *Muslim* (Nashville, TN: Thomas Nelson: 2015), 88.

psychological level. They developed a *dhimmi*-mentality of vulnerability, gratitude, and self-abasement:[19]

- vulnerable because they are not allowed to arm or defend themselves and because they may never testify against a Muslim in court, while a Muslim could bring baseless charges against them
- grateful because they should consider themselves so fortunate to receive protection
- self-abased, because they are constantly humiliated and have to live in fear

This *dhimmi* consciousness often shocked Western travelers to Muslim countries since the poor *dhimmis* seemed to have accepted the status quo and had become indifferent to change. They just kept a low profile and sought to stay out of trouble. However, with time, many forsook their Christian faith and converted to Islam, so as to pay less tax and no longer to be treated as *kufar*. They even expressed anger when Muslims were criticized, proving their loyalty.

And yet, over centuries, dhimmitude drained the very last bit of faith from many Christians in the Middle East and the Balkan. As Patrick Sookhdeo writes:

> To be treated as despised foreigners in one's homeland, to struggle daily with the humiliating and disempowering *dhimmi* regulations, and occasionally with outright persecution was a test of faith which, sadly, many Christians failed. "Apostasy" is a harsh word, but that is what it was. Where Christianity disappeared, it was mainly because Christians chose to convert to Islam for an easier life. [20]

Sookhdeo tells the story of Patriarch Ishu'-Yub III writing in anguished tones about the apostasy of Christians in Oman and the fact that Christian worship had ceased in the diocese of Mazon. The Omani Christians had given up their faith for material reasons and an easier life. In tears, the patriarch lamented:

---

19 For the psychological impact of dhimmitude, see Durie, *The Third Choice*, 179-181.

20 Sookhdeo, *Hated Without* Reason, 72.

> They have not been compelled by the sword, or fire or torments, but [were] merely seized with a desire for the half of their own possessions! Mad! – for apostasy has right away swallowed them up, and they are destroyed forever... Alas! Alas![21]

The reason why dhimmitude should be of great concern to us is not only because of how it affects our brothers and sisters in Muslim lands but also because it has already taken root among us in the West. Many Westerners suffer from *dhimmi*-consciousness already now, while scarcely five percent of their national populations are Muslim.

I experienced this reality when a congregation I once pastored sought to engage Muslims in dialogue for over ten years. The meetings were set up so that speakers from both sides could address the audience on a topic, and then answer questions from the floor. It struck me from the first meeting that Muslim imams felt free to criticize Christian beliefs,[22] which incidentally did not offend me, since I expected that. What troubled me deeply was that the Christian speakers were told by their organizers to stick to a positive proclamation of the gospel and not to say a word about Islam. Meanwhile, our Muslim friends, who received thousands of dollars from the Christians each time, for renting the venue and ordering food, were not required to submit receipts, since they were supposedly not accustomed to a culture of transparency and accountability! And, when some of the Christians wished to ask pointed questions about the ongoing persecution of Christians in Pakistan,[23] their own leader politely told them that such questions were beyond the pale.

In three different ways, these Christians have already succumbed to dhimmitude. Their attitude reminds one of a card left among the flowers in front of the house of the slain Dutch politician Pim Fortuyn in 2002,

---

21 Ibid.

22 E.g., that the Bible has been corrupted or that Jesus is not the Son of God and never died or rose again, to name but a few.

23 These were the days when Pakistani Christian Asia Bibi was sentenced to death by hanging under Pakistan's notorious blasphemy laws. The Supreme Court of Pakistan later acquitted her in October 2018, due to the massive outpouring of support from around the world.

saying: "In Holland everything is tolerated, except for the truth".[24] Many among us have already accepted *dhimmi* status, albeit unwittingly. This should deeply concern us all. Is fear already ruling us completely? It makes one think of Isaiah's poignant warning in chapter 51:12:

> I, even I, am he who comforts you.
> Who are you that you fear mere mortals,
> human beings who are but grass,
> that you forget the Lord your Maker,
> who stretches out the heavens,
> and who lays the foundations of the earth,
> that you live in constant terror every day,
> because of the wrath of the oppressor,
> who is bent on destruction?

24 See "Rotterdam, Capital of Eurabia" by Harry Antinodes, *Christian Renewal*, September 23, 2009.

CHAPTER 9

DAWA THROUGH VIOLENCE AND THREATS

In classical Islam, whatever serves the spreading of the *umma*'s faith is good. Whatever prevents it must be overcome with force. Hence, if the fear of violence serves the purpose of spreading Islam, then it cannot be bad, for to Mohammed and the first four caliphs the end *always* justified the means. I recall talking to a Muslim lady in Toronto during the second intifada,[1] asking her what she thought about Palestinians blowing themselves up among Israeli civilians to cause maximum mayhem and carnage. What this soft-spoken middle-aged Muslim lady very politely answered will stay with me for life. She said we are not allowed to judge. Allah alone knows the heart. It is not for us to judge whether it is good or bad to kill innocent civilians randomly.

Ultimately it comes down to this: Who do we believe God to be? What is God like? Is he the one beyond whom no greater good can be imagined,

1 The Palestinian uprising lasting from 2000 to 2005.

as Anselm of Canterbury once said?[2] Certainly not in the words of the Muslim lady just mentioned. Nor in the words of another woman, now an ex-Muslim, who once said in her testimony, "Every time I heard the words of the Quran (as a child) my heart became sad and fearful. The God of the Quran was very angry, demanding, and controlling." [3] He may even approve of suicide killings.

A Useful Tool to Weaken Resolve

Through the centuries, Islam saw violence and threats as an effective tool to further its cause, so that even moderate Muslims found it hard to argue against their own history. Fast forward to today, and one realizes how vulnerable we are. Violence and threats, when persistent, have become excellent tools in the political sphere because governments are often too weak and uninformed to resist. Add to that the fact that politicians in democratic societies are mainly concerned about re-election and least about our children's future, and one realizes how large the danger looms.

Most importantly, there is a dire lack of moral courage and conviction among many who lead our Western institutions today. This absence of moral courage and vision was clearly registered by the Soviet dissident Alexander Solzhenitsyn during a speech delivered at Harvard in 1978. He said that *the lack of courage* was the first thing he noticed in the West, coming out of the Soviet Union in the seventies. He was not very popular for saying it, but his words proved prophetic.[4]

It is hard *not* to notice how over the past decades, angry Muslim protests were often very successful in forcing governments or politicians to back down under pressure. One only has to think of the Salman Rushdie affair in Britain in 1989, or of the backlash to Italian Prime Minister Silvio Berlusconi's remarks in the wake of 9/11, as well as to Pope Benedict XVI's speech at Regensburg in 2006, or the mayhem the Danish cartoons evoked

---

2 *Anselm of Canterbury: The Major Works*, ed. by Davies and Evans (Oxford: Oxford University Press, 2008), 89.

3 Erwin W. Lutzer, *The Cross in the Shadow of the Crescent* (Eugene, OR: Harvest House, 2013), 39.

4 See "A World Split Apart (1978 / 2018)" on *Sober Minds*, soberminds.ca.

in European cities. In South Africa, the government had to apologize very quickly after the Synod of the Dutch Reformed Church in 1986 declared Islam a false religion somewhere in an internal committee report.[5] All around the world, governments, organizations, and individuals had to learn to yield in fear of Islam. It is that simple: threats work.

Targeted assassinations had a similar effect. One can still recall how the stabbing of Theo van Gogh in Amsterdam (with a warning pinned to his chest for Ayaan Hirsi Ali) left the Dutch nation reeling with shock. That murder came only two years after the assassination of another Dutch critic of Islam, Pim Fortuyn. And though the 2015 attack on the offices of *Charlie Hebdo* in Paris caused world leaders to march bravely through Paris in a show of strength, saying "Je Suis Charlie," we all know what the overall effect was: fear was struck into the hearts of Paris and Europe. Though I am firmly opposed to the public mocking of anyone's faith, as *Charlie Hebdo* did, not even that could justify targeted assassinations.

Nonetheless, the weakening of resolve continued unabated, until around 2015. Coinciding with the rise of ISIL and the massive refugee crisis in Europe, the pendulum began to swing back, albeit so slowly. As the brutal Syrian War turned a corner due to Russian intervention, sanity returned to many ordinary people of the West and even to some in high places. Civilizational suicide did not seem to be the most likely endgame anymore. Only time will tell if it was a matter of too little too late.

Why the Silence?

Few Muslims worldwide would like to associate themselves (at least openly) with Islamist terror movements and their affiliates. The same can be said in Africa regarding Boko Haram and Al Shabaab. The average Muslim thoroughly dislikes them. But that begs the question: why are they so silent? Why do they not oppose radical Islam much more? Is it because

---

5 Dr. Johan A. Heyns, professor of Systematic Theology and Ethics at the University of Pretoria and well-connected to the National Party government of the time, disclosed to his students that South Africa's Minister of Foreign Affairs, Roelf Botha, had received phone calls from Saudi Arabia, threatening South Africa that the Saudis would cut off oil supply to the country, should the DRC not back down on its statement about Islam.

many secretly share the same ideals? Or has violence been so much part of an age-old struggle for world domination—which will include the final "destruction of the cross"—that Muslims don't dare to oppose it? Do peaceful Muslims fear the consequences of voicing their concerns too much? We know that we humans tend to be like fish, swimming safely in the middle of the school, lest a predator take us out. Is that what is going on, or how should we understand the great silence?

Since the 9/11 attacks killed 2996 people in the U.S., major terrorist attacks in Europe *alone*, claimed by either Al Qaeda or ISIL, shook the cradle of Western civilization. These were the worst ones:[6]

Madrid 2004, killing 193
London 2007, killing 56
Paris 2015, killing 20
Paris 2015, killing 138
Brussels 2016, killing 35
Nice 2016, killing 87
Berlin 2016, killing 12
Manchester 2017, killing 23
London 2017, killing 11
Barcelona 2017, killing 24

These numbers only reflect the *death toll* in Europe, forgetting the thousands maimed and scarred both physically and mentally. The website of *thereligionofpeace.com* has kept a record of *all* Islamic attacks since 9/11 and has listed no less than forty thousand (40 000) worldwide. Why does the bulk of 1.8 billion adherents of Islam not rise against the shocking reality of these statistics? Is Islam then not the religion of peace?

One thing is sure; as it will take Westerners to address Western attitudes, Africans to address African attitudes, Asians to address Asian attitudes, Americans to address American attitudes, Russians to address Russian attitudes, Christians to address Christian attitudes, and Leftists to address Leftist attitudes. so it will take Muslims to address Muslim attitudes first of

6 "Terrorism in Europe," *Wikipedia* viewed on September 20, 2021, wikepedia.org.

all. This densely populated globe has no future unless we look at ourselves first and find the courage to speak out against our own group's aberrations, anomalies, evils, and folly. Outsiders may certainly hint and prod, but ultimately each sub-group of humanity needs to take responsibility for itself, exercising loyal self-critique, if we are going to coexist peacefully on this little planet. That's the best way to solve our problems as a global community.

But what if some don't want to stick the hand into their bosom? What if they instead have a centuries-long animus against others not of their creed, a strong proclivity for blame-shifting, and playing the victim card? Arab Muslim reformer Lafif Lakhdar mentions that both Islamists and racist right-wingers have "the inability to practice self-criticism."[7] We may add to this pitiful band of closed minds the woke Neo-Marxist left in the West.[8]

Islam's foundational documents contain a deeply-rooted religious rationale of oppression and violence against infidels and apostates, despite Mohammed and the Quran's concern for the poor and the needy among the *umma*. Moreover, ever since the twelfth century, any debate or discussion about these Islamic foundations was practically shut down. It happened in what is known in the Islamic world as "the closing of the gates of *ijtihad*."[9] *Ijtihad* basically means independent thinking on the basis of the Quran. When those gates closed, the Islamic golden age of reason and science was brought to an end,[10] as well as any questions about Islam itself. In a power struggle between the hardline Asharites and the moderate Mutazilites, the former won, closing down all reason independent of what the Quran and *hadith* actively commanded or forbade. That, beyond

7 Ulph and Sookhdeo (eds), *Reforming Islam*, 109.

8 British conservative columnist Peter Hitchens said that there is no citadel as impregnable as a closed mind. That tells us what battle we are up against in fighting political Islam.

9 *Ijtihad* represents the spirit of inquiry in Islam, i.e., independent reasoning, using the Quran and *hadith* as sources.

10 Sookhdeo, *Understanding Islamic Theology*, 46-48.

anything else, explains the silence and why speaking out is simply a bridge too far for so many within Islam.[11]

And yet, we should never lose hope. Some prominent Muslim leaders have spoken up in recent years. One example was the Egyptian leader Abdel Fattah el-Sisi addressing a crowd of Islamic clergy and scholars at Al-Azhar University in Cairo, asking them if they thought (like the extremists do) that billions of people around the globe need to be killed "so that they may live" (i.e., to fulfill Mohammed's dreams of a worldwide caliphate)?[12] Even more surprising were recently televised comments by Saudi Crown Prince Mohammed bin Salman that Islam urgently needs to reform and that 90 percent of the *hadith* is incompatible with modern society. What could this mean? It certainly sounds tremendously encouraging, because from our perspective, it is easy to conclude that most Muslims are far keener to ignore the problem of Islamic violence than to openly admit it.

Creating an Atmosphere of Fear

The moral of the story is that anger and violence work. I still recall driving my car, fresh in the wake of 9/11, hearing that Queen Elizabeth II said, "nothing these terrorists did will ever change the way we live our lives." I had sympathy for her, for she needed to comfort millions. But nothing could have been further from the truth. Fear began to grip the entire world by the throat. One only has to think of what happened to international air travel to realize that the Queen was too optimistic.

All the terrorist attacks mentioned above had one single purpose: to create fear, which will cause "the enemy" to yield. In the West, it means that we have to live under the dark cloud of excessive "political correctness," in which more and more Islamophobia laws can be passed through legislative assemblies to prevent anyone from talking about Islamist atrocities in the future. That means that *Islamist* extremism has, in effect, been sanctioned and that *dawa* is now firing on all cylinders.

11 That ordinary informed Muslims are well aware of the defeat of the Mutazilites and sound reason in Islam has become clear to me through several sources. Here is one: Mansour, *Minority of One*, 52.

12 See Hirsi Ali, *Heretic*, 70.

Such an atmosphere of fear creates a situation where tense Westerners (and Africans), bent on a program of appeasement, even begin to turn on each other, if anyone dares to raise the alarm. And suddenly, the age-old virtue of cherishing your heritage, culture, and faith has also now become taboo to our governing elites, in fear of a backlash from who-knows-where, so that even most Muslims scratch their heads about our pitiful suicidal temperament. On all sides, fear is winning because violence, on the one hand, and unatoned societal guilt, on the other, are working in tandem. That has been obvious everywhere for years, as Shelby Steele proved so eloquently in a column written for the *Wall Street Journal*, "White Guilt and the Western Past," published in 2006.[13]

Whether it is Belgian authorities changing the names of Christian holidays so as not to offend, or Danish school children obligated to read portions of the Quran but none of the Bible, or Germans offering a famous Reformation-era cathedral to Muslims for prayer, or Swedish politicians turning a blind eye to inner-city violence and the ongoing sexual harassment of women, or the British shunning tenacious reports of the grooming and raping of school girls, or a Christian school in South Africa denying the Son of God to appease Muslims, or Cologne police officers looking away when German women are groped, or American Bible-translators seeking to eliminate reference to the Son of God from the Bible, or a celebrity preacher claiming that all Abrahamic religions teach the same thing, or Christians in Canada refusing to raise the issue of persecution in their dialogue with Muslims, it goes on and on. On all sides, we are caving in, hoping that "neutrality" and appeasement will ultimately be the game-changer, transforming the tiger of Islam into a meek little kitten we can handle.

If ever there was wishful thinking, this is it: to fancy that political Islam will reform itself by our never opposing or criticizing it. It defies the laws of logic and the chilling facts of how Islam became the world's "fastest-growing religion." We know from physics that you can only stop a moving force with a more potent counterforce. How in the world do we then think

---

13 See "White Guilt and the Western Past" by Shelby Steele, in *The Wallstreet Journal*, Tuesday, May 2, 2006.

that gullibility and meekness will stop a force that promised from its inception to be victorious through terror?

Instilling fear through threats is also how Islam deals with dissidents within itself. By using a process called *takfir*[14] a moderate Muslim can easily be designated an infidel or an apostate by radicals. The significance of this is obvious. Once a person, community, or government has been labeled apostate through *takfir*, violence against them is fully justified, and few questions need to be asked.[15] That is why some brave advocates plead for *human rights* for ex-Muslims, because they have none. Why does no one have to fight for the human rights of ex-Christians, ex-atheists, ex-Hindus, ex-lesbians, or whoever? Because only ex-Muslims generally fear for their lives around the world.

And it doesn't matter how famous or ordinary you are. Princess Latifa Al Maktoum of Dubai disappeared in 2018. The world was told she was in the *loving care* of her family. But video material smuggled to the BBC proved otherwise. She was the prisoner of her father, the Emir of Dubai. Who knows what she had done to deserve that? After what must have been a horrifying experience, she escaped under daring circumstances, and was apparently seen somewhere in Europe, last reported to be in Iceland.[16]

Preventing Individuals from Leaving Islam

Nowhere does the instrument of fear work better than when Muslims want to leave the faith. It remains an open question how long Islam would last—let alone be the "fastest growing religion"—if its adherents were free to go. There is a growing concern deep within the Muslim-majority world about the number of Muslims secretly leaving, especially among the youth. An imam warns online that up to 24 percent of Muslim youth are leaving the faith. An American convert to Islam says that scores of Muslim youths disclose their unbelief to him confidentially since they are too afraid to talk

14 The act of declaring another Muslim an unbeliever.

15 A *takfiri* is a Muslim who accuses another of apostasy, causing many headaches to moderate Muslim authorities. See Mansour, *Minority of One*, 28.

16 "Princess Latifa: Dubai photo appears to show missing woman", *BBC News* website, May 22, 2021.

to their parents or imams. Another video says that a very high percentage of Muslims in the Middle East no longer care to attend a mosque. And *Al Jazeera Television* once reported that "if Malaysia allows conversions to Christianity [it] could trigger off mass conversions from Islam."[17] A prominent leader of the Muslim Brotherhood, Yusuf Al-Qaradawi, said:

> If they had gotten rid of apostasy punishment Islam would not exist today. Islam would have ended with the death of the Prophet; peace be upon him. Opposing apostasy is what kept Islam to this day.[18]

And yet amazingly, Muslims love to quote Surah 2:256 of the Quran, "that there is no compulsion in religion", while ignoring the very context of that chapter, which commanded early Muslims to slay those who fight against (i.e., resist) Islam.

Depending on where they find themselves in this world, the dangers posed to a Muslim leaving Islam may vary from death threats and imprisonment to bodily assaults and kidnapping, or at least the loss of friends, family, and employment. When telling her story, the female co-presenter of *Somali Christian Television* related what she faced from her family after being baptized as a believer. Though they were a close-knit family before, Shania's mother said that she would have killed her daughter with her own hands if she could, after hearing of her conversion to Jesus Christ.[19]

All of this is rather strange in the light of Islam's confidence that Allah is the only true God, full of mercy and compassion, and that you and I only need to be informed that we were all born Muslims. St. John's Gospel tells us in chapter 10 what "no compulsion" looks like. It means that, like sheep following their shepherd from the sheepfold out into the field—because they recognize and trust his voice—so Jesus' disciples through all ages followed him freely because they love and trust him as the Good Shepherd. All who came before or after him, pretending to be our shepherd, are

---

17 Lutzer, *The Cross in the Shadow,* 73. The occasion was when Lina Joy, a Malay woman, wanted her conversion to Christianity to be recognized by the Malaysian courts.

18 Hirsi Ali, *Heretic*, 55-56.

19 "Shania's Testimony with Al Fadi, on Let Us Reason..." *English Somali Christian TV*, on *YouTube.*

killers, thieves, and robbers. They are strangers whom the sheep will never trust and follow. The Good Shepherd does not have to threaten us with hellfire to follow him,[20] much less with a sword, or with *dhimmi*-status, or apostasy laws. We follow him because he spoke like no other, filled with grace and truth, coming down to us from the bosom of the Father. He then even laid down his life for us—to take it up again. For greater love, no one ever had, than to lay down his life for his friends.

Little wonder a young Muslim convert once told a pastor of the Moody Bible Church in Chicago that he accepted Christ after reading how Jesus asked his disciples in John 6:67, "Do you also want to go away?" "Amazing," he thought, "and how different from Mohammed, who would threaten you with death for leaving Islam?"[21] In other words, ours is a God who respects human freedom, which we saw as an essential part of the *Imago Dei*. The ancient *Letter to Diognetus*, dating from the second century, makes this abundantly clear. God does not force himself on human beings. The letter said: "He willed to save man by persuasion, not by compulsion, for compulsion is not God's way of working." This saying, wrote Italian scholar Marcellino D'Ambrosio, was so often quoted in early Christian literature that it became a popular proverb at the time.[22]

And yet, let it be clear to all, freedom of conscience and religion is now at risk all over the world, threatened by both the radical Left and Right,[23] and political Islam. Article 9 of the United Kingdom's *Human Rights Act* protects "the freedom of thought, beliefs, and religion" of its citizens. That basic human right of citizens in the *free world* always included the right to "change your religion at any time." However, please take note that "religious liberty" is not the same as "freedom of worship." There is a huge difference between the two. Christian migrants from other countries in the Arabian Peninsula are "free to worship" in designated areas under many

20 Jesus only threatened hardened sinners and hypocritical elites with the danger of hellfire.

21 Lutzer, *The Cross in the Shadow*, 72.

22 Marcellino D'Ambrosio, *When the Church was Young* (Cincinnati: Franciscan Media, 2014), 44.

23 Of which the Ukrainian Neo-Nazi website and Research Centre *Myrotvorets* is the most shocking current example, see myrotvorets.center

restrictions. Muslim authorities will not interfere, at least not according to law. But no Muslim in Arabia can change their religion and join them. That is the difference between the two ideas.

Here is the problem: How long will we still have "religious liberty" in the West if *dawa* continues to be successful? A reliable source told me that lobbyists are currently pushing the United Nations to replace its protection of "religious liberty" with "freedom of worship." That would be a massive loss for humankind and a huge victory for Islamic *dawa*.

The Penalties for Apostasy

A few countries still have the death penalty for any Muslim leaving Islam, like Mauritania, Saudi Arabia, and until recently, Sudan and Qatar. State executions for apostasy (and other crimes such as blasphemy, adultery, etc.) occur regularly in Saudi Arabia.[24]

However, most Muslim countries do not have a law calling for the execution of apostates, perhaps not even to punish someone for leaving Islam. Sudan recently scrapped its apostasy laws when it departed from the harsh ways of its former leader, Omar Hassan al-Bashir. That does not mean all is well though, since authorities will often seek another law to prosecute an apostate, to deter any defection from Islam. The rationale behind such prosecution is that a good citizen will be a good Muslim, for apostasy is seen as an unpardonable sin against Allah and treason against the state.[25]

Sharia sets out a list of punishments for apostates, like the dissolution of the apostate's marriage, loss of custody of children, loss of inheritance rights, etc. But even if no official punishment is passed, there is always the possibility of "honour killings" to restore a family's pride, which has begun to plague Muslim communities in the West as well. In her book *Heretic – Why Islam Needs a Reformation Now*, Ayaan Hirsi Ali provides a sorrowful litany of such honour killings, most of which occurred in Pakistan.[26] These honour killings are all about how social control of "commanding right and

24 See Hirsi Ali, *Heretic*, 157-159.

25 Sookhdeo, *Dawa*, 129.

26 Hirsi Ali, *Heretic*, 157-159.

forbidding wrong" is implemented by the *umma* on its members, often involving the close family or friends of the unhappy victim.

Authorities, on their part, often discourage conversion away from Islam by not resisting the harassment and persecution of ex-Muslims. If converts to Christianity (or to some other faith or atheism) manage to escape execution or imprisonment, they can nevertheless lose their jobs, be attacked, and even be killed, and often no one will be charged. At the very least, they can expect to be ostracized or undergo years of sorrow and separation from loved ones. Powerful accounts from *I Dare to Call Him Father*[27] in 1979 to *Seeking Allah, Finding Jesus*[28] in 2014, tell the heroic stories of disciples coming out of Islam to fôllow of Jesus.

Persecution of Liberal Muslims

Another form of fear-strategy is by keeping the faithful in line and disciplining any who dare to raise serious questions. Heresy in Islam is almost as bad as apostasy. A few Muslims worldwide dare to speak out and call for reform. One thinks of the female author, once called Osama bin Laden's worst nightmare, Irshad Manji; the courageous imam from Australia, tirelessly warning the West against radical Islam; and the brave but humorous Youtuber Mufti Abu Layth, whose home and family were attacked as recently as April 2021.[29] In *Reforming Islam – Progressive Voices from the Arab Muslim World*,[30] the brave voices of many moderate Muslim scholars can be heard cutting to the heart of the problems besetting their world.

An example of what can happen to a loyal critic of Islam is the case of Dr. Nasr Hamid Abu Zayd of Egypt. Abu Zayd did linguistic research on Muslim sources, which enraged Islamists in his home country.[31] Radicals declared he was guilty of blasphemy, and Muslim lawyers charged him with apostasy, although he said he was a faithful Muslim. He was found guilty by the *Cairo Appeals Court* in 1995 and was ordered to separate

27 Bilquis Sheikh and Richard Schneider, *I Dared to Call Him Father* (Kingsway, 1979).

28 Qureshi, Nabeel, *Seeking Allah, Finding Jesus* (Grand Rapids: Zondervan, 2014).

29 "Mufti Abu Layth's Home and Family Attacked by Terrorists", David's Wood's *Acts17Apologetics*, viewed May 17, 2021, on *YouTube*.

30 Edited by Ulph and Sookhdeo.

31 Sookhdeo, *Dawa*, 130-131.

from his wife. The ruling, based on the Islamic principle of *hisba*, which permits any Muslim to defend Islamic morals and behaviour, was the first in Egypt and served only to encourage Islamists.

All of the above should convince us how effective Islamic violence and threats are in the overall scheme of things, and that as Christians we should study the subtle psychological impact of it all on our own hearts and churches, lest we lose our calling to be a beacon of hope to this world.

Blasphemy and Muslim Mob-Justice

One of the most shocking cultural aspects in some Muslim-majority countries is the prevalence of random mob justice to punish anyone for supposedly committing blasphemy. It could happen in a flash. Somebody cries "blasphemy!" and before you know it an angry mob descends on a poor victim, stoning her to death or setting him on fire. Any motive could be the driver, like to settle scores or to get revenge for whatever reason. Since Christians have fewer rights before the law under *sharia*, and their testimony bears little weight, blasphemy laws put them at high risk.

A sad and widely reported case recently occurred in Sokoto, northern Nigeria, when a nineteen-year-old Christian student, Deborah Samuel, was accused of insulting Islam's prophet on social media before being stoned and set on fire, with the perpetrators filming the horrific murder. Her accusers demanded that she retract her words that Jesus helped her pass her exams. She refused, and then apparently said something in return about Islam's prophet on a student online group-chat, that aroused Muslim anger. For that one line on social media, she was then summarily killed. The Sultan of Sokoto unequivocally condemned the murder, but the chief imam of Abuja Central Mosque refused to do so.[32]

We are dealing here with jungle justice, based on *false charges*, but which, even if based on valid charges, remain inexplicably evil. It is a monstrous perversion of all justice. Consider that there are few crimes more strongly condemned in Holy Scripture than the sins of slander and false testimony. The ninth commandment, "You shall not bear false witness against your neighbour"

32 Achike Chude, "The killing of Deborah Samuel," *The Guardian — Opinion*, May 23, 2022, on guardian.ng

was primarily intended to safeguard justice in Israel and, by implication, truth-speaking in general. Whoever was found to be a malicious witness under the Mosaic Law was supposed to receive the very penalty intended to bring upon an innocent victim.[33]

The same law applied to all Israelites and foreigners, male and female. And if it was later believed among the Jews that a man's testimony bore more weight than that of a woman, then it was added to the Torah, corrupting the words of Moses.

The Old Testament contains several inspiring stories revealing the horror of false testimony. The account of poor Naboth, falsely accused by Jezebel, comes to mind, as well as the stories of Joseph in Egypt and Daniel in Babylon, who were both falsely accused by malicious witnesses. The Jewish apocryphal writing *Susannah* contains the story of a beautiful Hebrew woman falsely accused by four of her elders sometime during the exile, and how they ended up facing the death penalty for their heinous crime. And then, during the reign of Tiberius Caesar, humanity witnessed the worst case of them all when a Galilean carpenter-rabbi was falsely accused and sentenced to a horrifying death, having committed no crime in his entire life. In every case, the reader senses the evil of false testimony and how much God hates it.

Do most of the world's Muslims care about this? Or can anyone be charged with blasphemy, even for no reason, to suffer the most horrible consequences, with the perpetrators getting away with impunity? The world watched with bated breath as a young mother, Asia Bibi, awaited her execution for eight years, after being falsely charged with blasphemy in Pakistan.[34] Let it be known that there are countless more cases like hers. She was "lucky" to reach the headlines and to cause an international outcry.

Yet another heartbreaking story comes to us from Nigeria. It was reported by the American advocacy group *International Christian Concern*:[35]

---

33 See Deut. 19:18-21.

34 Robert Kenna, "Asia Bibi: Pakistani Christian on Death Row for Blasphemy Released from Prison," *Open Doors USA*, October 31, 2018, viewed on opendoorsusa.org.

35 Nathan Johnson, Jean Pauline Jones, & Jay Church, *Secular Sharia - Criminal Sharia Law and its impact on Nigeria's Christian Communities* (Silver Spring: International Christian Concern, 2021) 5-6, download.

On March 21, 2007, in Gandu, Gombe State, Nigeria, Christianah Oluwatoyin Oluwasesin, a schoolteacher and married mother of two, was brutally lynched by her students after being falsely accused of desecrating the Quran.

At Gandu Government Day Secondary School, the government teacher was in high spirits that morning as she traveled to her classroom to hand out final examinations. Since students had previously been caught cheating, she collected student belongings, per school policy, and placed them in front of the class. Unbeknownst to her, one of the students in the all-girls classroom had a Quran in her bag, causing an uproar as students began to shout, "Allahu Akbar."

Aluke Musa Yila, a fellow teacher, ran to the classroom upon hearing the commotion: "Soon after the bags collected by Oluwasesin were dropped in front of the class, one of the girls in the class began to cry. She told her colleagues that she had a copy of the Quran in her bag, that Oluwasesin touched the bag, and that by doing so she had desecrated the Quran since she was a Christian."

Multiple teachers ran to the classroom to assist Oluwasesin and escorted her to the principal's office for safety. She was hidden in the office bathroom, which was then locked to keep students out. Soon, though, the entire school was enraged, and outside Muslim extremists joined the unruly mob.

"They destroyed school property and were demanding that Oluwasesin must be given to them to be stoned to death," Yila said. "When we could not give in by releasing Oluwasesin to them, they started stoning us." Soon, Muslim extremists broke into the principal's office and dragged Oluwasesin out, insisting that they kill her.

Oluwasesin's husband recounted the events that followed with tears: "The students and outsiders, who joined, tied her up, beat and tortured her. One of the students later took a knife and slit her throat. They cut her into pieces and set what was left on fire. They burnt her car also and almost killed my son, Emmanuel. He was only ten months old then. A nice woman hid him in her long gown and saved his life." Authorities released every person suspected in Oluwasesin's murder without charge.

What more can be said? No words in the universe can describe the horror that such a crime evokes in the human heart. One can only look to the heavens and cry, "God, have mercy on the human race!" How is it possible that we can descend to such demonic depths of depravity?

Can a *hadith* of Abu Dawud (4361) possibly provide the clue?[36] A blind man once came to Mohammed, admitting to having stabbed his pregnant slave girl to death. The man claimed that she had reviled Islam's prophet, and wouldn't stop, even when he asked her. When she refused, he pushed a dagger into her stomach until she and her unborn child died. The blind man was terrified, but Mohammed's response was: "Bear witness that no retaliation is due for her blood."

Note that this hadith nowhere indicates that any investigation was made into the allegation of blasphemy.[37] We have to go by the blind man's words. How do we even know she mocked Islam's prophet? How do we know he did not kill her because they were arguing, or because she refused him sex, or because she burned his food? We only have her master's words to go by. But Mohammed says that is sufficient. No punishment is due for this murder.

Could this perhaps be why some radical Muslims feel justified in executing mob justice? Somebody yells: "Help, he insulted the Quran!" or "Help, she mocked Mohammed!" and no more questions are asked. The mob descends, and some poor victim suffers the consequences. If Mohammed did not investigate the charges against the slave girl, why should it be done today, even if one happens to agree with *sharia's* blasphemy laws? Little wonder Christians and Hindus in Pakistan must be careful not to get involved in an argument about *anything* with a Muslim. It can turn ugly in a moment for something you have never done or said.

---

36 "40 Prescribed Punishments (Kitab Al-Hudud)", on Sunnah.com.

37 I learned this first from Dr. David Wood when his *YouTube* channel *Acts17Apologetics* was still running.

CHAPTER 10

DAWA THROUGH JIHAD

We have seen that *dawa* is linked to *jihad*. Both have the same aim, to spread Islam and its dominion.[1] From the Muslims Brotherhood's world-view and strategy, we also learned that peaceful and militant means are interchangeable; whichever works best in a given situation should be employed until the goal is reached.[2] In all of this Mohammed's *sunna* of the seventh century plays a pivotal role. We saw how he underwent a metamorphosis during twenty-three years, first in his attitude and strategy toward the polytheist Arabs of Mecca and then toward the monotheist Jews of Medina.[3]

It was then that *jihad* became inherently part of Islam. The Arabic word *jihad* can be interpreted in various ways. It can mean a personal struggle for purity, or trying to correct wrong and support right by your voice and actions, or it could mean military war against non-Muslims and all who

1 Sookhdeo, *Dawa*, 117.

2 Ibid., chapter 6 "*Dawa* and Deception."

3 Ibid., chapter 7 "*Dawa* and Victimhood."

resist Islam.[4] Muslim apologists in the West have tried to convince us that *jihad* is mostly, if not exclusively, about the first two of these meanings,[5] but history, both distant and recent, tells a different story.

The End of Terror or a Shift in Strategy?

From a northern hemisphere perspective, it seems that Islamic terror has tapered off over the last few years, and it certainly did. It happened mainly due to the defeat of the ISIL caliphate in northern Syria and Iraq by a combination of Russian, Syrian, American, and Kurdish efforts. But has the problem of militant Islam subsided? Even in Europe, it is too soon to tell.

When we look at the continent of Africa, we realize that *dawa* has merely diverted its militant operations. The brutal terror campaign of ISIL and Al Qaeda merely shifted from the Middle East to Africa, where they linked up with Boko Haram and Al Shabaab. The *Global Terrorism Index* provides a comprehensive summary of key global trends and patterns in terrorism over the last fifty years. The GTI 2020 report says that deaths from terrorism in 2019 fell for the fifth consecutive year after peaking in 2014.[6] Deaths related to terrorism overall are down 59 percent from its last spike in 2014. That is terrific news. Moreover, one-hundred-and-three countries (or seven of the nine regions of the world) improved their GTI score.[7] But this is about where the good news ends. The report states that seven of the ten countries that saw the largest increase in terror are in Sub-Saharan Africa, the part of the globe that hardly features on the mainline news of the rest of the world.

> ISIL's affiliate groups remain active worldwide and have become especially prominent in sub-Saharan Africa, where deaths attributed to ISIL affiliates have increased. Twenty-seven countries experienced a terrorist attack caused by ISIL or one of its affiliates. The expansion of ISIL affiliates into sub-Saharan Africa led to a surge in terrorism in many countries in the

---

4 Ibid., 117.

5 See "Introduction." of *The Quran*, translated by Maulana Wahiduddin Khan, xiv - xvii.

6 *Global Terrorism Index 2020 - Measuring the Impact of Terrorism.* Downloaded, GTI2020Terrorism.pdf

7 We are considering deaths, incidents, injuries, and property damage from terrorism.

> region. Seven of the ten countries with the largest increase in terrorism were in sub-Saharan Africa: Burkina Faso, Mozambique, Democratic Republic of Congo (DRC), Mali, Niger, Cameroon, and Ethiopia. These countries face various ecological threats, are amongst the countries with the highest population growth and suffer from low societal resilience. The largest increase in deaths from terrorism occurred in Burkina Faso, where deaths rose from 86 to 593, a 590 percent increase.[8]

The report also cites the two most important trends in terrorism during the previous year: the proliferation of ISIL affiliates around the world and the rise of far-right terrorism in the West, both of which leave much room for concern. One may indeed ask why incidents of neo-Nazi far-right terrorism are rising? Does it perhaps also have to do with liberal governments sticking their heads in the sand about the problem of political Islam while, simultaneously, promoting woke madness? And, what does it mean that ISIL affiliates have spread so deep into Africa in particular, not to mention other parts of the globe? It should be clear that a premature elation about the drop in terrorist violence, primarily in Europe, has everything to do with a broad shift in strategy ever since the ISIL caliphate was defeated in the Levant.

Religious Cleansing

We have now come to the darkest part of *dawa*— the cleansing of the land, to make room for the people of Allah. My eyes were opened to this gruesome reality sometime in 2014. The saddest thing about it was this: It all happened with "our" broad Western approval, thanks to our main stream media's uncontested power to control the news.

A friend told me about Syrian Christians, whose extended family in northern Syria had just suffered terribly at the hands of ISIL. As we sat down with them, enjoying tea in their humble apartment, they told us how ISIL came through their family village near Raqqa in north-eastern Syria a few weeks before, raping, killing or carrying off twenty-two of their extended family members. They also showed me pictures of their beautiful

8 *Global Terrorism Index 2020*, 2.

church building, which President Assad once visited, now laying in ruins. The visit left an indelible impression on my mind of how cruel *jihad* is. And yet, through the entire Syrian War, our western media and governments supported the Syrian opposition for the supposed reason of getting rid of "an evil dictator."[9] Those in Syria who were worshiping the Triune God, as well as most Muslims who preferred living in a secular state, found themselves fighting a foe (supported by the West) that was going to impose *sharia*, raise the black flag over Damascus, and slaughter all Christians. Granted, the Americans did eventually support the Kurds to get rid of the jihadis north-east of the Euphrates, but only because that is where the Syrian oil-fields were. The Americans still occupy that part of Syria to this day.

Great was my surprise when I later discovered an article from Canada's *Maclean's* magazine published four years before the war, under the following headline: "Born Again in Syria".[10] The article reported how not only Catholic and Orthodox believers, but also Protestants and evangelicals, were free to worship without fear in Syria as recently as 2006. In other words, the country of the "evil dictator" was not as bad as we were all told until the eve of the devastating war. *Maclean's* confirmed what my Syrian friends told me, namely that Syria's three million Christians were not treated as *dhimmis* before the war, but were treated with respect. Yet four years later, the entire Western world felt it necessary to arm and support an insurgent army of Salafist jihadis, of whom 70 percent came from *outside* the country according to veteran German journalist Jürgen Todenhöfer.[11] They were fighting alongside so-called "moderate rebels" to bring about regime change in Damascus.

America and her allies, Israel included, did not move a finger to stop the advance of Jabhat al-Nusra, ISIL, the Islamic Front, and Ahrar al-Sham

9 The real reason had more to do with Damascus' refusal to allow a natural-gas pipeline to run from the Gulf to Europe through Syria. The War against Assad was planned in the U.S. after 9/11, well before the dictator's brutal crackdown of an uprising during the Arab Spring in 2011. See chapter 12.

10 Michael Petrou, "Born Again in Syria" *Maclean's*, January 30, 2006, p.18-19.

11 Jürgen Todenhöfer, *My Journey*, 164. Todenhöfer was the only Western journalist allowed to visit the Islamic State in Syria at the time.

toward Damascus. It waved through deliveries of cash and weapons to these organizations.[12] Had the Russians not intervened by mid-2015, Syria would have fallen to Sunni extremists, with the land thoroughly cleansed of every trace of Christianity and other religious minorities. So complete was the Western support for the jihadi-side that a whole page of letters appearing in Canada's conservative *National Post*, under the heading "What does the West do About Syria?", contained only one going against the grain, written by yours truly.[13]

Indeed, so complete was the media's deception that fellow Christians frowned when I publicly thanked God in prayer for Aleppo's liberation in 2016. Everyone thought the city "had fallen." Somehow, they never asked themselves afterward how it then came about that Aleppo's church bells only started ringing again *after* it "had fallen", and *after* a five-year lull. This sad example illustrates how little we in the West understand about *jihad* and how easily we fall for state propaganda, so that we even promote the slaughter of fellow Christians far away. Recently yet, a bashful female Syrian store attendant disclosed to me personally, almost whispering, that it is due to the Russian intervention in 2015 that peace returned to her country.[14]

Religious cleansing has been ongoing under the banner of Islam for ages. In *The Lost History of Christianity* Philip Jenkins tells the tragic story of *The Thousand Year Golden Age of Christianity and How it Died.* During the early fourteenth century, "wholesale massacres" by Islamic conquerors destroyed churches in the Middle East and beyond. Entire Christian communities were annihilated across central Asia. Jenkins quotes a contemporary of those times whose words are as sad as they

12 Jürgen Todenhöfer, *My Journey*, 235-236.

13 See "What does the West do about Syria?", *Letters, National Post*, February 13, 2013, A11.

14 The truth about the Syrian War eventually trickled through to those who cared enough to know, thanks to the heroic work done by some amazing women; Bolivian actress Carla Ortiz, Canadian activist Eva Bartlett, Hawaiian politician Tulsi Gabbard, as well as *by* Canadian journalist Aaron Maté.

are chilling: "The persecutions and disgrace and mockings and ignominy which the Christians suffered at this time, especially in Baghdad, words cannot describe".[15]

At Amida, on the banks of the Tigris River (today's Diyarbakir in south-eastern Turkey), where twelve thousand were carried into slavery by Muslim invaders, "the destruction of churches and monasteries was so thorough that fires reputedly burned for a month." Jenkins continues: "These persecutions had a greater effect on the Middle East than any other event since the conversion of the Roman Empire."[16]

The tragic scenes that swept through once famous Christian cities such as Alexandria, Jerusalem, Damascus, Antioch, Smyrna, Constantinople, and the like left Christianity so traumatized that our forefathers chose rather not to talk about it and left it out of our history books. Here is another heartbreaking report, coming to us from 1268, when the Muslim Mamluk general Baybars wrote smugly to the ruler of Antioch (who happened to be in Tripoli when his city was captured):

> You would have seen crosses in your churches smashed, pages of the false testaments scattered, and the patriarchs' tombs overturned. You would have seen your Muslim enemy trampling on where you celebrate the Mass, cutting the throats of monks, priests, and deacons upon the altars, bringing sudden death to the Patriarchs and slavery to the royal princes. You would have seen the fire running through palaces, your dead burned in this world before going down to the fires of the next, your place unrecognizable, the Church of St. Paul and that of the cathedral of St. Peter pulled down and destroyed.[17]

Religious cleansing began in Medina in the seventh century. Mohammed called for the digging of trenches in the sand of that desert town and called hundreds of Jewish men, all who have reached puberty, to step up to them. They would pay the ultimate price for not submitting to Allah; their wives and children looking on in horror.

---

15 Philip Jenkins, *The Lost History of Christianity*, 130.

16 Ibid.

17 Lutzer, *The Cross in the Shadow of the Crescent*, 98.

It befits us to realize that the doctrine of *jihad* and religious cleansing has never been revoked. It is still on the books. The land must be cleared for the caliphate to be established. What follows is a chilling reminder of what Christian families in Syria and elsewhere in the world woke up to in recent times, according to *Voice of the Martyrs*:[18]

TO THE FAMILY OF THE INFIDELS

IN THE NAME OF ALLAH, AND OF
HIS FINAL PROPHET MUMAMMAD
(PEACE BE UPON HIM).

The true religion of Islam WILL ARISE in your area;
you cannot stop Allah's will.
We have been watching your family, we have seen you go to
church, and seen you pray to your false God.
We know that you are infidels and we will deal
with you as our holy Quran declares;
In Sura 9 verse 5 it says TO SLAY the idolaters wherever you find them;
take them captive and besiege them.

It also says in Sura 9 verse 29 to FIGHT those who have been given
the scripture and (who) believe not in Allah or the Last day
or follow not the religion of truth.
If you and your entire family do not leave your false
religion and follow Islam, you will be killed.
Your sons will be slaughtered, and your daughters will become
Muslim wives, bearing sons who will fight for Allah in this region.
Your ONLY other option is to FLEE TONIGHT.
Leave your home and everything behind.

18 Ibid, 163.

Can we imagine waking up discovering such a notice pinned to your front door? As I am writing, we have good reason to fear that the same thing is happening in Afghanistan now that the Taliban has taken over. We saw that it happened to Armenian believers in Turkey early in the twentieth century. It happened in Syria and Iraq from 2011 to 2015. Thank God it could not be completed, and that there is still a remnant left worshiping Jesus and even growing in number again. Religious cleansing also came to Sudan and Somalia late in the twentieth century and has swept through large parts of Nigeria for the last decade. It is now spreading into Mali, Burkina Faso, Cameroon, the remote east of the Democratic Republic of the Congo, and even into the far north of Mozambique.

Its plan is always the same. To drive entire communities of non-Muslims from their tribal lands, to cleanse the earth from all *kufar* (infidels), tipping the balance of power by radically reducing opposition numbers. Africa's most populous Christian nation, Nigeria, is now beginning to tilt dangerously away from the cross to the crescent due to the brutal campaign of ethnic cleansing over the last two decades. Israeli news website *Arutz Sheva 7* reported in August 2021 that "Jihad murder has a successful trial run in Nigeria—and the media are ignoring it." It went on to say that the murder of 43 000 Christians in Nigeria over recent years is not deemed newsworthy by Western media outlets and that the country is "on the verge of genocide."[19]

How is this possible? Have we then forgotten what some of our Western leaders so piously said in the wake of the 1994 Rwandan genocide? President Bill Clinton confessed on television: "Had we gone in a hurry, we could have saved a third of the lives." The Rwandan genocide was over in the blink of an eye compared to Nigeria's. It was not religious but ethnic. But in Nigeria, another U.S. President, Barack Obama, or rather his State Department, went so far as to refuse to help the Nigerians in their fight against Boko Haram. The reason given was because of supposed human

19 "Jihadi-Murder is having a successful trial run in Nigeria - and the media are ignoring it." by Giulio Meotti, *Arutz Sheva 7*, August 9, 2021, on israelnationalnews.com.

rights violations in the Nigerian army, but it is more likely that it was the Nigerian refusal to sign up for America's enlightened LGBT agenda.[20]

Further south, an Islamic State insurgency is underway in Cabo Delgado, the remote northern province of Mozambique. *World* magazine reported that not even the risk to giant oil companies, like Exxon, Mobil, and Total, drilling off-shore, could compel Western action, so dangerous is the situation.[21] When mercenaries from the Russian Wagner Group went in trying to help, they were not only met by a brutal enemy in the warm African savannah, quickly severing eleven of their heads, but by the open scorn of the Western media.[22]

The ISIL affiliate in Mozambique is called *Ahlu Sunnah Wa-Jama* (ASWJ), which means "followers of the prophetic tradition". Yes, it is the tradition we mentioned many times, inspiring thugs to cleanse the land of infidels by burning, pillaging, raping, killing, and forcing young men to join them. In doing so, they target not only Christians but also moderate Muslims. Everyone is fleeing. American-based Iris Global Ministries evacuated some of its posts in Cabo Delgado, while Médecins Sans Frontières (Doctors without Borders) also withdrew due to the attacks. *World* reported in 2020 that "the provincial capital Pemba now resembles a warzone."[23]

We are faced with a bleak picture, but thanks to God, that is not the end of the story. Extremist Islam has a way of not only playing perfectly into the hands of the devil but also into the hands of Almighty God. One of the core reasons why many Muslims get "fed up" with Islam is because of what is being done and said in the name of Allah. Many Muslim refugees who have arrived in Europe in recent years embraced our Saviour for this very reason. The church in Syria not only got a new lease on life but is being blessed with spiritual revival and many new converts from Islam; in Iran,

---

20 Philip Obaji Jr, "U.S. to Nigeria: No Guns to Fight Boko Haram", April 14, 2017, *The Daily Beast*, on thedailybeast.com

21 Onize Ohikere, "Brutal and Brazen." *World*, June 27, 2020, 74-79.

22 Ben Hill, "Vlad's Cowards", *The Scottish Sun*, April 1, 2021, on thescottishsun.co.uk

23 Ohikere, "Brutal and Brazen," 79.

where millions are turning against the Shia extremism of the Ayatollahs, thousands continue to find hope and healing in Israel's Messiah.

Persecution of Christians

During the twentieth century, Communism turned out to be the foremost persecutor of Christianity. When we look at the past two millennia, however, Islam towers above all others for having shed more Christian blood and having destroyed more Christian churches than any other adversary.[24] This begs the question: Why? Why were Christians (and Jews) Islam's favourite target for so long?

Before we seek an answer to this question, let us briefly look at the sheer magnitude of the tragedy. That militant Islamists are singling out Christians in their attacks has become abundantly clear in recent years in Africa and beyond. The horrific attacks on Garissa University in Kenya in 2015 (leaving 148 dead) and on Sri Lanka on Easter Sunday in 2019 (leaving 269 dead) were supposed to send a chilling message to all Christians of the world: "We are coming for you!" Reports in recent years from many countries in South-East Asia, the Middle East and Africa have all confirmed this very clearly.

It has become a pattern: When the terrorists arrive, Christians are asked to identify themselves, while others are allowed to go. Then the Christians are summarily summoned to say the *shahada* or to face the consequences. The sad reality, however, is that the targeting of Christians is almost systematically denied. In *The Next Jihad* a Jewish rabbi and Christian pastor provide the grim details of how not only the Nigerian government but even an American ambassador to the country collaborated in camouflaging the fact of a deliberate cleansing of Christians from Nigeria by their clever political rhetoric. They made the conflict sound like a mere battle between herders and farmers for grazing space and fertile land; not to deny that the latter issue also plays a role in Nigeria's crisis. Sadly though, the sheer number of deaths and destruction, of pastors killed, schoolgirls kidnapped, and houses, churches, and schools burned will dispel all doubts about what is really going on. The authors state that "denying the religious element in

24 Johnstone, *Future of the Global Church*, 21-65.

Nigeria's conflict defies credulity." And yet, someone of the stature of Mr. John Campbell, a senior fellow at the Council on Foreign Relations, could still write in 2019, "When Christians or Muslims are killed in the Middle Belt (of Nigeria), it is not clear exactly why."[25]

The situation in Nigeria serves as a solemn reminder of what *jihad* is all about, and it is going on all the time. When Boko Haram kidnaped 276 mostly Christian girls from Chibok in 2014, it still made the news headlines. Not anymore. The world has moved on and left Nigeria and Africa behind. That became clear in February 2018 when another 110 girls were kidnapped from their high school in Yobe State. After the government paid millions in ransom money, all but six of them were released, since five reportedly died during the raid. The sole surviving schoolgirl who did not return to her parents was Leah Sharibu. And so, while the West was celebrating the fame of a Jenifer Lopez or a Kim Kardashian, a solitary schoolgirl in the hands of Boko Haram militants showed us what a true heroine looks like. Her friends related to the media why she was not among them...

> Boko Haram told Leah to accept Islam, and she refused. So they said she would not come with us... [W]e begged her to just recite the Islamic declaration and put the hijab on and get into the vehicle, but she said it was not her faith, and so why should she say it was. If they want to kill her, they can go ahead, but she won't say she is a Muslim.

May Jesus, the Son of God, have mercy on this girl if she is still alive. Trying to deny the glaringly obvious fact—that *Christians* are deliberately being targeted, raped, killed, and kidnapped, more than any other group in the world—is far worse than hypocrisy. To look the other way after the Armenian genocide, after Nanjing, after the holocaust, after Srebrenica, and after Rwanda is unspeakably evil and sad. Have we learned nothing yet? Just listen to what a single update from *Barnabas Aid* sounded like on May 26, 2021.

25 Moore and Cooper, *The Next Jihad*, 39.

- Two hundred strong Muslim mobs terrorized Christian villagers in Punjab, Pakistan
- Armed men kill 15 at baptism in northern Burkina Faso
- Eight killed in attack that left church destroyed in Kaduna, Nigeria
- Church minister killed, another abducted, in attack on northern Nigerian Church
- Thousands flee as Myanmar army attacks town in majority-Christian Chin state
- Muslims in Malawi demand Christians leave "Muslim territory"
- U.N. Human Rights committee urged to act over Christian persecution in Turkey[26]

We can only thank God that the denial is not total. Many do still care. The American Office of International Religious Freedom is a massive force for good. And in January 2021 *Forbes Magazine* published the following data gained from *Open Doors* online.

> The newly published data reveals that, during the reporting period between October 2019 and September 2020, more than 340 million Christians were living in countries where they might suffer high levels of persecution and discrimination because of their faith… Among this number, 309 million Christians were living in countries where they might suffer very high or extreme levels of persecution. As Open Doors emphasizes, "That's one in 8 worldwide, 1 in 6 in Africa, 2 out of 5 in Asia, and 1 in 12 in Latin America."
>
> Open Doors' research identified that during the reporting period, 4,761 Christians were killed for their faith, 4,488 Churches or Christian buildings were attacked, 4,277 Christians were unjustly arrested, detained or imprisoned, 1,710 Christians were abducted for faith-related reasons. On average, 13 Christians are killed every day for their faith, 12 churches or Christian buildings are attacked, 12 are unjustly arrested, detained, or imprisoned,

26 *Barnabas Aid* email, May 26 2021.

> and five are abducted for faith-related reasons. In the 21st century, it is still not possible to practice religion or belief safely.[27]

Some people out there are concerned. Thank God that it bothers even secular folk that *every single day*, on average, thirteen Christians are being killed for their faith, twelve churches are being attacked, twelve Christians are either unjustly arrested, detained, or imprisoned, and five are kidnapped. Most of it, but not all, results from Muslim persecution. If nothing is done, we will see the eradication of Christianity from some parts of the world in the not-too-distant future. Little wonder Moore and Cooper can ask poignantly in *The Next Jihad*: "Is this the kind of world we want to live in?"[28]

We still need to answer the question, why? Why are Christians their target? Let me attempt to explain:

1. It *was* by design

   The oldest Muslim building on earth, the *Dome of the Rock*, was completed in 691. It is abundantly clear from the beautiful Arabic calligraphy in the ambulatory of this historic building how those Arab marauders invading Jerusalem were motivated from the beginning to say "not three but one" and never to call Jesus the "Son of God" but only the "son of Miriam." That makes one wonder why this new religion was so fixated on Christianity's core beliefs?

   The Arabs, rising against the Byzantine Empire in the seventh and eighth centuries, had to invent a sufficiently monotheistic religion to unite all their tribes and to lure weak adherents of Judaism and Christianity over. Even a very brief and sanitized contemporary biography of Mohammed tells the uninformed reader how both a Jew and a Christian featured prominently in the prophet's life, helping him to realize that he was indeed sent from God as the final messenger

27 Ewelina U Ochab, "One in Eight Christians Worldwide Live in Countries Where They May face Persecution", *Forbes*, January 13, 2021, on forbes.com

28 Moore and Cooper, *The Next Jihad*, 117.

of Allah.[29] These sorts of stories were skillfully used to convince Jews and Christians to come over, which, by and large, did not happen, as Mohammed had hoped. That is why he and his successors turned against them as Islam's main religious contenders in the Middle East and the Roman world. Islam had to impose itself by military force if it hoped to eliminate the rival political power of Byzantium, for Islam was far more than a religion. It was very clearly a political ideology pursuing universal objectives.

2. It *still is* mostly by design.
   Another reason why Christians are so actively persecuted by Muslim radicals is that both Islam and Christianity are missional in outlook. This is especially the case in Sub-Saharan Africa, where Christianity completely surpassed Islam in terms of winning that part of the continent for Christ with lightning speed since the mid-1800s. That stirred a sense of shame in the Muslim mind, where some of their scholars would have asked, "Why did it happen?" From our perspective, it almost seems as if God protected Africa for centuries from the Muslim north by a massive sand barrier—the great Saharan Desert—until Europeans, with advanced naval technology, could sail around Africa to begin evangelizing the vast continent from the south upwards. Within a generation or two, Sub-Saharan Africa turned Christian due to the tireless labours of thousands of missionaries,[30] all of which took the followers of Mohammed by complete surprise.

I suspect there might also be a deep sense of insecurity within Islam, knowing that Christianity has been there all along—six centuries before Islam arrived—and that none of its bold claims that the *Injil* (gospel) has been corrupted or that Jesus never died and rose again, or that the Quran was eternally preserved, can really be proven. It is all based on assumptions,

29 Abdurrahman Al-Sheha, *Mohammed the Messenger of Allah* (Riyadh: Islam Propagation Office, 2005).

30 Three of my direct ancestors, Johann Böhm (1833 – 1918), Gustav Trümpelmann (1841 – 1923), and Christoph Sonntag (1862 – 1919) sailed from East Prussia to Southern Africa for Christian mission work in the 1800s.

compelled by the sword, and divorced from any historical data. Muslims are scared of "critical thinking" since they know it will cause the house of Islam to shake, while the house of Jesus has weathered three centuries of criticism and has only come out stronger. Add to all this what was once mentioned to me by a young Christian from Aleppo, that most of his compatriots know deep in their hearts that their ancestors in Syria were forcibly converted centuries ago. The same applies to the Berbers of North Africa. What Hussein Mansour says somewhere in his book, that even as a Muslim growing up in Egypt, he always knew that it was the Copts who were the true Egyptians—the Muslims came mostly from elsewhere. And yet these Coptic Christians were those exemplifying real joy, tolerance and love. If such anecdotal claims are valid, how will it not nurture a deep sense of insecurity and even inferiority? The Holy Spirit says in Gal. 4:21-31 and I John 3:11-15 that *envy* often lies at the root of persecution. That is what the legacy of Cain, King Saul and the Pharisees tell us also.

Add to this the amazing testimony of so many Christians martyred by Islamists, like the twenty-one orange-clad Copts slain on the Libyan beach by ISIL in 2014, and the insecurity only increases. Why can a seven-year-old Iraqi Christian girl, Myriam of Qaraqosh, pray and sing so passionately for the bloodthirsty jihadis that swept through her village in 2014, that God might forgive them?[31] What is her secret? In other words, there is the power of the sword and the power of the Holy Spirit, *and never the twain shall meet.* A god that has to make and keep you his worshiper through violence and threats is very insecure, and his followers know it.

Radical Muslims stereotypically see Christians as representatives of the West. They hate the West for at least three reasons. Bernard Lewis well explains the *first* in his book *What Went Wrong?* [32] A deep sense of shame pervaded the Muslim world when "backward" Europe surged ahead in the late Middle Ages, leaving the Islamic world behind in its wake, in every aspect of civilization. *Secondly*, we have seen how Sayyid Qutb portrayed America (and the West) as morally depraved and decadent since the late

---

31 "Myriam's Story and Song," *SAT-7 Kids, YouTube*, February 26, 2015.

32 Bernard Lewis, *What Went Wrong?* (New York: Oxford University Press, 2002).

1940s, a theme many other Muslim thinkers have picked up since him.[33] And *lastly*, the West is hated for its recent wars and aggression against Muslim lands. For instance, whenever another random drone attack leaves scores of innocent dead in a Middle Eastern village, supposedly to target jihadis, it nurses deep-seated grudges against the West. All of the above means only one thing: local Christians will face the music. That is why someone like Rev. Victor Atallah of the Middle East Reformed Fellowship warned already before the invasion of Iraq in 2003, that local Iraqi Christians would be the first to suffer due to an American invasion. And they were. A CNEWA Canada report stated in 2004: "Persecution has been a fact of life for Iraqi Christians since the insurgency started in 2003." What makes this situation so sad is that of the one million Christians in Iraq, 150,000 fled to Syria, only to face another war over there, also fuelled by Western powers since 2011.[34]

What Motivates Islamic Terror?

It is hard to know what percentage of Muslims are positively inclined to Islamic terror since opinion polls cannot always reflect the heart's true convictions. We do believe, however, that it is a minority. A minority of 1.8 billion people is still a huge number though. We know from the history of revolutions that it takes only a tiny minority of very devoted people, consumed by their ideology and willingness to die for their cause, to radically overturn the *status quo*. So let us look at a list of reasons that can motivate Islamic terror:[35]

1. The *military* example of Mohammed and the first four caliphs continues to inspire and radicalize many Muslims worldwide.[36]

---

33 Similarly, Russia, despite its affinity for Europe, has feared the rise of decadent Western thought and culture since the early 1800's. See Paul Robinson, *Russian Conservatism* (New York: Cornell University Press, 2019), 190-191.

34 *Iraqi Christians Under Attack*, A Special Report from CNEWA Canada, Ottawa.

35 See also Patrick Sookhdeo, "The Motivation of Terrorists and Suicide Bombers", in *Understanding Islamic Terrorism* (McLean, VA: Isaac Publishing, 2009), 107-127. The list is not given in order of priority, nor do all the reasons play a part in every act of terror

36 Nabeel Qureshi pointed out that with the help of the computer it has now become much easier to trace the accurate trajectory of Mohammed's life, becoming ever more

2. Utopian dreams of a worldwide caliphate under *sharia*, coupled with a deep sense of duty to Allah, continue to inspire many to bring it about.[37]
3. The longing for the reward of seventy-two virgins, and other delights in paradise, inspires many young men to die in *jihad*.[38]
4. The sense of shame (*fitna*) experienced vis-à-vis another culture or faith, Christianity in particular, can fuel resentment.[39]
5. The desire to reclaim lands lost to the West and Christianity after the Islamic golden age, may also be a motivating factor.[40]
6. The rediscovery and propagation of *dawa* by multinational Islamic organizations since the second half of the twentieth century, also helps,[41]
7. as does the spiritual and moral collapse of the West, Islam's number one rival for the last five hundred years.[42]
8. There is the fear that decadent Western values and critical thinking may infiltrate and destroy Muslim foundations. The porn-plague in the Middle East comes from the West.[43]
9. The death and destruction caused by American and/or NATO foreign policies, and its forever wars over the last three decades, fuels anger and resentment.[44]

---

violent towards its end. See Qureshi's "Is Jihad in the Quran and the Life of Mohammed?" in *Answering Jihad - A Better Way Forward*, 40-54. Sources like the *hadith* are also now more readily available online.

37 See chapter 4, "*Dawa* as a Divine Command with a Worldwide Scope."

38 The Somali lady mentioned in chapter 1 told me that scores of young men in her home country couldn't wait to be enlisted for the next suicide operation due to the promise of seventy-two virgins in paradise.

39 See chapter 7, "The *Umma* and Victimhood."

40 Think of Osama bin Laden's many messages to America and to the West.

41 See chapter 3, "The History and Agents of *Dawa*."

42 See chapter 5 under "The Conversion of Society and Culture."

43 As a young ISIL recruit from Europe told German journalist Todenhöfer in Raqqa: "Too much promiscuity, too many one-night stands. Everyone with someone else. That can't be what life's about". Jürgen Todenhöfer, *My Journey*, 220; See also Mansour, *Minority of One*, 49.

44 Ever since 9/11, it has been painful for most Americans to come to terms with this fact. The U.S.' humiliating exit from Afghanistan will hopefully bring the post-Cold War era of American exceptionalism to an end.

10. Economic and social deprivation experienced in Africa or the Middle East can be a breeding ground for terror.[45]
11. The legacy of heroes, called *shahids*, who have died in suicide operations, inspires many.[46]
12. Extensive training and oaths sworn to terrorist leaders and cells (as a result of being radicalized) will naturally contribute toward terror.[47]

Preliminary Conclusion

All of this begs the question: How should we, as Christians respond? That is what part two of this book hopes to address. Can we afford to live any longer as if nothing is happening? Even Prince Charles of Britain went on air on the BBC pleading with governments and churches to act before Christianity was wiped off the map in the Middle East.[48] One only has to look at global demographic projections for the rest of the twenty-first century to realize how foolish our nonchalance would be. Everywhere in the world populations are shrinking, while the Muslim-population is steadily rising, and Africa's is skyrocketing. Researchers tell us that four out of ten Christians will likely live in Africa by the mid-twentieth century. But will that be mostly under Islamic *sharia*? Or will they be free? And what if some western European countries have become Islamic states in the meantime?

Much of African Christianity today is a mixed bag, ranging from true vibrant Christianity on the one side, to nominal Christianity, the Prosperity Gospel, syncretism, cults, and liberalism on the other. Moreover, many of the mother denominations of the West that once brought the gospel

---

45 Soon after 9/11, the lack of "social mobility" was widely named as the main cause of Islamic terror in the West. It has since, however, been shown as a wholly inadequate theory. See Anna Bekele "Islamist Activism Through the Lens of Social Science" in Bekele and Sookhdeo (eds), *Meeting the Ideological Challenge*, 113-134.

46 Palestinian suicide terrorists receive lavish funerals, which spurs others to follow in their footsteps.

47 Once someone has been set on a trajectory toward committing terror, it is psychologically almost impossible to turn them around.

48 "Easter 2018: Prince Charles supports persecuted Christians", *The Catholic Tablet*, March 30, 2018, *YouTube*.

to "dark Africa", are now peddling a diluted form of Christianity that is mostly useless for any spiritual warfare. All of this suits the Muslim world well. Compromised Christians are soft targets for Islamic *dawa*. They easily convert to Islam to escape harassment, shame and discrimination, or for whatever benefits they may gain.

From a human perspective, the true church of Jesus in Africa looks very much like an orphan. Her mother is on life-support far away in Europe or elsewhere, and her adversary, who has all the money and the power in the world, is mighty as a dragon (see Rev. 12). And yet, her God, who is all-mighty and all-knowing, will not leave nor forsake her, but cover her under his wings, to use a Biblical metaphor. The true body of Christ in Africa (and beyond) is strong and is growing with leaps and bounds, even though she is often materially poor. She is constantly winning over new disciples from Islam, Atheism and Animism, regardless of the cost to personal safety and welfare. The reason they keep on coming is simple: Only the risen Lord Jesus can deliver us from the bondage of sin and death, and from the darkness we are in.

This is so abundantly evident in Africa that a correspondent for *The Times of London* could once observe—after traveling from Algiers to Lilongwe with a 4X4—that what Africa now needs more than anything else, is the God of the Christian gospel![49] Why did Matthew Parris write that? Because it was only among Christians that they truly felt safe, whenever they camped out somewhere on their long African safari. It was the Christians whose eyes sparkled with hope and joy. Matthew Parris is a self-confessed atheist.

But why is this so? Here is one answer. Just over a century ago, the famed philanthropist and missionary-doctor to central Africa, Albert Schweitzer, wrestled with the question: "What is civilization?"[50] He had been wrestling with that question back in Germany already, witnessing in silence how Europe was steadily losing it. Few, however, shared his concerns. Now, as he was sailing up a river in Gabon on the equator, faced with the realities of Africa,

49 Matthew Parris, "As an Atheist I Truly Believe Africa Needs God" *The Times*, December 27, 2008, on thetimes.co.uk.

50 See Albert Schweitzer. *Out of My Life and Thought* (Baltimore: Johns Hopkins University Press, 2009), 147-155.

and overcome with emotion, as he was thinking constantly of young men dying in the trenches of World War One, it dawned on him "unforeseen and unsought": "Civilization is reverence for life!", which meant: "love, devotion, and compassion in suffering, the sharing of joy and common endeavors."[51] All of a sudden, the path through the jungle became clear; Schweitzer had found the answer. *Civilization is reverence for life.* That is why Parris and his friends felt safer among Christians. What Schweitzer did not realize fully yet, was that apostolic Christianity alone was the sole guardian of that sublime ethical principle. And that is why overcoming the challenge posed by Islamic *dawa* will be so immensely critical in the twenty-first century: for essentially, Islamism has very little reverence for life… or for truth.

51 Ibid., 158.

PART II

HOW SHALL WE OVERCOME?

CHAPTER 11

THE WAR OF IDEAS AND THE STRATEGIES THAT FAILED US

There can be no doubt that the free world is facing an unprecedented challenge in multi-faceted Islamization. It is a challenge that won't go away and that won't ultimately be won by military force. The Islamists know it well. Saudi sheik Abd al-'Aziz bin Salih al-Jarbu said, "The battle with the disbelievers is a battle of beliefs... It is not even due to their hostility toward us! Rather, it is a battle based on belief and religion."[1]

Likewise, after the 7/7 bombings in London, British Prime Minister Tony Blair said, "What we are confronting here is an evil ideology [...] It is a global struggle and a battle of ideas, hearts, and minds, both within Islam and outside of it..."[2] Dr. Robert R. Reilly, a senior fellow at the American Foreign Policy Council, wrote a few years later: "From my experiences in the Cold War and since 9/11, I have formulated a few brief principles for the conduct of the war of ideas": These principles according to Reilly are:

1 I have lost the source of this quote.

2 Tony Blair, "Pulling the jihadis up by their roots", *National Post*, July 18, 2005, A17.

(1) do not go into a war of ideas unless you understand the ideas you are at war with, (2) do not go into a war of ideas unless you have an idea, and (3) wars of ideas are conducted by people who think; people who do not think are influenced by those who do. Try to reach the people who think.[3]

Sobering words indeed. Reilly's comments echo those of the Chinese military strategist quoted before:[4]

> If you know the enemy and yourself,
> you need not fear the result of a hundred battles.
> If you know yourself but not the enemy,
> for every victory gained, you will suffer defeat.
> If you know neither the enemy nor yourself,
> you will succumb in every battle.

We desperately need to realize that we are engaged in *a war of ideas* and, secondly, that some ideas have radically failed us. That is how simple it is. Without knowing our adversary, ourselves, and the nature of the conflict, we are in for a decent clobbering in the West and Africa. All that will be needed to turn our lands into Muslim caliphates under *sharia* will be for political Islam to stay the course.

Let us, therefore, look at four strategies (ideas) that failed us and why we may in no way promote or support them any longer. For information about the first three, I am indebted to papers published in 2015 under the title: *Meeting the Ideological Challenge of Islamism: How to Combat Radical Islamism*. For the fourth failed strategy, I depend on an interview by Ayaan Hirsi Ali with a Swedish journalist, Paulina Neuding.

Failed Strategy # 1: Ignoring Theology

In his essay "The Role of Religion in the Battle Space since 9/11", Dr. Patrick Sookhdeo deals with some of the most significant failed strategies followed by America and her allies in recent decades. Sookhdeo begins by highlighting three quotes from our political leaders:

---

3 Robert Reilly, "Information Operations: Success and Failures," in *Meeting the Challenge*, 47.

4 "Sun Tzu > Quotes > Quotable Quotes," *Good Reads*, on goodreads.com

> Islamic terrorist attacks serve a clear and focused ideology, a set of beliefs and goals that are evil but not insane. Some call this Islamic radicalism, militant Jihadism, and still others Islamo-fascism. Whatever it is called, this ideology is very different from the religion of Islam.
>
> — US President George W. Bush, Oct. 2005 [5]

> This is a religious ideology, a strain within the worldwide religion of Islam, as far removed from its essential decency and truth as Protestant gunmen who kill Catholics or vice versa, are from Christianity.
>
> — British Prime Minister Tony Blair, July 2005 [6]

> ...we reject the notion that al-Qaeda represents any religious authority. They are not religious leaders, they are killers; and neither Islam nor any other religion condones the slaughter of innocents.
>
> — US President Barack Obama, May 2010 [7]

These quotes illustrate clearly how consistently these leaders of the Anglosphere refused to admit any connection between Islamist ideology and Islam itself, and how their advisors forgot all about theology in trying to understand the problem. The Islamists were bemused. Here is one clear response:

> "I am astonished by President Bush when he claims there is nothing in the Quran that justifies jihad violence in the name of Islam. Is he some kind of Islamic scholar? Has he ever actually read the Quran?" [8]

After 9/11, serious misunderstandings about the role of Islam in Islamist terror continued for at least a decade in the corridors of Western power. Almost all our leaders failed to recognize that the terror of Al-Qaeda, its affiliates, and other Islamic extremist groups, is deeply rooted in a legitimate reading of classical Islam. Their ideology of terror is rooted in

---

5 Sookhdeo, "The Role of Religion..." in *Meeting the Challenge*, 11.

6 Ibid.

7 Ibid.

8 Abu Qatada, jihadist cleric, as quoted by Mark Durie in *The Third Choice*, 155.

"orthodoxy," to use a Christian term. Sadly, the rejection of this fact was virtually wholesale.

The former Deputy Chief of the CIA's Counterterrorism Center, Henry A. Crumpton, tasked with defeating Al Qaeda and Osama Bin Laden, is one such expert who failed to see it. He saw Al Qaeda as a non-state actor, divorced from Islam. Crumpton showed little understanding of Bin Laden and Al Qaeda's rootedness in Islamic theology.[9]

The 9/11 Commission Report serves as another example of this fatal delusion. It stated famously: "The enemy is not Islam, the great world of faith, but a perversion of Islam…" The report did not realize that the *rejection* of militant *jihad* and the failure to strive for a worldwide caliphate is the real "perversion of Islam" for many traditional Muslims.[10] Crumpton and others were correct in stating that the US is not at war with Islam, yet they missed the obvious fact that Islamic terrorism is a valid interpretation of Islam and has been such for fourteen centuries. It is not a perversion of Islam.

All of the above illustrates how fierce the war of ideas raged in and beyond the so-called *War on Terror*. Is that why a former Secretary of Defense, the late Donald Rumsfeld, could indicate that America is so far behind in understanding this battle of ideas.[11]

But why are we so far behind? And why do we have no answer for their ideology? The answer is simple. We have ignored the link between Islamist ideology and Islamic theology. Dr. Sookhdeo proves this from the primary sources of Islam; the Quran, the *hadith*, and *sharia*. The Quran not only has the famous sword verse of Surah 9:5, but its violent Medina sections (originating from the last ten years of Mohammed's life) also abrogate (revoke) the more peaceful Meccan sayings from an earlier time. That means the peaceful verses should be ignored and the militant ones followed. Here is what Surah 9:5 and 29 say:[12]

---

9 Sookhdeo, "The Role of Religion…", 12-13.

10 Ibid., 15.

11 Ibid., 15.

12 As quoted by Sookhdeo.

> When the sacred months are passed, kill the idolaters wherever you find them, and lie in wait for them in every place of ambush.

> Fight those who believe not in God or in the Last Day, nor hold that forbidden which hath been forbidden by God and His Apostle, nor acknowledge the Religion of Truth, even if they are the People of the Book, until they pay the jizya with willing submission, and feel subdued.

The late Dr. Nabeel Qureshi pointed out in *Answering Jihad: A Better Way Forward* that the internet has made it much easier for radicalized Muslim youths to put the Quranic surahs in chronological order so as to get a clearer picture of their prophet's life and aims, and how he became ever more militant towards the end.[13]

This is why an ISIL affiliate in northern Mozambique can call itself *Ahlu Sunna Wa-Jama* (ASJW), which means "followers of the prophetic tradition." The simple fact is that a straight line can be drawn from the prophet's life to the terror group. All Muslims know this. Yet, imagine what the world would say if a so-called Christian terror group, burning, raping, and killing unsuspecting poor Africans like ASJW, would call itself "followers of the Jesus-way"? It would sound as insane as plucking hand grenades from mango trees. But forming an Islamic terror organization inspired by Islam's holy book and prophet's life is not so far-fetched. This is precisely why the well-known Egyptian scholar Nasr Hamid Abu Zayd (1943-2010) could state that it is *impossible* to condemn Islamic terrorism based on theology (i.e., the Quran and the *hadith*).[14]

The *hadith* contains various collections of the words and deeds of Mohammed, i.e., his *sunna* or way of life. Regarding the question of violence, it not only fully backs the *Quran* but goes much further and illuminates the profile of Mohammed's example much clearer. It is that example which faithful Muslims must follow. It records Mohammed's involvement in raids, wars, and assassinations in great detail, in which Christians, especially Jews, were also targeted. Influential Islamist Abdallah 'Azzam (1941-1989) pointed out that Mohammed was involved in either sending

13 Nabeel Qureshi, *Answering Jihad* (Grand Rapids: Zondervan, 2016), 145-145.

14 Sookhdeo, "The Role of Religion..." 16-17.

out a military expedition or leading one himself (often against unsuspecting caravans) on average every other month since his public life began.[15] That is the image that informed Muslims have of their founder. The stark difference in image with the "founder" of Christianity couldn't be greater.

Consider also that memories of the rapid advance of Islam during its first three to five centuries are etched into the collective Muslim consciousness. Every Muslim is obliged to strive for a worldwide caliphate. The great sin both secular Muslim governments and the West are committing is usurping Allah's sovereignty and legislative authority by not striving for the caliphate and *sharia*, wrote Sayyid Qutb.[16]

A telling example of just how far the US has fallen behind in this war of ideas, and of grasping the role of religion in the battlespace, is the fact that the U.S. State Department replaced its once powerful and popular *Voice of America* to the Arab world with the hopelessly weak *Radio Sawa*, airing little more than pop-music to its Arabic audience since 2002, wrote Robert Reilly.[17] There could scarcely be a more poignant example of how *not* to wage the war of ideas.

In summary: culture is based on religion, not vice versa. Separating political Islam from Islamic sources, even from Islam itself, is an exercise in futility through which decades have been lost in the war of ideas. Unfortunately, that was not the only failed strategy.

Failed Strategy # 2: The Problem is Violence

A second critical mistake that was made, closely related to the first, is the notion that the enemy is simply *violent* Islamic groups. That much was already inherently evident in the remarks of Presidents Bush and Obama above. The enemy is *a perversion of Islam*, said the 9/11 Commission report famously. That led the report's writers to assert that Al Qaeda's violence can be separated from Islam. The US and its allies, or so it was believed, should seek to destroy terror networks and focus on addressing the perceived grievances that were thought to give rise to them.

---

15 Ibid., 17.

16 Ibid., 18.

17 Ibid., 15; See also Reilly, "Information Operations...", 49-52.

Sookhdeo shows how the Brookings Institute as an influential think tank urged U.S. policymakers back in 2010 to engage with nonviolent Islamists by separating "hardliners" from the "moderates." That may sound plausible, but whom are we talking about here? The real "moderates" would call Islam away from its dream of worldwide political domination. The only problem is that such Muslims will not be considered to be faithful by the "real" ones, i.e., those who take the Quran and the *hadith* seriously. And yet, these are *not* the moderates that counter-terrorism experts had in mind or that the Brookings Institute was necessarily thinking of. They thought of the other *Islamists*. The following quote from Mr. James Clapper, U.S. Director of National Intelligence in the Obama Administration, serves as an excellent example of this approach:

> The term Muslim Brotherhood is an umbrella term for various movements... which has eschewed violence and decried Al Qaeda as a perversion of Islam. The Muslim Brotherhood has... no overarching agenda, particularly in pursuit of violence, at least internationally.[18]

Clapper suggested that the Muslim Brotherhood is a safe actor to engage with since it does not support violence, at least not openly. But does the Brotherhood really disagree with violent organizations about their goal? One only has to read the writings of its best-known advocates, such as Sayyid Qutb and Hasan al Bana, to realize that it is wishful thinking.[19] Does the Brotherhood even renounce violence in achieving its goal? By no means. That's why the line should *not* be drawn between peaceable Islamists and militant Islamists, as the Brookings Institute suggested, but between all Islamists and those Muslims who reject the classical ideals of Mohammed and the first caliphs. The simple truth is that the so-called peaceable Islamists are as implacably opposed to western notions of freedom and democracy as their violent comrades.

Here is another example of the problem. CIA analyst Emile Nakhleh consistently emphasized the *means* Muslim organizations use (whether violent or not), disregarding whatever *aim* they may have in mind.

---

18 Michael Youssef, *Jesus, Jihad and Peace* (Franklin, TN: Worthy Publishing, 2015) 20-21.

19 See Waller "The Muslim Brotherhood...", 67 ff.

Whoever uses violence is our foe; whoever does not is our ally. Nakhleh, a Palestinian Christian of origin, failed to realize that *all* Islamists share the same goal: a global caliphate under *sharia*, whether they actively use or promote violence or not. The nonviolent actors often pose a far greater threat than violent ones, says the American historian and president of the Middle East Forum, Daniel Pipes.[20]

During the Obama years, America supported the Muslim Brotherhood in Egypt to replace the Mubarak regime. This was an example of misguided engagement with the wrong kind of Muslims. During their short and bloody reign, the Brotherhood in Egypt made great strides toward the establishment of an Islamic state under *sharia*,[21] which is precisely why the people of that country stood up *en masse* against President Morsi and his cadres. Sookhdeo continues: "It makes little difference whether the Islamists engaged are violent or nonviolent because it is their share in Islamist goals that are the ultimate challenge to the West."[22] As we have said, peaceful strategies of Islamists are often much more dangerous and successful than violent ones since they are so subtle and hard to censure. The very reason why some Muslims are called Islamists is because they strive for the establishment of Islamic hegemony under *sharia* across the globe. That is hardly a goal that any freedom-loving citizen or leader could ever be at peace with.

Failed Strategy # 3: Engaging our Enemy's Enemy

A common idea is gaining great popularity in politics: "My enemy's enemy is my friend." It's a saying that often proved useful also in African tribal wars. It has become a standard foreign policy tool in the West for many decades, unfortunately. It is by far the worst of the failed strategies we have been looking at and is having a devastating impact not only on geopolitics

20 Sookhdeo, "The Role of Religion...", 14.

21 Hussein Mansour, supporting the Arab Spring in 2011 and hoping it would bring democracy, vividly describes the take-over by the Muslim Brotherhood in his book *Minority of One*, 162 ff.

22 Ibid., 25.

and security issues across the globe (Africa in particular) but also on the sanity and moral integrity of the entire collective West.

It is a strategy that comes with ancient papers. Early in the nineteenth century, when the young nation of the United States of America was faced with a huge foreign policy dilemma (eventually leading to the Barbary Wars), she learned how to use her enemy's enemy to bring about change. There was one difference though— the enemy's enemy in those days was a reputable entity.[23] No more so today.

This is how it goes: We groom (at first secretly) a little striped cub in the hope that it would one day take over from the other cats we don't like, since they stand in the way of our "national interests." The idea is that we can control the tiger once it is full-grown, but it hardly ever turns out that way. There are multiple examples over the last half a century illustrating this devastating strategy, some of them quite vivid in my memory, having

23 North African Muslim pirate vessels were causing a real headache for American ships in the Mediterranean and even the Atlantic. One after the other, the vessels were needlessly attacked, captured, and robbed on the open sea. The Muslim sheiks then demanded ludicrous amounts of money in exchange for their growing number of American hostages. The crisis dragged on for years and got so bad that the US consul in Tripoli, William Eaton, came up with a wild proposal. He proposed to President Jefferson's Secretary of State that the Americans ally themselves with the exiled brother of Tripoli's bashaw, Hamet Qaramanli. The latter, who lived in exile far away from his wife and children, was the rightful heir to the throne that his brother Yusuf had stolen by murdering their other brother. Eaton had met with Hamet in Tunis and discussed his secret military plan. Captain William Eaton, an experienced soldier, was convinced he could solve America's problem in North Africa by aligning himself with Hamet, attacking Tripoli across the desert from the east. At the same time, American ships launched an assault from the sea. Jefferson did not immediately fall for this daring raid but later agreed. After much preparation, the American and his Muslim ally began their march from Egypt in 1805, all along the Mediterranean coast. Having managed through exceptional bravery to defeat the coastal city of Derne on their way to Tripoli, Eaton called for supplies and reinforcements. Tripoli was within reach, and victory was within sight. The next thing Eaton learned was that the Americans had reached a deal with the bashaw in Tripoli and that he should abandon his campaign and ditch poor Hamet. Eaton had no choice but to follow orders. The betrayed Hamet and his men, who joined the campaign rather reluctantly, were left behind heartbroken and outraged. See Brian Kilmeade and Don Yaeger, *Thomas Jefferson and the Tripoli Pirates – The Forgotten War That Changed American History* (New York: Sentinel, 2015) 138-140, 171-175, 195-197.

grown up not far from the Rhodesian border in South Africa in the sixties and seventies.

In Zimbabwe (formerly Rhodesia) the British chose to support (among others) Mr. Robert Mugabe's revolutionary Marxist ZANU despite its well-known terror campaign and atrocities against black and white civilians. The West thereby sidelined moderate and peace-loving African Christian groups, as well as the pro-western Rhodesian government of the time. Well before he was knighted by her majesty Queen Elizabeth in 1994, Comrade Mugabe could spur his Shona comrades on with Maoist rhetoric and quotes from Lenin "to sweep the enemy completely from our land... by torrents of blood, tears, and anguish."[24] These were the days when Western liberals, who had never seen the carnage caused by a landmine or a car bomb, could say, "One man's terrorist is another man's freedom fighter." In the case of South Africa, liberal Western governments, following the lead of Sweden and The Netherlands in the early seventies, decided to throw their weight behind the Marxist-inspired African National Congress (ANC), ignoring its Soviet ties, blatant human rights abuses, torture camps, and well-known affinity for political violence.[25] The West betrayed the popular Christian-based Inkatha Freedom Party,[26] because it was still too close to their "enemy," the pro-western white regime in Pretoria.

The outcome of all the backroom deals, open lies, propaganda, brutal economic sanctions, and political bullying, both in Zimbabwe and South Africa, is there for anyone to observe. Zimbabwe was turned into a failed state twenty years after independence, while South Africa is at the brink of

---

24 Peter Stiff, *Cry Zimbabwe* (Alberton, RSA: Galago Books, 2000).

25 See Martin Bosma, "Mythe: we konden het niet weten" in *Minderheid in Eigen Land* (Amsterdam: Bibliotecha Africana, 2015), 208-210; and Harry Booyens, *Amabhulu* (North Vancouver: Cliffwood Fogge, 2014), 417, 447, 460-461, 498-499.

26 An IFP election poster of 2000 still warned voters how support for a radically anti-Christian, violent, and openly Marxist movement like the ANC would cost South Africa dearly in years to come. See also Anthea Jefferey, "The Balance of Forces in the Run-Up to the People's War" in *People's War,* 41-71. The Western powers also knew about the ANC campaign of terror against Inkatha's political leaders and supporters in Kwa-Zulu Natal in the run-up to the 1994 elections. In one notorious incident, ANC snipers fired from a high-rise in Johannesburg (Shell-House) on Inkatha supporters marching down below, just before the 1994 elections, killing nine and injuring dozens

total collapse, and very likely to be literally shrouded in complete darkness soon. Virtually every citizen of these two countries craves to leave due to the lawlessness, graft, and incompetence of its many kleptocrat elites of the last few decades. Who knows what these countries could have been today had the world not meddled so much in their affairs or if the West had opted for supporting non-revolutionary, secular, and Christian-based political movements instead?

Other Western experiments supporting "our enemy's enemy" are well documented. Sookhdeo mentions several examples from the Middle East over the last few decades. We begin with Afghanistan. Few know that the U.S. has been positively engaging Islamists worldwide for quite a while. During the Soviet-Afghan war of 1979-1989, Operation Cyclone provided $630 million a year to empower violent Islamists, including Osama bin Laden, helping them destroy secular-nationalist groups. According to a former U.S. government official and academic, Peter Mandaville, U.S. diplomats had regular meetings with Islamists during the eighties and into the nineties.[27] Even Tora Bora, the cave complex in the inhospitable mountains where Bin Laden supposedly took refuge, was once built with the help of the CIA in support of the Taliban to fight the Soviets.[28]

With the arrival of the powerful tool of social media, neo-conservative groups in the U.S. began to plot and plan the so-called Arab Spring, supposedly to bring about "democracy" in Middle Eastern countries. It is well documented that neo-conservatives in Washington set out to bring about regime change in seven different Middle Eastern countries and that 9/11 served as the ideal pretext for it.[29] What these neo-cons really wanted, of course, were pro-American vassal states. In chapter 14 we will see how the crowds on Tahrir Square thanked Facebook and Mark Zuckerberg for the successful uprising against the Mubarak regime, before mayhem

27 Sookhdeo, "The Role of Religion…" 37. Many Islamist groups received funding through the United States Agency for International Development (USAID) and the National Endowment for Democracy (NED).

28 Megan Stack, *Every Man in This Village is a Liar* (New York: Anchor Books, 2010), 22-24.

29 See the now famous interview on *YouTube* with Maj. Genl. Wesley Clarke on the television programme *Democracy Now* in 2007.

broke loose and the Muslim Brotherhood took over.[30] The cynical project to export "democracy" to countries that never had the chance to fully grasp its crucial underpinnings backfired badly, Syria being the prime example. A popular uprising in that country, also fueled from the outside, led to Operation Timber Sycamore, which armed and funded all sorts of terror groups to fight against President Assad's regime.[31] This happened in the Middle Eastern country that probably had the most religious freedom in the entire Muslim world before the Arab Spring of 2011.[32]

All of this was yet again done in the name of the sacred doctrine to engage "our enemy's enemy." One must ask what could be worse than chopping off heads, destroying villages, kidnapping children, smashing historical artifacts, and burning down Christian churches, for that is what the Free Syrian Army's partners did in the Syrian War fighting Assad. And yet, "we" ended up funding and supporting them, with our Western media playing the double role of either denying or excusing this grim reality. Upon closer scrutiny, it became pretty obvious that seven out of ten Sunni militants fighting against Assad came from *outside* the country,[33] sponsored by Western, Saudi, and Qatari funds. If we were so concerned about evil despots, why was no Western military action ever considered against someone like Robert Mugabe, who committed far worse crimes than Assad, and who *really* fought against his own people? What explains all of this, other than the geo-political aspirations of a superpower and its vassals?

Eventually, Syria's situation became so bad that its government asked an erstwhile ally for help. Had it not been for the Russian intervention in mid-2015, all of Syria would have been a smoldering wasteland under a

30 Hirsi Ali, *Prey,* 159.

31 See Sookhdeo, "The Role of Religion..." 38-39.

32 Michael Petrou, "Born Again in Syria – Evangelical Christian churches have been drawing Arabs across this Middle east nation," Macleans, January 30, 2006, 18-19. According to Oliver Stone in his documentary *The Untold History of the United States*, neo-conservatives in Washington DC planned and engineered the entire Arab Spring (see *YouTube*). Tim Weiner, the author of the definitive book on the history of the CIA, *Legacy of Ashes*, said that while the organization's focus has always been regime change since the 1950s, its persistent weakness was its understanding of the countries it is was dealing with, due to its ignorance about its language and culture.

33 Jürgen Todenhöfer, *My Journey into the Heart of Terror.* 164.

black flag today, without any churches worshipping the Triune God. That would have been the chilling outcome had the West succeeded in its political aims. The irony is too big to miss: the West secretly supported Salafist jihadis to promote "democracy"—with one eye on Syria's oil wealth—while the Russian president declared openly that he wanted to save Syria's church from extinction, in addition to stopping the spread of Islamism and helping an old regional ally.[34]

And then came Libya, probably the worst example of all. By the time Western powers got involved in arming and supporting a civil war in Libya,[35] that country's dictator had done everything required to cooperate with the West. He had paid compensation for downing a Pan-Am Boeing over Scotland, and had given up his nuclear aspirations. Libya was a flourishing and stable country by African standards, but there was a problem: certain Western leaders wanted Ghaddafi out.[36] And so, NATO powers fueled civil unrest and war, in which the Libyan leader was eventually killed like a dog, with Hilary Clinton famously boasting about it to her colleagues. Today, Libya is a failed state, with the country's south in Al Qaeda's hands and weapons flowing freely through the Sahel into Sub-Saharan Africa. Over the last decade, the ever-worsening security situation in many African countries is a direct result of turning Libya into a militant Islamist hotbed: yet another horrific example of the failed and immoral strategy of "engaging our enemy's enemy."

The examples don't end here. In his book, *Devil's Game - How the United States Helped Unleash Fundamentalist Islam*, author Robert Dreyfus devotes a chapter to "Israel's Islamists." Dreyfus tells the story of how Israel started *Hamas*. During the seventies, the Israeli domestic intelligence agency *Shin Bet* thought it could use *Hamas* to hem in the *Palestinian Liberation Organization* (PLO). The founders of *Hamas* were all members of the *Muslim Brotherhood* (another organization Israel had secret ties

---

34 This sad reality was recently again confirmed to me by a shy Syrian lady, serving us in a furniture store.

35 See Sookhdeo, "The Role of Religion...", 38.

36 In a video that went viral, current Italian PM Giorgia Meloni reminded France's Emmanuel Macron of this sinical plot.

with). Yet the Israelis thought they could use these radical Islamist organizations against the PLO to stifle Communist influence in the region. Thus, radical Islam was secretly funded with Israeli shekels. Several people in Israel and beyond were concerned, so that David Long, former Middle East expert at the State Department, thought "they were playing with fire." He said: "I didn't realize they would end up creating a monster."[37]

The grim legacy of "engaging our enemy's enemy" is still ongoing[38] the latest example even more unfathomable. The many rumours of NATO funding and even training self-confessed radical neo-Nazi fascists for years in Ukraine are now proven to be true. According to Jacques Baud, a former member of Swiss strategic intelligence, extreme right-wing militants of nineteen nationalities, numbering 102 000 in total, and comprising forty percent of the Ukrainian forces by 2020 (according to Reuters), were "armed, financed and trained by the United States, Britain, Canada and France", regardless of urgent warnings by the *Jerusalem Post* and many other news outlets.[39] Washington and London helped launch these neo-Nazi militias when they instigated a *coup d'ĕtat* in Kyiv in February 2014.[40] Again, NATO powers were willing to make a compromise of mammoth proportions in seeking regime change, this time in Moscow itself. Any amount of racial hatred is justified, it seems, if the enemy is Russia. All the warnings of the Global Terrorism Index regarding the rise of Neo-Nazi white extremism (see chapter 10) were conveniently set aside.

The full global impact of this horrific, immoral intelligence strategy by the West, to side with pure evil in defeating its foes, is yet to be fully assessed: Marxist terrorists in Africa (and in Latin America), Islamist terror in the Middle East and now, Neo-Nazi militias in Ukraine. It brings

---

37 Robert Dreyfus, *Devils Game* (New York: Owl Books, 2005), 191-198.

38 See Genl. Michael Flynn on *Al Jazeera Head-to-Head*, "Who is to blame for the rise of ISIL?", *Al Jazeera* website.

See "Retired "Colonel Richard Black: US Leading World to Nuclear War," *Schiller Institute, YouTube.*

See "How to Start a Revolution – Joaquin Flores, Herland Report TV" *Herland Report, YouTube.*

39 Jacques Baud, "The Military Situation in Ukraine," *The Postil Magazine*, April 1, 2022.

40 See "Ukraine of Fire: Oliver Stone Documentary" *Glenn Diesen, YouTube.*

to memory a sermon preached by the Very Reverend John Da Costa, Anglican Dean of Salisbury, in the wake of a horrific terror act committed by Joshua Nkomo's ZIPRA operatives in 1978. The terrorists not only shot down a passenger plane after taking off from Lake Kariba but went so far as to brutally kill all its survivors in the forest. Da Costa, mentioning all the main statesmen and dignitaries of the West *by name*, continued with a tone of immense sorrow and righteous indignation from the pulpit of St. Mary's: "One listens for a loud condemnation... one listens, and the silence is deafening..."[41] That cowardly silence has only gotten worse over the years, for how can you truly weep over terrorist atrocities if you deem the perpetrators your allies? Incidentally, 1978 was the very same year in which Soviet dissident Alexander Solzhenitsyn came to Harvard, telling us that we had lost both the moral high ground and the virtue of courage.

Failed Strategy # 4: Bargaining on Naiveté and Ignorance

All the aforementioned failed strategies relate to foreign policy. Let us now turn to domestic policy. We will find no better example than the country of Sweden, which prided itself for so long on being the moral compass of the free world. Sweden serves as a sad example of how our collective Western attitude of naiveté and ignorance, coupled with a deep sense of moral superiority, has led to the betrayal of our citizens to a terrifying and uncertain future.

The West looked up to Sweden as the moral superpower of liberalism, being so stable and prosperous, setting the world standard in gender equality. Yet sadly, some cities of that very country have been plunged into levels of violence that nobody thought possible only twenty years ago. What has happened? Why is the number of gun-related deaths in Sweden the highest in Europe? Why are so many children in Sweden waking up during the night to the sounds of automatic gunfire or hand grenades exploding nearby? Why can't paramedics enter certain areas without police protection? What went wrong with Sweden?

An excellent source for finding an answer is the Swedish journalist and activist Paulina Neuding. She is the editorial writer with the center-right

41 Hannes Wessels, *A Handful of Hard Men* (Philadelphia: Casemate, 2015) 152-153. The sermon is available on *YouTube* as *The Deafening Silence – September 8, 1978.*

Svenska Dagbladet. Her work has appeared in the *New York Times*, *Politico*, and *The Spectator*. Ayaan Hirsi Ali spoke to her about her experience as a journalist in Sweden over the last decade and more.[42]

Paulina was born in Sweden as the daughter of Jewish immigrants who fled antisemitism in Poland during the late sixties. They were among the first groups of immigrants that came to Sweden, a "very well organized" country marked by "high trust, [and] high levels of social cohesion." The neighborhoods where the Jewish refugees settled were all very safe, and they all interacted well with the Swedes. There were no forms of exclusion for whatever reason.

As Paulina grew up, she joined the Liberal Party. Like everyone else, she believed in free immigration until she realized things were not going so smoothly. Being the child of Jewish immigrants, they were the first to sense a problem when nobody else wanted to discuss it. Gender inequality and antisemitism increased as more and more new immigrants arrived. Ayaan Hirsi Ali asked Neuding why she thought it was such a sensitive topic. Her response is telling: "For two reasons, I think there's a genuine fear to stoke populism, racism, and xenophobia, but there is also fear of being accused of all these things. I think those are the two main drivers."

For example, when a decent Swedish journalist, Per Brinkemo, raised the impact of clan culture on Sweden, he was immediately accused of racism. Neuding continues:

> People would not believe that there are people in this world who are not Swedish and don't organize their societies according to the Swedish way... Everybody is like us, and if they aren't like us, they want to be like us and become Swedes.

The naivete is obvious. Neuding says things opened up for a while when the Swedes began speaking freely about honour killings. That happened after the horrific honour-killing of Fadime Sahindal by her father.[43]

---

42 "Paulina Neuding on Crime in Sweden", *The Ayaan Hirsi Ali Podcast* - 036, on ayaanhirsiali.com

43 Sahindal was a Kurdish woman who spoke to the Swedish Parliament about the oppression she was living under. She was killed soon after. Her death had a sobering effect on the collective psyche of the Swedes.

All that openness disappeared, however, as soon as the clouds of political correctness moved back in, blocking out the sunlight of bravery and honesty. When Neuding dared to write about antisemitism in Malmö, she was accused of generalizing or ignoring the scourge of right-wing extremism. And yes, she was even called a racist, "the lowest thing you can be." Sweden's largest newspaper compared her with Anders Breivik, the Norwegian monster who gunned down sixty-nine teenagers on Utoya Island because of their pro-immigration views. Only twenty-eight at the time, Neuding was deeply traumatized by the media's response and felt the severe cost of speaking out. Thanks to people standing by her, she did not lose her job.

A sudden change came about in the fall of 2015. Though she does not mention it, it was in the summer of that year that millions of refugees walked into Europe as a consequence of the war in Syria. Until then, everyone said limiting immigration for moral and legal reasons was impossible. No one was even willing to discuss the matter. But since the fall of 2015, Sweden began to impose identity checks at the border. Neuding says the whole establishment shifted. "Let's be rational," they said, "we know that we have to limit immigration." A country that was in the grip of a collective psychosis for so many years had changed overnight.

So, what caused the change? Neuding is confident that it happened when the problem of inner-city violence began to affect the children of the Swedish middle-class. When white middle-class children were robbed and humiliated by gangs of immigrants on their way from school or to play soccer, their parents woke up. They were shocked to face their sobbing kids and yet to hear them begging passionately not to report matters to the authorities. It was, in other words, a class issue. When poor immigrants or other lower-class children suffered, it was not deemed serious enough. But when her own middle-class children came home weeping, Sweden suddenly woke up from her deep winter sleep.

Neuding explains that Swedes have a strong sense of collective opinion, which does not allow them to discuss controversial matters publicly. At the same time, you may freely hold to and discuss your personal views with friends in your living room. After the fall of 2015, everything changed, due to the sharp rise in gun violence and other social problems. As Neuding spoke, Sweden already had more than sixty hand grenade explosions that year. The count for the previous year stood at 241. Neuding concluded:

> Suppose this can happen in a country like Sweden because of bad policies. In that case, that tells us how careful we have to be when it comes to the issue of integration and immigration and how important it is to have a rational discussion about these things. I'm not saying that an immigrant commits every single crime. That's a straw man that we'll probably hear after this. But there's an over-representation. And there's a huge problem in immigrant neighborhoods, which are increasingly marked by crime. And the victims of those crimes are mostly other immigrants. It's immigrant children who wake up at night from bombings. And we can't allow that to go on.

That is what political correctness, naiveté, and ignorance brought about in Sweden, so that *The Telegraph* can now call that beautiful country a gangster's paradise.[44] God only knows what all this credulity and cowardice will bring about for the rest of Europe, and whether valour and common-sense will ever return.

These then were the four failed strategies. No one serious about facing the challenge of political Islam may dare to ignore them. Behind them lies the moral collapse of the collective West. This is how far we have fallen and how grave the situation has become. We all have a sacred duty to speak up, to save our nations from the brink, and to influence public opinion. Otherwise, our children will face a very bleak future. May God Almighty grant us genuine faith and love ere it is too late. May he send many a young shepherd-boy to step into the fray, not fearing the nine-foot giant mocking us so relentlessly.

44 See chapter 5.

CHAPTER 12

THE GREATEST VIRTUE NEEDED: COURAGE

We have looked at four strategies by Western powers that have failed emphatically, even though they have not yet been abandoned as such.

> Refusing to own the real source of Islamic terror.
> Refusing to acknowledge the common goal of all Islamists.
> Refusing to shun all terrorism and tyranny but instead often empowering it.
> Refusing to face the simple reality caused by uncontrolled immigration.

If Christians want to become a real force for good in this war of ideas raging so fiercely, then we will have to take note of these failed strategies. We will have to take a Biblically responsible position on each of them and learn to absorb our radically one-sided mainstream media with much more caution. Preaching the gospel while inadvertently supporting such strategies through our tacit approval or cool nonchalance will render us harmless soldiers of the cross at best or secret agents of evil at worst.

And why should we be taken seriously in our own countries if we hardly ever push back on policies that put the most vulnerable at risk—if not us all? Shall we be viewed as ambassadors of a Messiah who was said to bring deliverance and justice to the poor, if we do not care how many bruised reeds are being broken and how many smoldering wicks are snuffed out, far and near? Let us dare to stick out our necks for what is right and true, to expose and to oppose evil, knowing that "...there is nothing concealed that will not be disclosed, or hidden, that will not be made known" (Matt. 10:26). For if we faithfully follow the Lamb, refusing to call evil good, and good evil, we will encourage the righteous and stifle the plans of the wicked. Our silence, though, will only do the opposite, for tyrants have always loved an uninformed and silent public.

The Deepest Source of Our Paralysis

But what shall we say of these failed strategies, and what can we as Christians learn from them?

First of all, what is the reason why politicians and so-called experts refused to make the connection between militant Islam, or Islamic extremism, and Islam itself? On the surface, it has everything to do with political correctness. How dare we criticize another man's faith or religion? We are Westerners, the champions and guardians of religious pluralism. Moreover, we carry the seemingly unbearable burden of our past colonialism, when we too often looked condescendingly down on another man's faith and culture. How dare we now say anything, even if it is true? In fact, for the super "woke" among us, it is totally reprehensible that Caucasian British missionaries could tell the native peoples of India two centuries ago, that they should not burn their widows alive on the funeral pyres of their deceased husbands![1]

What's more, we believe in the separation between church and state. Hence our deep-rooted reluctance to draw the mosque and the Quran into any debate about terrorism.

But the real reason for our obvious failure to connect things with Muslim religious sources lies deeper. We are afraid. We are dead scared of the firestorm it might create if we dare to criticize another man's faith or

1 Interview with Vishal Mangalwadi, "India, Europe & Biblical Revelation | Vishal Mangalwadi | EP 257" on *The Jordan B. Peterson Podcast – YouTube*, April, 28, 2022.

religion. So, we avoid it at all costs because the virtue of courage is at its lowest ebb ever in the history of the West.

Christians often look at reality through the same fuzzy lenses as their politicians and leaders and are unfortunately not much less dominated by fear. It is very easy to prove this vis-à-vis Islam. Bible-believing Protestants would have no qualms criticizing certain doctrines of Catholics (going deep into history) or confronting the views of Mormons, Hindus, or Marxists, for that matter. We will go after the origins and consequences of their ideas and expose them. But when it comes to Islam, we fall silent, perhaps in fear of stirring up Islamophobia. And with that, the debate is over.

But that is not the deepest source of our paralysis yet. It is not that we fear Muslims in the first place; we fear each other. We fear division among ourselves so much that we prefer retreating into a little corner of silence, considering this or that issue as too "political". But, like Israel's pseudo-prophets, we have become dumb dogs that cannot bark, since we have muzzled God's Word when it comes to the most urgent issues of the day, turning a blind eye to injustice and oppression (see Is. 56:10). It is for this reason that hardly any Evangelical leader of note spoke out against the invasion of Iraq in 2003. Even when it was admitted that the whole war was based on "failed intelligence", or that the repeated claims about WMDs were simply a pretext for war, hardly a single Evangelical voice cried out. Meanwhile, trillions of dollars were wasted, Islamic terrorism was boosted, a whole country was plunged into chaos, and thousands of soldiers returned with PTSD. But that did not concern most of our pastors or parishioners too much.

But there are other reasons as well, speaking as Protestants. Our paralysis to engage our Muslim friends in this battlespace of ideas also stems from a misplaced piety. We have been telling ourselves for a few centuries now that the Biblical message concerns mainly personal salvation—some call it the salvivification of the Christian message—which is most likely an unfortunate by-product of the Protestant Reformation. The European reformers emphasized justification and assurance of salvation so much in an attempt to (rightly) correct the medieval works righteousness of Catholicism, that Protestants later came to believe that the Biblical story is all about the "salvation of our souls." One only has to scan the hymn sections of most Christian songbooks to become acutely aware of this fact, i.e., that a vast majority of hymns center on individual salvation and "spiritual issues", with few focusing on this world and our calling to be faithful disciples of Christ in it.

What is more, the gospel brought to Africa often taught that the "Kingdom of God" is all about a disembodied future abode beyond the clouds. Though that sort of hereafter may not be all that exciting, it is at least far better than the murky shadowlands of the deceased ancestors (the so-called living-dead) which traditional Africans believed in ever since they could remember. Compare all of that with the Islamic ideal, an earthly caliphate under *sharia*, and one can see (in one sense) how radically ill-prepared Christians are for taking their Muslim adversaries to task in this war of ideas. For if all the gospel is about is "going to heaven," why bother taking a stand for truth and righteousness here on earth?

So, what shall we do? Shall we run? Shall we cower in fear, or what? Or shall we compromise and yield wherever Islam and the Left push and threaten, hoping for better times? Shall we flee like the sons of Ephraim in the day of battle, forgetting our covenant with God and his mighty works (see Psalm 78:9-10)? Worse yet, shall we change sides like cowards, when we spot the enemy at the gate? Or shall we live by our precious clichés, that "God is in control" while sticking our heads in the sand, selling our children out to the schemes of the prince of this world? Shall we here in North America dream that life will continue as always and that the grim realities of Africa and Europe will never reach our shores? And above all, shall we as a Christian church in the West continue in our confused and fragmented state—through majoring in all the minors—while we ought to have been "standing firm in one spirit, with one mind, contending side by side for the faith of the gospel, not being intimidated in any way by our opponents" (as Paul wrote in Phil. 1:27-28, NEB)?

In hindsight one might say that it would have served Protestantism well, had a reformer like Martin Bucer of Strasbourg (1491-1551)—who emphasized evangelical unity instead of dogmatic partisanship—received more attention during the early reformation period of the 1500s. Then perhaps a book like Ephesians, instead of Romans, would have become the rallying cry of the Reformation, with its emphasis on God's grace, the unity of the church and Christian piety, instead of putting all the emphasis on "doctrinal"[2] purity. Moreover, Ephesians also summons us to take up the full armour of God for the day of battle![3]

We will have to face our innate fear and preponderance for crawling into our shells at a foundational level, if we hope to become a force for good like Christians of former ages. To engage the evils of our time, both in our own camp and elsewhere, we desperately need the supreme Christian virtue of courage and bravery. The opening chapters of the book of Joshua tell us how crucial faith and courage were in the battle between light and darkness. Later on, we marvel at the heroic bravery of a mere shepherd-boy standing up to a Philistine-giant in the name of Yahweh. This David became the very prototype of our Messiah, who stood up against the whole world, and conquered! And then we have not even spoken of Daniel closing the mouths of lions, and of many others. Was it not for the bravery of the pre-exilic Hebrew prophets, the cries of the needy and the poor would have been drowned out by the temple songs of Jerusalem. Who can read Amos, Micah, Isaiah or Jeremiah and not be touched by their passion for truth and justice in Judah's towns and Jerusalem's courts? They knew that injustice and oppression for whatever reason were "a blot on God's conscience" to use the words of Abraham Heschel.[4] That's why they refused to retreat into a safe corner to avoid all controversy until the storm was over. Jeremiah's big crime, for that matter, was that he dared to talk openly about the future implications of Jerusalem's corrupt politics and lack of moral integrity, when no one else dared to do so. Nor shall we forget how the disciples gathered in an "upper room" somewhere in Jerusalem, to pray for boldness when they were threatened no longer to even mention the name of Jesus.

But then, someone may say Israel was a theocracy; we live in the gospel age. That is undoubtedly true, but it makes little difference in the end. The Hebrew prophets were called to point Israel back to Yahweh's covenant

2 The word "doctrine" acquired a different meaning in the post-reformation era, from what it had in the New Testament and Patristic eras.

3 Cf. Interview with Dr. Willem van't Spijker, "Geleerd en bescheiden," *Terdege*, date unknown.

4 Abraham J. Heschel, *The Prophets* (New York: HarperPerennial, 2001), 253.

with Moses, and the apostles were called to point the whole world to the person, work, and commands of Christ. And to use Christ's own words, we were called to be a city on the hill, and a lamp in a dark place, which by implication also means that we must be willing to bear witness to the truth like he did before Pilate, for if the salt has lost its saltiness, what shall it be good for, asked Jesus? It is only ready to be trampled underfoot by men.

An Honest Look in the Mirror

Genuine bravery and courage must include an honest look in the mirror. Some very valid cultural criticism has been leveled at the West, not only from the Muslim world but also from other circles. Are we willing to listen? While we do not have to take everything for our account, we should at least allow the sacred texts of the Judeo-Christian tradition to help us weigh the critique and call for radical change where necessary. If we expect to be taken seriously as Christians, then we must realize where things have gone wrong in our culture, and where the church shared in the blame for the sad unraveling of the West, by either supporting or implicitly approving the policies and ideas that have pulled the seams of our culture apart. And, if we dare to go deeper, let us explore the devastating impact of our most celebrated Western prophets: men like Nietzsche, Marx, Freud, Sartre, and Foucault. Can any civilization feasting on such an intellectual menu expect to survive?

Muslims often equate the West with Christianity. In their collective memory, Europe was not only the cradle of Western civilization, but also Christian, as the crosses on so many European national flags testify still today. Where was the church's much-needed protest (except for a few selected issues) across a broad spectrum of increasingly decadent moral values, destructive philosophies, and selfish foreign policies over the last several decades? And remember, all of this came on the back of two devastating World Wars fought among "Christian nations", from an outsider's perspective.[5] To this day, the West is staggering like a drunken harlot in

5 Let it be known, though, that these two cataclysmic wars came about not *because* of Christianity, but because of the systematic destruction of the Judeo-Christian foundations of Europe from within, since the late seventeen-hundreds.

the dim streetlight of her fading greatness, due to the hangover of these cataclysmic wars. In an effort to atone for our sins the West has cast almost every moral virtue and common-sense principle that once made her great to the dogs. Evangelical scholar David Wells called it all "the loss of center," which amounts to ripping the hub out of a bicycle's wheel.[6]

Thus, if we are going to survive as a church and a civilization, we will have to take a deep look at ourselves, so as to build on what was good and to reject what was useless and evil. Consider by way of example: what must unsuspecting Muslims think of us, flying to our shores, when they are introduced to an avalanche of decadent-nihilist Hollywood in-flight entertainment on our airline carriers? So much rudeness, vanity, and sensuality are thrown right into their faces before they have even set foot here. It might all seem perfectly normal to us, but for them, it is not. For if we call that "freedom" which enslaves our children and destroys our culture, let us not think we shall ever win this war of ideas with a civilization as mighty as Islam.

During the mayhem that engulfed the US' final withdrawal from Afghanistan, the prominent Slovenian philosopher Slavoj Zizek remarked:[7]

> Decades ago, Ayatollah Khomeini wrote: "We're not afraid of sanctions. We're not afraid of military invasion. What frightens us is the invasion of Western immorality." The fact that Khomeini talked about what a Muslim should fear most in the West should be taken literally: Muslim fundamentalists do not have any problems with the brutality of economic and military struggles. Their true enemy is not the Western economic neocolonialism and military aggressiveness but its "immoral" culture.

In *The Crisis of Islam – Holy War and Unholy Terror*, the late Princeton scholar Bernard Lewis mentioned how one of the founding members of the Muslim Brotherhood was first radicalized by what he saw in America back in the 1940s: "Sayyid Qutb's stay in the United States seems to have been a crucial period in the development of his ideas concerning the

6 See David Wells, *The Courage to be Protestant* (Grand Rapids: Eerdmans: Grand Rapids, 2008), 97-133.

7 "Slavoj Zizek: The true enemy for Islamists..." *RT Question More*, August 20, 2021, on tr.com

relations between Islam and the outside world."[8] He was shocked by the American way of life, principally its sinfulness and depravity, and by what he saw as its addiction to sexual promiscuity.[9] Qutb also observed,

> ... churches in America operate like businesses, competing for clients and for publicity, and using the same methods as stores and theaters to attract customers and audiences... success is what matters, and success is measured by size...

What a sad report (though no doubt biased) written a century after Alexis de Tocqueville's praise of America's high moral standards. Qutb's denunciations of the US were so vehement, wrote Lewis, that he was obliged to leave his post at the Egyptian Ministry of Education by 1952 to join the Muslim Brothers of Egypt.

No More Excuses!

The upshot of it all is that there is little room and time left for vain excuses, if we are going to prevail in this cosmic battle of ideas. Someone who thought long and hard about our innate proclivity for finding excuses when the battle heats up, was the French existentialist philosopher Jean Paul Sartre.[10] He did so as he reflected on the horrible time of the Nazi occupation of France, aiming some vehement denunciations at his fellow countrymen for their cowardice, hypocrisy, and collaboration with the Nazis. What bothered him most was how many shirked their *responsibility* to join the resistance. They cited the following reasons:

> "What can I do about it?" – an appeal to impotence.
> "I did not start the war, did I?" – an appeal to innocence.
> "Everyone else is doing it." – an appeal to the herd.
> "I am just looking out for myself." – an appeal to self-preservation.

---

8 Bernard Lewis, *The Crisis of Islam* (New York: Random House: 2004), 78-79.

9 These were the times of the notorious Kinsey Reports on the sexual behaviour of males and females in America, which overturned traditional Christian values and inspired Hugh Hefner's *Playboy* magazines.

10 Robert C. Solomon, "No Excuses: Existentialism and the Meaning of Life" in *The Great Courses* (Chantilly, VA: The Teaching Company, 2000), 68.

"I couldn't help it." – an appeal to helplessness.

"I was afraid" – an appeal to fear.

Sartre argued against all such excuses by saying that we are "absolutely free." The atheist philosopher meant that since we have been "cast into this world" by fate, we are responsible for everything we do. Responsibility is key. Without exercising it you are not free. How sad that modern-day Christians have to learn this from an atheist, for we seldom hear this emphasis in our own circles. It has become commonplace for us to use even good theology to avoid our responsibility, when God's Word is calling for brave action.

Others much closer to the Christian tradition than Sartre, also called for a greater sense of individual responsibility, if we hope to see a better world. Of the three brothers in Fyodor Dostoevsky's famous 1880 novel *The Brothers Karamazov*, Dimitri's life is an empty pursuit of selfish happiness and sensuality, while Ivan dreams of intellectual pride, in his cynicism of everything sacred. Both of them lack any sense of real accountability and both lives end in despair.[11] It is only the youngest, Alyosha, who truly cares for his family and community, whose life has any sense of meaning and beauty about it. But such a life, Dostoevsky reminds us, is rooted in God's love and in an understanding of life's deepest secret, as summarized in John 12:24. When the Bible says that "perfect love casts out fear," (I John 4:18) it means so not only in a vertical sense, but also horizontally, for fear and sincere brotherly love cannot occupy the same space. Therefore, love does not dodge responsibility for my neighbour's good, but responds to the divine call, even at the expense of my own reputation or life.

Closer to our times, Canadian psychologist Dr. Jordan Peterson summons young men to take responsibility for their own lives and those around them if they want to find lasting meaning in this life.[12] The courageous South African public servant Thuli Madonsela likewise stressed the importance of taking moral responsibility for your immediate surroundings as one of the major

---

11 Fyodor Dostoevsky, *The Brothers Karamazov*, translated by Andrew R. McAndrew (New York, Bantam Classic, 2003).

12 See Jordan Peterson, "Rule 6: Set your house in perfect order, before you criticize the world" in *12 Rules for Life: An Antidote to Chaos* (Toronto: Random House Canada, 2018), 147-159.

qualities of true leadership.[13] Indeed, true leadership doesn't hide behind vain excuses. Shall we ever forget how Athanasius stood up against the whole world defending the deity of Jesus Christ? Or how William Wilberforce fought twenty years against the entire political establishment in London to ban the immensely lucrative transatlantic enterprise of slavery? Or how the "small woman" Gladys Aylward laboured to ban foot-binding in China, and William Carey widow-burning in India? And what about Dietrich Bonhoeffer walking right into the eye of the storm, out of a comfortable life in New York, to join the protest of the Confessing Church in Nazi Germany? And then we have no time to mention Luther, Solzhenitsyn, Martin Luther-King and many others, not to forget Canadian Jordan Peterson's own heroic stand against the super-woke madness engulfing the West in our own day.

Finding excuses so as not to act responsibly and courageously is so common to man that it is always inspiring to hear of someone who overcame it. The story of American neurosurgeon Dr. David Levy is an inspiring contemporary example. Levy, a devout Christian, became convinced in his own heart that he should pray for his patients before surgery. Such a conviction in the heart of a medical specialist in the intense secular environment of a Californian hospital, is already a miracle of itself. How much more to have the faith and courage to put it into practice! But that is what Levy did after overcoming a heap of excuses in his own heart.

He tells his story in *Gray Matter - A neurosurgeon discovers the power of prayer... one patient at a time.*[14] When he finally took the courage to pray for a female patient, he had to battle the following excuses in his heart:[15]

> "It could be seen that I am lacking confidence"
> "Patients may be offended"
> "If I prayed and it went badly, it could ruin people's faith"
> "I was trained to respect the gulf between medicine and religion"
> "I would lose my reputation in the medical community"

---

13 Adriaan Groenewald and Ellis Mnyandu, *Thuli Madonsela on Leadership*, e-book (Candid Media Group: 2016), 172 of 561.

14 See chapter 2, "How I began praying with patients" (Carol Stream, IL: Tyndale House, 2011).

15 Ibid.

> "It could suggest that my knowledge and skills were inadequate"
> "It would introduce an unnecessary element into an already stressful situation"
> "It would alter the typical doctor-patient relationship"

Has Dr. Levy become a rare example? The apostle Paul wrote to Timothy long ago that God has not given us a spirit of fear but of power, love, and self-control (II Tim. 1:7). We can also think of the twelve spies returning from Canaan. Two had faith; ten had none. Ten were overpowered by fear and could only think of excuses. Two remembered God's promise and were absolutely positive (see Num. 13). Courage and bravery, coupled with wisdom, was the one thing Jesus instilled in his apprentices when he trained them for their future mission in Matthew 10. This is indeed what we as Christians need if we are going to take personal responsibility for the world we live in, particularly in our battle against the ideas of Islamic *dawa*. We need Biblical bravery, and lots of it, as we trust in him to whom *all power has been given in heaven and on earth* (Matt. 28:18). Thank God that is exactly what Jesus promised will happen to his disciples of all times, when the Holy Spirit fills them: they will receive divine power to speak and act boldly without fear (Acts. 1:8). All of this underscores the vital importance of prayer, for only those who diligently ask receive the Holy Spirit (Luke 11:5-13).

Here is another example of Christian courage. *Kyk Hoe Slinger Hulle* ("Look How They Stagger")[16] was a 1946 Christian novel based on real events, exposing the abhorrent "dopstelsel" (dop system) in the Western Cape. Many wine farmers in those days paid their brown workers (at least in part) with wine. That caused widespread alcohol dependency and social misery among the "Cape Coloureds" as those were called working on these wine farms. The main character in the novel, Hendrik Karsten, decided one night that he could no longer resist the Holy Spirit to speak out against this social evil. But he was up against many obstacles. His wife urged him "not to get involved" and to rather focus on "spiritual things". His pastor advocated for a neutral position in his quest to keep the peace. Moreover, the larger business and farming

16 Jik, *Kyk Hoe Slinger Hulle* (Christen-Studentevereniging van Suid-Afrika, Stellenbosch, 1946).

community was not interested in trouble. And there was Hendrik's fear that the church would be divided if he should speak up.

Then God gave him the nerve one night at a church-council meeting. The immediate fall-out was big. His neighbour-farmer, and strong supporter of the *dopstelsel*, got so angry that he resigned from the council, bringing their fragile relationship to an abrupt end. The council meeting ended in disarray and sorrow, the pastor going home a broken man. Yet, as Hendrik knelt by his bed in prayer that night, he had peace with God. He lay his head on the pillow, knowing he had no choice but to obey his Maker. In the short-term, things looked bleak, but down the road, a light was shining. It was all for good, for the evil system was later abandoned, and brown families were saved from self-destruction and even brought to Jesus in repentance. Hendrik's integrity was honoured by the whole community, and even the pastor came to his senses. A simple novel but a powerful lesson.

That is just how life is. We bring a sacrifice now for a hopeful future later, or we avoid it now and pay a far higher price down the road. There is no escape from facing difficult challenges. Time is hardly ever so kind as to solve them for us. Looking for a comfortable life is lethal; it's the opposite of being a disciple who has taken up his or her cross. Solzhenitsyn hinted in his famous speech of 1978 that the pursuit of happiness killed America. Our love affair with comfort and ease is killing our children's future. Yes, we are in for a mighty battle, but praise God, it's a good one, and there shall only be one outcome: the triumph of the Lamb and his redeemed. One day we shall finally sing, standing around the throne,

> "Salvation belongs to our God,
> Who sits on the throne,
> And to the Lamb"
>
> — Rev. 7:10

Therefore, let us be watchful, standing firm in the faith. Let us act like men, and be strong. And let all we do, be done in love (see I Cor. 16:13-14).

CHAPTER 13

THE SURPASSING BEAUTY OF CHRISTIANITY (I)

Nothing will steel us better for believing and defending the faith that was "once delivered to the saints" (Jude 3), than by comparing it with the "faith" that some would like to impose on the world by force. In doing so I have selected four topics for comparison. My purpose is not to be exhaustive but to illustrate the contrast between the two faiths looking at only four themes: women, leadership, justice and conquering evil.

Women

What exactly is the position of women in Islam compared to Christianity? In his seminal work *Democracy in America*, first published in 1835, Alexis de Tocqueville stressed that any society is only as free as its women are. When our women live in fear, our children live in fear. When our women are abused, our children will be abused. But when our women and children are free, in the best sense of that word, then our societies will be free and flourishing.

Let us consider for a moment what we mean by freedom. Politicians will typically say that freedom is that which holds Western civilization together or at least used to, but the late British conservative author Roger Scruton also reminded us that: "... taken by itself freedom means the emancipation from constraints, including those constraints which might be needed if a civilization is to endure. If all that Western civilization offers is freedom, then it is a civilization bent on its own destruction".[1]

Freedom, in the Christian sense of the term, is not the sort of freedom seeking emancipation from all constraints but a freedom that will maximize human flourishing. It is freedom liberating us from our self-destructive sinful bent, desiring to obey the voice of God speaking through Scripture. It is the freedom of "faith working through love" (Gal. 5:6), for "love does the neighbour no harm" (Rom 13:10). It is noteworthy to mention that every one of the Ten Commandments were given to protect either God's honour or my neighbor's life and dignity from me, i.e., from *my* insolence, arrogance, lust, vengeance, greed, lies or whatsoever. God had to protect himself and my neighbour from me. All of this is abundantly clear in the teaching of Jesus too. Little wonder that societies flourish where his commands are believed and obeyed. So let us then turn to our first topic of comparison: women.

In 2011 television audiences in the United States were shocked by CBS journalist Lara Logan's ordeal while reporting on protests in Cairo's Tahrir Square. This is what the South African-born reporter went through,[2]

> We were filming in the square... [Richard Butler] knelt down to change the battery [on his camera] and we stood around him, surrounded by the crowd who were excited, but calm and happy. The last person I had interviewed had just said, "Thank you Mark Zuckerberg, thank you Google, thank you Facebook—this is your revolution."
>
> As we stood with the crowd... our young Egyptian fixer turned to me in a panic, his face totally white with panic and fear and he said, "We have to go now, NOW—RUN!" So we started to run and get ahead of much of the crowd. I was running with him and our team security person, Ray.

1 Roger Scruton, *The West and the Rest* (Delaware: ISI Books, 2002) viii.

2 See Hirsi Ali, *Prey*, 158-160.

> It was confusing because I thought the men/boys running with us were trying to help and they were telling me to slow down and wait, and I could feel people's hands between my legs grabbing my crotch violently, and I was worried about the team… We seemed to get far from the mass of people but there were still many men around us who were saying they were helping, but I began to realize they were slowing me down and also grabbing me and then the mass of the crowd had caught up to us and began to tear at my body and my clothes and stick their hands inside my shirt and my pants. I was stripped naked, my clothing was shredded and [I was] violently raped with sticks, flag poles, hands—at a certain point I lost track… I could feel my bra strap tear and the air on my skin and their nails as they tried to tear my breast from my body. My legs were distended as they tore my body in different directions as the mob seethed.

Lara was beaten, gang-raped and sodomized, until she almost died. Hussein Mansour, who was also on Tahrir Square that night, wrote that he found the look in the eyes of these men the most terrifying thing he had ever seen, and likened it to that of a hyena chasing its prey.[3] The same Mansour tells us how Egyptian men fantasize about Western women, due to all the Western pornography they absorb.

Lara Logan later learned that this is "a form of social control in Egypt. That women do not want to go out without men if they knew this could happen to them… [and] that women of course bear the burden because the government uses this to remind them to cover themselves."

This is what north Africans call *taharrush gamea*, the rape game. It has been recorded in Algeria and Tunisia since the 1960s.[4] On New Year's Eve of 2016 it came to Cologne, when 661 German women reported being sexually assaulted that single night, as they went out to celebrate the dawn of the New Year as always.

Before probing the roots of these shocking events, we need to pause briefly at some popular explanations as to why something like this could

3 Mansour, *Minority of One*, 170.

4 Ibid., 160.

happen. Ayaan Hirsi Ali says in her book, "[to] be sure, this kind of thing is not unique to Muslim societies", but it is severe.[5] She suggests that this is common to all societies, though it is worse in the Muslim world. In a panel-discussion[6] on her book *Prey,* with Peter Robinson from the Hoover Institution, two of Ayaan's conversation partners went much further. They suggested that the problem (of random male sexual assault on women in public) has always been among us. It is only now more readily reported due to the rise of the Me-Too movement. They also suggested that these sorts of sexual attacks happen where there is a male-dominant demographic ratio. In other words, it occurs where (young) men are in the majority, and since there were so many young men out there in Cologne or on Tahrir Square, what can you expect?

I listened to this part of the panel discussion with horror. My mind went back to my youth and upbringing in South Africa. I asked my wife if she was ever sexually assaulted in public in the slightest way, when she still went to the dances. I knew what her answer would be. I also knew that I didn't have to ask my old female schoolfriends the same question.

Then my thoughts turned to accounts I read about two shipwrecks in the Atlantic. The more famous one sank off the coast of Newfoundland in 1912, the other one off the southern tip of Africa near Aghullas in 1852. In both cases, eyewitness reports had it that women and children were first let down into the rescue boats and that men subsequently perished in far greater numbers. Here is the story of HMS *Birkenhead.*

> The *Birkenhead HMS* was *en route* to Algoa Bay, carrying British troops and some civilians when it struck a submerged rock off Danger Point. The lower compartments were flooded as water poured in through the breach, and many soldiers drowned before they could even reach the deck. Captain Robert Salmond gave the evacuation order, but instructed his men to "hold fast" so the women and children could board the lifeboats first. The conduct and courage of the soldiers onboard would go down in legend as

5 Ibid., 153-154.

6 "Ayaan Hirsi Ali's Prey: A Panel-Discussion on Europe, Islam and Women's Rights," *Hoover Institution*, July 1, 2021, *YouTube.*

> they obeyed the captain's orders without question. Survivors later testified that they had never seen embarkations – let alone evacuations – carried out with such composure. The troops and sailors suffered heavy casualties, but thanks to their bravery, all women and children aboard the wreck survived. Rudyard Kipling paid tribute to the bravery of the *Birkenhead's* crew in his poem *Soldier an' Sailor Too*, and the phrase "Birkenhead drill" became synonymous with standing strong in the face of death.[7]

That was the cumulative effect of Christianity on Western society, regardless of all our many faults. The stories that have become common in recent years, of woman and children being trampled by young men in a wild stampede, is the clear consequence of a human race forsaking its Maker and living by its worst instincts. And dare we say, it is also the sad result of feminism celebrating its ultimate triumph by casting aside that old notion of "the weaker vessel."

All of this escapes Ayaan Hirsi Ali (and her friends), who thinks the high levels of respect that women in Sweden enjoyed until recently, was due to humanism and liberalism, forgetting how the Vikings still burned their widows before the gospel arrived in those Nordic regions not so long ago. The simple and *irrefutable* fact is that it was mainly due to the impact of Christianity that women were so safe for so long. Indian author Vishal Mangalwadi argues that among Christians in India, women are generally much safer, while they may otherwise be fair game for sexual predators.[8] The same is generally true in Africa as well.

But let us return to the shocking events on Tahrir Square and in Cologne. We must ask ourselves, why is the problem of sexual assault so severe in Muslim societies? For what happened to Lara Logan on Tahrir Square and to hundreds of German ladies on *Silvesternacht* is by no means an exception. If it were, Hirsi Ali and her team would not have bothered putting up

---

7 Matthew Flax, "Famous Shipwrecks of the Cape of Storms – HMS Birkenhead" in *The 200 Best Experiences in the Cape*, viewed on March 12, 2022, insideguide.co.za

8 Vishal Mangalwadi, *The Book That Made Your World* (Nashville, TN: Thomas Nelson, 2011), 276-277.

with all the meticulous research in writing her book *Prey - Immigration, Islam and the Erosion of Women's Rights*. The crisis is massive and has arrived in the West in many shapes and forms, from sexual assault to mandatory burkas, from forced marriages of young girls to honour killings and FGM.[9]

The grim proof of it all is not only found in the sobering statistics of Hirsi Ali's important book. It is also seen in something else incredibly sad, happening on our watch. Hirsi Ali draws attention to it in the opening pages of *Prey*, where she writes,

> We in the West are used to seeing women everywhere around us. We see them as colleagues in the office, sitting next to us on the bus, as patrons in restaurants, jogging on the streets, and working in shops...[10]

And we take it all for granted. I recall coming back home in 1994, when we briefly lived in the Netherlands, surprised to see a middle-aged woman taking her dog for a walk by midnight. That is how safe it was. It was normal for her. But in many European cities, women won't dare do that anymore. As Hirsi Ali wrote, "in some parts of Western cities and towns these days, you may notice something strange: there are simply no women around— or very few". She continues,

> Walking in certain neighborhoods in Brussels, London, Paris or Stockholm, you suddenly notice that only men are visible. The shop assistants, waiters, and patrons in cafés are all men. In parks nearby it's only men and boys playing soccer. In the communal areas of apartment buildings, its men talking, laughing, and smoking... What happened to the women? Why are they no longer sitting at the sidewalk cafés or chatting in the streets?[11]

Why are they all home or out of sight? The answer is simple. They feel too vulnerable, yes, they are scared. They don't want men calling out to them,

9 Ayaan Hirsi Ali's narration of her own circumcision as a young girl in "Under the Talal Tree" was one of the most shocking things I have ever read. See her *Infidel* (New York: Free Press, 2007), 31-34. It is still being widely practised by Muslims in Africa and beyond.
10 Hirsi Ali, *Prey*, 3.
11 Ibid.

"Hey, baby, give me your number" or "Nice ass" or "What are you doing here?" says Hirsi Ali. To put it bluntly, the culture of the rape game has come to town. Hirsi Ali provides the staggering numbers of rising sexual assaults that followed in the wake of the two million immigrants flooding Europe in 2015. But Europe should have been warned. Across the English Channel, the shocking truth of thousands of British girls who were systematically raped by South Asian grooming gangs, was kept under cover for years by the police and the press to avoid the "racist" label.[12] England threw its lower-income schoolgirls under the bus for political correctness.

So, what lies behind it all? Hirsi Ali provides the answer. The *modesty code* defines the distinction between all modest and immodest women.[13] All modest women avoid being out alone after dark. Most importantly, modest women are expected to dress modestly. We know what that means, for we see it all the more in Western cities. Her ankles or arms may not be seen, sometimes not even her nose or mouth.

There are four categories of modest women: virgins, married, divorced, and widows. A virgin is a young girl living in her father's home, waiting to be married off. She may leave the home, but only in the company of family members, and she must be home before dark. She is eligible to be married from her first period.[14] Once a girl or woman is married, she must maintain the norms of modesty in her husband's home. If a man sends his wife away,[15] she returns to her father's home or another male guardian until she marries again. It is still not proper for her to go out at night.

Modest women are considered protected. They maintain the modesty code in return for protection from the menfolk. Any man who misbehaves towards them will face grim consequences. His family, the neighborhood, the mosque, or the government will ensure that.

12 See Hirsi Ali on grooming gangs in the UK, *Prey*, 215-222, 266-267.

13 See Hirsi Ali, "The Modesty Doctrine" in *Prey,* 141-161.

14 Mohammed set the example by marrying a six-year-old, consummating the marriage when she was nine.

15 The Quran allowed men to marry and then divorce prepubescent girls. See Robert Spencer's commentary on Surah 65, *The Critical Qur'an* (New York: Bombardier Books, 2021), 412.

But then there are the immodest women. If a woman is perceived to have broken the code, the protection of her family is withdrawn. But how does she break the modesty code? If, as a virgin, wife, divorced woman, or widow, she goes and works outside the home or moves around freely in public; or if she ignores the dress code or dates a boyfriend not approved by her parents or guardians, she is deemed immodest. She has no male relatives to protect her. She is fair game and may even become the target of an honour killing planned by close relatives, which is becoming all too common in Western countries. Any woman without a veil or a *wali* (guardian) is fair game. It is open season when she walks around in public, where many Muslim men are around. From this perspective, Western women have been viewed for centuries as immodest whores who "glowed with ardor for carnal intercourse... offering themselves for sin." [16] Poor Lara Logan was one of them.

Consider that Surah 2:223 of the Quran tells Muslim men, "Your wives are your fields. Go then into your fields as you will", and it is not hard to imagine how they will look at a female "infidel," especially if she is pretty, walking around alone without a burka. Lara Logan found that out the hard way, and so also the many European women whose stories are recorded in *Prey*.

It is crucial to realize that not all modern-day Muslims approve of this. But, they are powerless to go against this culture since it has been so firmly rooted in the Islamic tradition for centuries. That point is powerfully made in the documentary *Banaz: A Love Story*.[17] It is the true story about the honour killing of a young Iraqi Kurdish woman Banaz, whose body was later found buried behind her parents' house in England. The film relates how most people from the Kurdish community recoiled with horror and disgust at the idea of an honour killing. Still, when push came to shove, they couldn't stop the minority who occupied the "moral high ground" on the issue. It is hard to combat evil if a people's moral compass has been bent out of shape for so long.

16 Ibid., 151.

17 *Banaz, A Love Story, YouTube.*

The evil of Islamic misogyny also has another deep-seated root: *polygamy*, which predates Islam. Hirsi Ali argues that cultures that practice polygamy "impose extreme modesty on women, and exclude them from public life."[18] What Hirsi Ali asserts should be obvious to common sense: If the more wealthy and powerful men can have multiple wives, then many ordinary, less powerful men will have none.

In those parts of the Middle East, North Africa, and South Asia, where societies tend to be more stable and where social order is enforced, young men are subject to stringent controls, at least regarding Muslim women. But when they go to Western countries, or when Christians or other "infidels" appear on their streets, the reins are lifted, and the consequences are dire. The shocking legacy of Nigeria, Egypt, and Pakistan's ongoing assault on Christian women and girls is there for anyone to study.

Polygamy is never good for anyone, least of all for women. It only benefits the wealthier and more powerful men. Somewhere in her autobiography *Infidel*, Ayaan Hirsi Ali describes the misery her mother had to put up with due to the fact that her traveling father had wives in different places. It is a miserable existence and utterly degrading to any woman.[19] A Canadian woman, Yasmine Muhammed, tells of the misery living in the basement with her mother and siblings, while this other man (not her father) lived with his *favourite* wife and children upstairs on the first floor. Meanwhile,

---

18 Hirsi Ali, *Prey*, 141.

19 A Muslim is allowed four wives at a time. Muhammed was allowed to have thirteen. To prevent jealousy, he spent one night with each of them. One night it was his wife Hafsa's turn, but she was visiting her father. She returned unexpectedly to find Mohammed in the arms of Maria, his Coptic concubine. Bitterly upset, she threatened to tell his harem. Mohammed promised to stay away from Maria, but Hafsa confided in Aisha, who also despised the Coptic girl. The scandal spread, and Mohammed found himself ostracized from his harem. That is supposedly the background to Surah 66, absolving him from keeping his promise to stay away from the attractive maid and encouraging him to discipline his wives if they complain too much. Needless to add, the prophet promptly obeyed the angel's word, and the wives all fell in line. See Robert Spencer's commentary on Surah 66, *The Critical Qur'an*, 415, and Vishal Mangalwadi, *The Book That Made Your World*, 279-280.

like many other Muslim women in Canada, her mother casually claimed her monthly benefits from the government as a *single* parent.[20]

What exactly is the impact of polygamy on men? It is obvious that in polygamous societies—where poverty is common and fathers often wed their daughters off to the highest bidder—many (young) men will be left without the prospect of marriage.[21] Hirsi Ali quotes American social scientist Dan Seligson, who argues that polygamy gives rise to more violent and less prosperous societies.[22] The upper strata of wealthy and powerful men monopolize the most desirable mates. Hirsi Ali continues, "the surplus of unmarried males scrambling for an artificially reduced pool of marriageable females spurs the growth of crime and violence."[23] Seligson says,

> The commodification and objectification of women begins with polygamy. When one man takes two wives, he leaves another man without one. This creates scarcity, and we humans hoard resources when they are scarce. [24]

This raises the social temperature, creating a hostile, angry culture, says Seligson. If we consider this data against the backdrop of the gender-ratio of refugees pouring into Europe since 2015, the picture gets even more chilling. By 2017 two thirds of asylum seekers in Germany were male. Across Europe, there were 2.6 male migrants for every female in 2015; in Italy, the ratio was seven to one, and in Sweden, ten to one. The ratio later stabilized across Europe to 2.1 males for every female asylum seeker.[25]

It is clear that the modesty doctrine and polygamy have had devastating consequences for Muslim culture. Let us now look at what the Bible teaches about women. What sets Christianity apart from everything else, also when it comes to women? Why did women in the Roman Empire

---

20 "Yasmine Muhammed on Divorcing a Terrorist" on *Ayaan Hirsi Ali Podcast 027*, ayaanhirsiali.com

21 Hirsi Ali, Prey, 145-146

22 Ibid., 147.

23 Ibid., 147.

24 Ibid., 148.

25 Ibid., 142.

flock to the fledgling Christian movement in such large numbers when the church was openly persecuted? The answer is simple: They heard and knew that only the risen Nazarene could save them and their families from self-destruction. In the teaching of Jesus and his apostles, three *impenetrable blockades* protecting marriage, the family, and society, were firmly established and divinely sanctioned.[26]

The *first* and most foundational blockade was the prohibition against all sinful lust. "For you have heard that it was said: you shall not commit adultery" said Jesus in his Sermon on the Mount, "but I say to you that anyone who looks at a woman lustfully has already committed adultery in his heart" (see Matt. 5:27-30). In condemning sinful lust for the reasons he did, Christ stood completely alone in history. No, he does not condemn all sexual desire as evil, à la the ancient Gnostics, some mistaken church fathers or Mohandas Gandhi[27] for instance. The Song of Solomon and many other Bible passages explicitly sing the praises of marital romance. Jesus is condemning adultery and the ubiquitous desire to reduce a woman's body to an object of lust and fantasy. In doing so he protects her against *me*. And he protects me against my sinful self, for my unrestrained lusting will eventually dishonor not only my neighbor, his wife (or daughter), and my own wife and family, but will bring God's displeasure upon us, for whoever rejects sexual morality, rejects God (see I Thess. 4:8). Dare anyone disagree with the Man from Nazareth? Who would like to deny that unrestrained sinful lust lies at the root of our modern-day plague of adultery, divorce, sexual abuse, abortion, pornography, sex trafficking, rape, pedophilia, and incest ravaging our world?

The *second* Christian blockade protecting marriage and society is the prohibition against easy divorce. This, too, comes uniquely from Jesus' teaching. It seems certain that many Jews in his day misinterpreted Moses'

---

26 I first learned this from Indian author Vishal Mangalwadi. See his chapter on "The Family" in *The Book that Made Your World* (Nashville: Thomas nelson, 2011).

27 See Mohandas Gandhi, *Autobiography*, 204-211. In seeking to break free from all sexual desire, Gandhi began to pursue *brachmacharya* at age 35, which involved abstaining from all intimate relations with his wife for life since sex was viewed as inherently unclean. The Bible presents human sexuality in marriage as a gift from God while tirelessly warning us against the fire that will consume us if we pursue sex beyond its holy margins.

ancient ruling to regulate divorce, by taking it as an excuse to send your wife away for almost any reason. In Muslim culture, someone can send his wife packing by repeating "talaq" three times— "away!" For very little reason, a Muslim man can do so in a fit of rage, rending a mother of three or four homeless in a matter of minutes. Indian Muslim women have been fighting a fierce battle against this horrible practice for years.

In Christ's day, divorce was seemingly rampant among the Jews too. Hence the question of the Pharisees to Jesus: "Is it lawful to divorce one's wife for just any reason?" Jesus' response was as simple as it was sublime. He pointed "to the beginning" (see Matt. 19:3-9). In doing so, he did not condemn all divorce, for that would place marriage above God, which some mistaken Christians unfortunately do. No, he stood alone against a culture of easy divorce, and especially against *divorcing your wife so as to marry another*. Nothing erodes a woman's security, dignity, and the glory of God more, than when men can send their wives away for any reason. The roaring sixties that glorified easy divorce while calling monogamous marriage a prison-house did not produce greater happiness, but only countless broken hearts and great financial ruin.

The *third* barricade protecting the family is Jesus' implicit rejection of polygamy. Vishal Mangalwadi writes: "Monogamy was not the Jewish, Hindu, Buddhist, or Islamic conception of marriage. It was a peculiarly Christian idea. It spread worldwide in the nineteenth century, mainly through the Western missionary movement."[28] So how did that come about? Because Jesus said long ago: "Have you not heard, in the beginning, He made them male and female? Therefore shall a man leave his father and his mother and be joined to his wife, and they shall become one flesh" (Matt. 19:4 ESV). Not the example of Abraham, Jacob, or David, but that of Adam and Eve in the garden shall be your pattern. Mangalwadi shows how polygamy downgrades all women and enslaves society. In Jesus' eyes, marriage shall only be between one man and one woman, period. Anything beyond that will never have God's blessing, nor will it cause human flourishing. Mangalwadi also shows how all efforts to introduce monogamy in India failed and how scared the British rulers were to challenge it. Even India's first Prime Minister, Jawaharlal Nehru, deeply

---

28 Mangalwadi, *The Book*, 275-276.

convinced of how polygamy degrades women, failed to pass it into law during his tenure.[29]

Add to the three divine barriers mentioned above the apostolic command to love one's own wife as Christ loved his church (Ephes. 5:21-31), and that male and female are equal in the body of Christ (Gal. 3:28) *and* in marriage, or James' exhortation to care for the widows and orphans. It is easy to see why Christian culture, applying New Testament ethics, would rise far above cultures allowing unrestrained sexual lust, fornication, easy divorce, homosexuality, polygamy, gender inequality, widow burning, etc. Add to this the early church's stand against female abortion and infanticide in the Roman world, and it is clear why women flocked to the church in such great numbers during the first three centuries.[30]

This, and not Modernity, lies at the root of the equality, respect and freedom women experienced in the West for so long. Widows received a future—from the Nordic regions of the Vikings to the tropic villages of India—not because of Rousseau or Kant, but because Jesus died and rose again and sent his ambassadors to all nations. When their husbands died, pagan widows had to follow on the burning pyre, for they were seen as a liability. But in the church of Jesus, they heard, "we will always be loved and cared for," so the church in Rome at one time cared for no less than one-hundred-and-sixty widows. And never mind how much Roman society liked to normalize every form of sexual perversion, the fledgling Messianic Christian community all around the Eastern Mediterranean maintained uncompromisingly: "Whoever lives in whatever sin of sexual immorality, will not inherit the Kingdom of God" (cf. I Cor. 6:9). By the same token, salvation, forgiveness and a new life were freely offered to all who wished to repent and come to Christ.

---

29 Ibid., 281. Mangalwadi shows that neither the *wali* and the veil from Islam, nor Hinduism's open sexual perversion displayed on the temple walls of Khajuraho, promoted in the erotic fantasies of Kama Sutra and Tantra Yoga, or the seductive image of Hinduism's most popular goddess Khali, brought any freedom to Indian women.

30 See Rodney Stark, *The Rise of Christianity* (New York: HarperOne, 1996), 104-107. See also Rodney Stark, "Appeals to Women" in *The Triumph of Christianity* (New York:HarperOne, 2011), 122-136.

That, then, is the radical contrast between Christianity and Islam on women. Who will dare to disagree that women and children—living where the barriers against sinful lust, easy divorce and polygamy were firmly established—were truly happy and free? Who will deny that a culture tolerating or promoting polygamy, FGM, child marriage, wife-beating, honour killings, modesty distinctions, and the rape game would send icy chills down every woman's spine? The contrast is simple and huge. When a powerful king in Israel saw a gorgeous lady bathing and called for her to come to his bed, his actions were eventually severely rebuked by a brave prophet, and the Holy Spirit smote his conscience. That king gave us the most poignant penitential song of all, Psalm 51. But when a powerful Arabian warrior saw a beautiful young lady one morning covered only by her chemise (his daughter-in-law in fact), he received a revelation from Allah that he may have her for his pleasure, and we got Surah 33 of the Quran. He alone was allowed to have thirteen wives, while other men were only allowed four.[31] The difference between the stories of King David and Islam's prophet could not be greater and explains everything in a nutshell.

Sadly, the mighty barriers of Jesus and his apostles have been demolished, one after the other. Western nations no longer care for marriage or the family. *The Geneva Consensus Declaration on Promoting Women's Health and Strengthening the Family* of 2020 is currently signed by thirty-seven countries, including Brazil, China, Egypt, Georgia, Hungary, Indonesia, Oman, Pakistan, Poland, Russia, Uganda, Zambia and the like.[32] Sadly the names of Western countries are glaringly absent among the signatories. How have the mighty fallen! Some are now saying that the legalizing of polygamy and pedophilia is around the corner in the West, as our societies continue to "slouch towards Gomorrah." Only divine intervention can still save us from ourselves.

31 Mohammed's marriage to Zaynab, wife of his adopted son Zayd, and Allah's revelation that he may have her, and that adoption should be abolished, forms the background to Surah 33:4-5, 37, 50-51, according to the best Muslim commentators. See Robert Spencer, *The Critical Qur'an*, 292-294.

32 Ryan Foley, "37 countries sign pledge to uphold pro-life, pro-family policies…", *The Christian Post*, November 18, 2022, christianpost.com

Justice

The next theme that we need to look at is justice. Justice and equity are crucial for the peaceful future of any civilization. During the *Black Lives Matter* protests in 2020, a slogan on a banner somewhere read, *No Justice, No Peace*. That is essentially true, whatever one thinks of BLM. When justice is being systematically trampled upon, it is just a matter of time before everything unravels, unless a dictatorship can keep things in check. That applies everywhere, from the home to the state. Peace and harmony can't flourish without equity. That is why the virtues of the just ruler of Psalm 72 are sung so highly. He wants justice to roll down like water and righteousness like a mighty stream (see Amos 5:24). Such justice, however, is founded upon a very sure foundation, "the commands of the Lord" (Is. 48:18). When it goes, everything goes.[33]

The Biblical patriarch Abraham was once bold enough to ask the "judge of all the earth", whether he was going to do right? When God sent angels to inform Abraham that he was going to destroy the cities of the plain, since the cries of their egregious debauchery and perversity had reached his ears in heaven, Abraham asked Elohim (Gen. 18:23-25):

> "Will you sweep away the righteous with the wicked? What if there are fifty righteous people in the city? Will you really sweep it away and not spare the place for the sake of the fifty righteous people in it? Far be it from you to do such a thing to kill the righteous with the wicked, treating the righteous and the wicked alike. Far be it from you! Will not the judge of all the earth do right?"

Will not the judge of all the earth do right? Why could Abraham pray like this? Because he believed in something the Old Testament calls *mishpat* (justice), or *tzedakah* (righteousness). He could not accept that the God of

---

33 Francis Schaeffer warned in the seventies that America is headed for what he called "sociological law", where the whims of the majority will decide from one decade to the next what is right and wrong, and therefore also what is just and fair. He said, "if there are no absolutes by which to judge society, then society is absolute." See *How Should We Then Live* (Westchester, IL: Crossway, 1990), 224.

all the earth could do anything unjust. That was a thought too abhorrent to fathom.

The direct consequence of this sublime truth for the political realm is found in the famous dictum that "no one is above the law." That was what the *Magna Carta* of 1215 was essentially saying when it famously stated: (1) justice could no longer be sold or denied to freemen who were under the authority of barons; (2) no taxes could be levied without representation; (3) no-one would be imprisoned without trial; and (4) property could not be taken from the owner without just and fair compensation.

The concept of natural law was commonly accepted in Judeo-Christian civilization as the basis for all national, civic, and criminal law. It was the foundation upon which sound jurisprudence rested.[34] The idea of natural law was understood as the process whereby human beings, through sound reason, could reach a high degree of consensus on what is morally right and wrong and, consequently, also just and unjust. St. Paul expressed this idea when he said in Romans 2:14-15:

> Indeed, when Gentiles, who do not have the law, do by nature the things required by the law, they are a law for themselves, even though they do not have the law. They show that the requirements of the law are written on their hearts, their conscience also bearing witness, and their thoughts sometimes accusing them and at other times even defending them.

The basic principles of justice are found all through Scripture. Here are only a few:

- "You shall not give false testimony against your neighbor." (Ex. 20:16)
- "Do not spread false reports. Do not help a guilty person by being a malignant witness. Do not follow the crowd in doing wrong. When you give testimony in a lawsuit, do not pervert justice by siding with a crowd, and do not show favouritism to a poor person in a lawsuit." (Ex. 23:1-3)

---

34 It is what CS Lewis argued for so eloquently in *Mere Christianity* under "The law of human nature," see CS Lewis, "Mere Christianity" in *The Complete CS Lewis Signature Classics* (New York: HarperSanFrancisco: 2002), 11-13.

- "Do not pervert justice; do not show partiality to the poor or favouritism to the great, judge your neighbour fairly. Do not go about spreading slander among your people. Do not do anything that endangers your neighbour's life. I am the Lord." (Lev. 19:15-16)
- "When a foreigner resides among you in your land, do not mistreat them. The foreigner residing among you must be treated as your native-born. Love them as yourself, for you were foreigners in Egypt. I am the Lord your God." (Lev. 19:33-34)
- "Acquitting the guilty and condemning the innocent - the Lord detests them both" (Prov. 17:15).

The reason why the Hebrew prophets were so audaciously bold about justice and righteousness, challenging both the king's court and the religious leaders, was "because the suffering of man is a blot on God's conscience" writes Jewish scholar Abraham Heschel, and because it is in relations between man and man "that God is at stake."[35] He continues: "Life is clay and righteousness the mold in which God wants history to be shaped." That is precisely why the prophet Micah could cry out:

> "He has shown you, O mortal, what is good.
> And what does the Lord require of you?
> To act justly, to love mercy and to walk humbly with your God."
>
> — Micah 6:8

Ezekiel's scathing rebuke of the false prophets, who maintained nothing was wrong when everything was wrong, and all was right when nothing was right, shows us exactly what goes wrong when justice stumbles in the gate and truth perishes on the city square:

> "... you have disheartened the righteous falsely, although I have not grieved them, and you have encouraged the wicked, that he should not turn from his evil way to save his life."
>
> — Ezek. 13:22 ESV

35 Abraham Heschel, *The Prophets* (New York: HarperPerennial, 2001), 253.

That is what corrupt justice systems do everywhere: they dishearten the righteous and empower the wicked, which is why the Proverb-writer could say: "When the righteous increase, the people rejoice, but when the wicked rule, the people groan" (Prov. 29:2 ESV).

All of this forms the backdrop to the arrival of the Messiah, the Lord's Servant, of whom Isaiah prophesied that he would "bring justice to the nations" (Is. 42:1). When he was suffering under the most appalling perversion of justice ever recorded, Jesus reminded the High Priest (whose servant had just struck him in the face for no reason), "If I said something wrong... testify as to what is wrong. But if I spoke the truth, why did you strike me?" (John 18:23).

Jesus appealed to the most elementary principles of justice, i.e., the difference between right and wrong and the hard evidence required to establish wrong. Allegations and accusations are no proof of wrongdoing, and they could very well be evil in themselves, seeking to condemn the innocent falsely. The sad story of Naboth's vineyard in his own scriptures should have reminded the High Priest of that. All of this should also have been ingrained in the collective consciousness of Judeo-Christian civilization in the West, but alas, only some quivering remnants of the same remain. And now Islam is knocking on our door.

So, what is Islam's concept of justice? We recall what was said earlier when we discussed dhimmitude, how there are two systems of justice in the same country for Muslims and non-Muslims, all based on *sharia*. We also recall how the Muslim World League stated emphatically that the *Cairo Declaration of Human Rights in Islam* supersedes the *United Nations Declaration of Human Rights*. Nonetheless, to find an answer to our question, we could do no better than to turn to possibly the most renowned Muslim scholar of all time, Mohammed al-Ghazali, who died in the year 1111. American author Robert Reilly discussed Al-Ghazali's legacy in his brilliant work *The Closing of the Muslim Mind*.[36]

---

36 Robert R. Reilly, *The Closing of the Muslim Mind* (Wilmington, DE: ISI Books, 2017), 67-90.

Al-Ghazali was the most prominent spokesman for the Asharites in their long battle with the Mutazilites during the Middle Ages. The latter argued for the place of reason and theology in Islam and also promoted a more benign view of Allah, which meant that he is not only known through, but also bound by his eternal, unchangeable attributes. The Asharites, on the other hand, wanted nothing to do with reason, philosophy, and theology and argued in favour of a distant, harsh, and arbitrary God who was not bound to any eternal attribute or virtue. For them, there is no place in Islam for reason, only for blind obedience to *sharia*.

The Asharites went so far as to deny all causality in physics and metaphysics, hence the title of Reilly's book *The Closing of the Muslim Mind*. Nothing that happens occurs as a consequence of something else. To believe that would make God subject to the laws of nature. He is sovereign and subject to nothing. The fact that the beheaded victim's head fell in the sand has nothing to do with the swinging of a sword moments before. It is a sovereign act of Allah. The fact that the body stopped breathing is likewise no consequence of the severed head; it is a divine act of Allah. The absurdity of this position is impossible to fathom, and yet it has a strange and distant bedfellow in Christianity among those who promote blind divine determination, to uphold the absolute sovereignty of God.

Nonetheless, Al-Ghalazi's views are both startling and chilling when it comes to the topic at hand. He argues that "[no] obligations flow from reason but from Sharia." All acts are in themselves morally neutral. Allah is pure will. Good and evil are only conventions of Allah. Some things are *halal* (permitted), and others *haram* (forbidden) simply because he says so and for no other reason. It would be good if he declared murder, lying, or stealing good. God is a supreme monarch, subject to nothing, neither to our notions of justice or injustice. As Reilly says, Allah is beyond good and evil and is, in this sense, Nietzschean. In Plato's *Republic*, Thrasymachus long ago claimed that "right is the rule of the stronger." And so, as Allah is the strongest, his rule is always right.[37] This is why Jihadis shout "Allahu Akbar!" after committing their atrocities.

37 Reilly, *The Closing...*, 71.

It is not hard to imagine what kind of society such a Nietzschean view of God would produce. He, for sure, is not the God to whom Abraham could cry out: "Will not the judge of all the earth do right?" Nor is he the kind of God whom his people could worship as the One who is good and whose lovingkindness endures forever. Neither is he the kind of Saviour of whom we dare say that he is the same, yesterday, today and forever (Heb. 13:8). All such speech betrays confidence that God won't act contrary to who he is or to what he has promised. But that is exactly what was so abhorrent to the Asharites.

This led British Muslim author Ed Husain to conclude, "there was no such thing as morality in Islam; it was simply what God taught. If Allah allowed it, it was moral. If he forbade it, it was immoral."[38] Reilly rightly concludes that the significance of the Asharite position can hardly be overstated. "Undermine the integrity of reason, and you subvert the foundation for freedom of conscience" says Reilly, adding that there is no Arabic word for conscience.[39]

That all of this would result in a total loss of justice should be obvious. As we have seen, justice is inseparably bound to the principle of right and wrong, or good and evil, and the innate God-given human ability to know it. The Quran, however, states in line with the Asharite position in Surah 2:284, "He forgives whom he pleases, and punishes whom he pleases." Al Ghazali says: "There is nothing Allah can be tied to, to perform, nor can any injustice be supposed of him, nor can He be under any obligation to any person whatsoever." The God of Scripture reminds his people, though, even when they pass through deep trials of suffering due to their own rebellion, that his eternal covenant-promise of love will never fail, if only they would return and seek him with all their hearts. There is nothing arbitrary in this God. He is forever faithful to his promises, provided we walk uprightly before him, for his warnings are just as serious.

For Al Ghazali though, eternal criteria of justice would imply that God is bound to obligations, to which he is not. As the Quran states in 21:23, "He cannot be questioned concerning what He does." He is under

38 Ibid., 74.

39 Ibid., 77.

no obligation to reward obedience or to punish disobedience. Al Ghazali puts the following words in God's very mouth, "These to bliss, and I care not; and these to the Fire, and I care not."[40] Al Fakhr al-Razi (1149-1209) went so far as to declare, "It is possible according to our religion that God may send blasphemers to paradise and the righteous and worshipers to (eternal) Fire, because our ownership belongs to Him and no one can stop Him."[41]

This austere theology of the Asharites has been consistently maintained through the ages, all of which made the famous German philosopher G.W.F. Hegel to conclude that "the activity of God" in Islam "is perfectly devoid of reason."[42]

Unfortunately for the world, it is the same version of Islam that survived in the mainline Sunni position of today, for the Asharites are the spiritual ancestors of Sunni Islam. Strangely though, the recently deceased doyen of Middle Eastern studies in the U.S. could write,

> Al-Ghazali was no radical. In a series of tracts, he defended the mainstream Sunni positions against the esoterism of the Shi'a and the rationalism of the philosophers. In the same time, he leveled sharp criticism against some of the intellectual trends of the time...[43]

But what are the implications of all this? How important is this radical difference between the Judeo-Christian and Islamic views on justice for humankind? I will let the award-winning author and celebrated historian Tom Holland answer the question. In the closing chapters of his book *Dominion, How the Christian Revolution Remade the World*, Holland comes to the following remarkable observations and conclusions (in my own words).

Christianity has this strange inherent quality (over time) to auto-correct. The revolution that began on the cross, when God chose the weakest thing in the world to shame the mightiest, repeats itself again and again.

---

40 Ibid., 80.

41 Ibid., 82.

42 Ibid., 82.

43 Bernard Lewis, *The Middle East* (London: Phoenix Press, 2002), 240.

Holland has numerous examples to prove his point, some of which I will present here in my feeble paraphrase of his sterling prose. The overt racism left in Christian America after slavery was banned, was confronted by a man who got his inspiration from the Bible. Martin Luther King stirred the conscience of America with a message of Biblical love, not that Bohemian love sung about by John Lennon.[44] And so we can go on. The same Bible that convinced Evangelicals that homosexuality was wrong, convinced them to love gay people genuinely. The same Bible that told Christian men that they were the head of their homes also convinced them to view their wives as equal to themselves and to love them as Christ loved his church. The same faith that inspired Dutch farmers to take the gospel into Africa and then much later to implement apartheid, later inspired the non-Whites to throw off the yoke of apartheid. And not only that, it was the gospel that taught these same Afrikaners to repent of their political sins, for Mandela to forgive, and for De Klerk to hope that there would be pardon for his people under Black-majority rule after 1994. Holland continues,[45]

> Repeatedly... it was Christianity that had provided the colonized and the enslaved their surest voice. The paradox was profound. No other conquerors, carving out empires for themselves, have done so as the servants of a man tortured to death on the orders of a colonial official. No other conquerors dismissing with contempt the gods of other peoples, had installed in their place an emblem of power so deeply ambivalent as to render problematic the very notion of power.

For, beneath this Christian concept of justice lies the singular truth found only in the Bible, which was never taught as clearly by anyone, as by Jesus the Messiah. The notion of every human being possessing equal dignity was not remotely evident outside Christianity.

> A Roman would have laughed at it. To campaign (today) against discrimination on the grounds of gender or sexuality, however, was to depend on large numbers of people sharing in a common assumption: that everyone

44 See Holland, *Dominion*, 490-491.

45 Ibid., 504.

> possessed an inherent worth. The origins of this principle – as Nietzsche had so contemptuously pointed out – lay not in the French Revolution, nor in the Declaration of Independence, nor in the Enlightenment, but in the Bible.[46]

Holland then turns to Islam, which has nothing in its history or sources to auto-correct. That much someone like Pres. George W. Bush did not realize when he launched his regime-change wars on Middle Eastern countries. President Bush, a self-confessed Evangelical, sincerely believed that the terrorists of 9/11 had hijacked not only those planes but Islam itself, and that most Muslims would welcome freedom from their dictators and the core values of the West. Bush's "assumption that the concept of human rights was a universal one was perfectly sincere... He took for granted that his own values... were values fit for all the world." writes Holland.[47]

What the Iraqis saw was something else, however. They saw that the Americans and the West were willing to impose their "liberating" values with brute force. And so, once the dust had settled on the initial "success" of toppling Saddam, the Americans were not welcomed with high-fives but with a bloody insurgency, the main inspirer of which was Abu Musab al-Zarqawi. Al-Zarqawi did not dream of human rights but of a sword to descend from heaven on Allah's enemies and to destroy the cross. While in jail, he was taught by his radical Salafist tutor that,

> to be a Muslim was to know that humans do not have human rights. There was no natural law in Islam. There were only laws authored by God. Muslim countries, by joining the United Nations, had signed up to a host of commitments that derived not from the Qur'an or the Sunna, but from law codes devised in Christian countries: that there should be equality between men and women; equality between Muslims and non-Muslims; a ban on slavery; a ban on offensive warfare.[48]

---

46 Ibid., 494. This principle does *not* mean that the Bible ever or anywhere condones what it would deem sinful living, but simply that even the greatest "sinner" should be treated with love and respect, as bearer of God's image.

47 Ibid., 507.

48 Ibid., 510.

America's wars to impose democracy and so-called Western values was a call to duty for many Muslims who despised these values, to restore the pure revelation of their ancestors, the *Salaf*. For the Salafists, "The only road to an uncontaminated future, was the road that led back to an unspoiled past."[49] That is the impetus that gave us the Islamic State. And that is how Islam's sources and history default. Like Nietzsche, the Islamic State looks upon Western civilization's concern for the weak and for the individual's rights with utter contempt. The cross had to be redeemed from Christianity and given back to the Caesars, as a fitting means of punishment, for the Quran states: "The penalty for those who wage war against God and his messenger, and who strive in fomenting corruption on the earth, is that they be killed or crucified…"[50] And that is exactly what the Islamic State does with Christians. They crucify them.

Even though the Islamic State by no means represents the mainstream of Islam today, there can be little doubt that Salafism has grown considerably in recent decades, and that their views and desires approximate what Islam was originally meant to be. A worldwide caliphate under *sharia* is where they want to go, where justice in the Judeo-Christian sense of the word, human rights, and the dignity and equality of the individual before the law, *will have no place at all.* Let all the freedom-loving people of the world take this to heart, as well as those who (with Tom Holland) believe that "God chose the weak things of the world to shame the strong."[51]

49 Ibid., 512.

50 Quran, Surah 5:33, as quoted by Holland in *Dominion*, 513.

51 Ibid., 542.

CHAPTER 14

THE SURPASSING BEAUTY OF CHRISTIANITY (II)

We have looked at the radically different views of Islam and Christianity on women and justice. In this chapter, we will look at two additional themes: leadership and the struggle between good and evil.

Leadership

How do Islam and Christianity compare concerning the important notion of leadership? How will we fare under someone who is driven by genuinely Christian principles from the core of his being? And how will we fare under a leader who is driven by those values that belonged to Islam from its inception? We know how many leaders in this world *claim* to be either Christian or Muslim when they are, in reality, driven by a host of other core-motives and incentives. But what will it look like if someone is truly beholden to the most enduring values of his worldview and religion? We must go back to the beginning of both faiths to find an answer.

In Mark 10, two of Jesus' disciples, James and John, came and asked Jesus if they could sit at his left and right hand in glory. They were thinking of positions of power once the Messiah had taken control in Jerusalem.

That their request went diametrically against the entire grain of the gospel, they could not see at the time. How many times did Jesus not emphasize that they must repent and have a child's attitude to enter the kingdom? But they were dreaming of positions of power. Jesus, however, used this opportunity to teach his disciples something precious, namely to beware of the mindset of the rulers of this world, who love to lord it over people to exercise authority over them. Instead, whoever wants to become great among us, Jesus said, must become a servant. Mark then adds possibly the most important words in his gospel: "For the Son of Man did not come to be served, but to serve, and to give his life a ransom for many" (Mark 10:45).

Again, right after the Last Supper, on the eve of Christ's crucifixion, a silly dispute arose among some of his disciples, according to Luke 22. They now argued among each other who of them was the greatest. From our perspective, it seems incomprehensible that they could argue about such a vain thing at such a solemn moment. But that is only because we have been saturated for centuries with the story and impact of Jesus of Nazareth, who humbled himself to the death of the cross. And so, in Luke 22:25, Jesus said:

> "The kings of the Gentiles lord it over them, and those who exercise authority over them call themselves Benefactors. But you are not to be like that. Instead, the greatest among you should be like the youngest and the one who rules like the one who serves. For who is the greater, the one who is at the table or the one who serves? Is it not the one who is at the table? But I am among you as one who serves".

Add to this the moving scene in John 13, also at the Last Supper, of how Jesus got up to wash his disciples' feet, to Peter's utter astonishment. The indelible impact of a serving Messiah, offering up his life for his own in love, was captured twenty years later by Paul in the famous Christ-hymn of Philippians 2. It tells us how God the Son emptied and humbled himself, taking upon himself our very flesh, yes, coming to us as a servant, humbling himself to the Father's will, even to the point of dying on a Roman cross. And for Paul, *that* is why Jesus was exalted and received a Name above every name. And that is the pattern that all Christians should follow, of not seeking themselves, but in humility to put others first.[1]

This was the metaphor, the theme, and the definitive inspiring narrative, that shaped the leaders of the early church. There was no room for selfish ambition, pride, wrangling about who is the greatest; there was no room for all manner of backstabbing and power trips among Christ's apostles. Servant leadership is what Jesus called for, to the very point of laying down one's life for the sheep as the Good Shepherd did. And indeed, that is what happened with almost all of the apostles, according to tradition, except for John, who was buried near Mary in Ephesus after he returned from his banishment to the Isle of Patmos.

One has to read Galatians 2 to see how careful the new convert Saul of Tarsus was, not to cause a rift in the early church. When the risen Messiah, against all expectations, inserted Saul (now called Paul) into the team of those proclaiming the crucified Nazarene as Lord of all, it was done with the utmost care by both God and men. We read how James, Peter, and John gave Paul and Barnabas the "right hand of fellowship," symbolizing respect for each other's calling and sphere of labour. When two apostles later had a brief altercation in Antioch due to one of them "not walking according to the gospel," it would have stunned all, but thank God the issue was soon settled. The only other dispute we read about was between Paul and Barnabas. They disagreed whether or not to take John Mark along on a missionary journey. It caused such a rift that Paul and Barnabas went their separate ways. Later in Paul's writings, we learn that the division was healed, as Paul referred to John Mark as a beloved brother in the Lord.

That a leader in the church is not one to be served, but to serve, was beautifully exemplified in the lives of so many characters of the early church until this whole image became sadly distorted through the influx

---

1 This idea of glory and power through service and even suffering received its climatic adoration in the heavenly throne-room scene of Rev. 5, where myriads of angels and celestial beings fell prostrate before the Lion of Judah. It is the ultimate scene of service and suffering crowned with power and glory by God. Amazingly the all-powerful Lion of Judah, who alone is worthy of taking the scroll out of God's right hand, looked like "a Lamb as if it had been slain". From this scene, endless praise has been reverberating throughout the universe ever since.

of worldly power and money, and the subsequent rise of the papal system, several hundred years after Christ. But that is not how it was from the beginning, and every informed Christian over two millennia knows this instinctively. But alas, what do we see in the house of Islam? We see the polar opposite. Let the children of men beware.

In looking at the inception of Islam, we will skip over the life of Mohammed himself. Interestingly enough, he did not indicate who should succeed him. He did not give detailed instructions (as Jesus did to his disciples) about the time after his departure. That incidentally is the direct cause for the massive rift between the Suni and Shia through the ages until today. In his book, *The Tragedy of Islam*, Australian Imam Mohammed Tawhidi has a chapter entitled "Islamic Leadership: Murder, Invasions, and Terrorism." I am greatly indebted to him for what we are about to learn. He writes that "[d]uring the early centuries of Islam, a culture of war and violence existed amongst the Arabic nations as a form of conflict resolution, a show of strength, and in many cases self-defense."[2]

Please note we will see in the paragraphs to follow how Islamic rulers led their people and settled their conflicts. Remember, there was no agreed-upon principle for who should succeed Muhammed as ruler over the Muslim nation. In most cases, the leading figures of the Islamic religion *fought over* the caliphate says the Australian imam. The first three caliphs were, in fact, all fathers-in-law of Mohammed: Abu Bakr, Omar, and Uthman. The first two were so busy fighting over the caliphate that they failed to prepare properly for Mohammed's funeral.[3]

Tawhidi continues, "in my opinion, the culture of terrorism in Islam was officially introduced by Abu Bakr, our first caliph, and father-in-law of prophet Muhammad. He legalized it and gave it a religious coating by using violent verses of the Quran, which he interpreted to his own benefit."[4] Tawhidi argues that Abu Bakr introduced the gruesome practice

2 Tawhidi, *The Tragedy of Islam*, 36.

3 Ibid., 136.

4 Ibid., 133.

of the beheading or burning alive of his enemies, a practice carried on by ISIS and their affiliates today.

Let us look at one example of Abu Bakr's cruelty. After becoming the first caliph of the growing caliphate, Abu Bakr needed finances, so he depended on Muhammad's chief tax collector, Malik ibn Nuwayrah.[5] Unfortunately, Malik was not a great supporter of Abu Bakr since many Muslims at the time disapproved of his arrogance and self-appointment. Therefore, Malik refused to attend the ceremony of his installment, which infuriated Abu Bakr. When Malik also refused to collect taxes for the caliphate, Abu Bakr sent his right-hand man, Khalid Ibn al-Waleed, with four thousand troops to straighten him out. Even though Khalid's army protested against his cruelty, he encircled Malik and a few of his followers, and murdered them in cold blood during the night. Within the next twenty-four hours, Khalid also raped Malik's widow Layla, and took her as his own wife.

Amazingly, many Muslims since then until today have defended Khalid's actions and have nicknamed him the "Sword of Allah" while claiming that his sexual intercourse with Layla was through a legitimate marriage. It is important to remember that in fundamentalist Islam, you can marry a woman by raping her first, even if her husband was killed moments ago by your own sword. You may also divorce her again within months.

Mohammed Tawhidi continues, "[c]ountless Islamic sources testify that Khalid also cooked Malik's head in a saucepan and ate from it after he had beheaded him. He did that to place more fear in the hearts of the Arab tribes."[6]

When the world saw ISIS militants placing their victims in cages and burning them alive, they wondered where this culture emerged from. Islamic jurists ruled that it is forbidden to kill with fire (something only Allah is allowed to do, according to Sahih al-Bukhari, the most reliable and authoritative *hadith* collection in Islam). The only problem is that Sahih

---

5 For the full account, see Tawhidi, *The Tragedy of Islam*, 138-139.

6 Ibid., 140. Omar, the second caliph, appointed this same Khalid as the leader of the Islamic armies during his caliphate. Tawhidi writes: "Today, ISIS commits the very same crime by beheading its opponents and eating the heads of its victims after cooking them in pots. The caliph of ISIS adopted the name 'Abu Bakr al Baghdadi,' that is, 'Abu Bakr of Baghdad.'"

al-Bukhari 's *hadith* was compiled two-hundred-and-fourteen years after the death of Muhammed, contradicting the verdicts and rulings of the first caliph of Islam, who punished with fire, says the Australian imam.[7] During his brief two-year reign, caliph Abu Bakr burned hundreds of people alive. He was the same man who gave his six-year-old daughter, Aisha, as a wife to Mohammed when the latter was a man in his fifties.

Tawhidi concludes his comments on Abu Bakr by saying: "Muslims, Islamic governments, and caliphates will never be able to escape this bloody and violent history. It is ours, forever engraved. It is part of our being and existence." His only hope is that Muslims will turn against much of their own history.[8]

This brings us to Islam's second "rightly guided" caliph, Omar. Abu Bakr appointed him on his deathbed, despite the remonstrations of many Muslims, due to Omar's "murderous history, evil reputation, and corrupt nature."[9] Omar's terrorism, says Tawhidi, was the worst in Islam. Under his bloody reign, the Islamic caliphate spread fast through military conquest. What is more, Omar ibn al-Khattab was also a misogynist of the worst kind, as illustrated in the shocking story of the murder of his daughter.

Omar had seven wives. Because he was ashamed that one of them had given birth to a baby girl, this wife (whatever her name was) decided to hide the infant from Omar for some years, hoping that his heart would somehow mellow with time. However, when Omar finally saw his daughter, he remained silent. He took her into the desert and began to dig a grave. While doing so, the little girl, at one point, gently cleaned the sand from his beard, oblivious to her father's intentions. Once Omar had finished, he got out of the grave and told his daughter to stand on the edge and to look inside. He pushed her from behind, and she rolled down to the bottom. He then quickly covered her tiny body with the desert sand, something he later regretted much with tears.[10]

7 Ibid., 141.

8 Ibid., 143.

9 Ibid., 145.

10 Ibid., 147-148.

Omar also earned a reputation for being a torturer of women. More than once, he was seen beating a slave girl with a whip until the thing dropped out of his hand. He not only beat his wives, he physically abused other women too, and loved to quote Mohammed, who supposedly said, "A man should not be asked why he beats his wife."[11] Though Omar is called the "Prince of Believers" today, Tawhidi begs to differ, for the second caliph of Islam was also known to have raped Atiqa, the daughter-in-law of Abu Bakr.[12] He proposed to her after her husband's death. When she refused, he raped her and walked away. The man was, in fact, as sensual as you can get. According to leading Islamic scholars, Omar had slave girls serving him and his companions "with their heads uncovered and their breasts shaking."[13] He had no time for compassion either. He prohibited people from mourning the dead. Even Mohammed's widow, Aisha, was not allowed to weep over her husband's passing. Tawhidi says Islam has never been ruled by such a savage tyrant, who continued his predecessor's gruesome practice of beheading his enemies and even burned down his own son's home out of malice. Omar eventually died at the hands of a Zoroastrian Persian who stabbed him.

Tawhidi asks some crucial questions at the end of his account of Omar's life, Islam's second rightly guided caliph:

> If Caliph Omar was a bloodthirsty, child-killing and woman-murdering individual, why did our ancestors allow him to reign over them? Why did they not revolt and rise against his tyranny? The Muslim population was still small in comparison with surrounding nations, and Muslims of that era could have easily regained control and elected a more reasonable leader. Our ancestors are partly responsible for remaining silent throughout the many centuries of corrupt Islamic leadership.[14]

The third caliph of Islam was Uthman bin Affan, another father-in-law of Mohammed, who came to power in the year 644. His reign lasted sixteen

11 Ibid., 150.

12 Ibid., 153.

13 Ibid., 154.

14 Ibid., 167.

years. Uthman tried to be a modest man and a good leader, but his example also left much to be desired.

Years before becoming caliph, he married Ruqayyah, the daughter of Mohammed, who bore him one child. Ruqayyah fell ill during the famous Battle of Badr, causing Mohammed to give Uthman permission to stay home and care for her. Uthman, however, was upset that he would miss out on the spoils of war and ended up beating his sick wife to death. He slept with her maid the same night he killed her. Thus, Mohammed's father-in-law, who became his son-in-law, broke the prophet's heart, causing him to weep excessively, according to Muslim sources.[15]

During his caliphate, the Islamic Empire became extremely wealthy through all its expansive conquests. Uthman not only stole much of this money but spent it for the benefit of family and friends. Uthman was eventually murdered when Aisha, the wife of Mohammed, called for his death. She could never forget how he stole her inheritance from her father. Muslim tradition has it that the greedy Uthman was struck in the head, soaking the Quran he was busy reading with his own blood.[16]

The fourth caliph of Islam was Mohammed's cousin, Ali. Shia Muslims believe that Mohammed had appointed Ali as the first caliph, but his father-in-law usurped the position for his own benefit, hence the deep rift between the Shia and Suni until today. Ali was much more loved by all Muslims than the former three. No doubt he lived a much better life. Aisha, however, could not stand him since she wanted her adopted son, Abdullah bin Zubayr, to be the new caliph. So she went up with three thousand warriors to Basra in Iraq to wage a civil war against Ali, which led to twenty-one thousand casualties. Ali's caliphate eventually ended when he was struck by a poisoned sword while praying in 661.[17]

The contrast between early Christian thought on leadership and early Muslim practice of the same could not possibly be greater. It resembles

15 Ibid., 168.

16 Ibid., 170.

17 Ibid., 174.

the two sides of the moon when it shines at its brightest. Therefore, let all Christians who aspire to leadership make sure to read Ezekiel 34 very carefully. Before we can lead with integrity, we must share Yahweh's sorrow about the lack of faithful leaders. We must hear God's echoing cry, "I saw, but there was no man..." (cf. Is. 59:14-17). We must groan for what has gone wrong in the world and very often in the church too. And we must realize how utterly unfit and unworthy we are, asking ourselves whether we are willing to suffer for a cause much greater than us. Otherwise, all dreams about leadership are selfish, hollow, and dangerous.

Overcoming Evil

The last idea we would like to discuss is perhaps the most important: How to overcome evil. It is here where the true faith revealed by the living God distinguishes itself most clearly and magnificently from every man-made religion and humanistic ideology.

The desire for revenge has been a basic human impulse since the fall. The Genesis account of the brutal massacre of the sons of Hamor by Jacob's sons—after the patriarch did nothing to come up for his daughter Dinah when Shechem so shamelessly raped her—reminds us how powerful this impulse is, and that it never brings forth any good (see Gen. 34). That's why Abigail is pictured as such a noblewoman because she dared to stop David in his tracks, when he was bent on taking revenge on her wicked husband Nabal, who needlessly insulted David and his men (I Sam. 25). The Bible does not approve of human vengeance. It allows the state to punish evildoers, but only through a process of due justice. A famous catechism from the Reformation era calls "the desire for revenge" the root of murder, urging us to lay it aside in repentance.[18] Whoever allows room for revenge will never rid his heart and home of the lethal poison of hatred and bitterness. Where passions for revenge are left to flourish, societies are plunged into never-ending cycles of violence and counter-violence.

So how must our desire for revenge be quelled and overcome? We all know how powerful it can sometimes be. In her book *Unveiled,* Yasmine

18 The Heidelberg Catechism, Lord's Day 40, *The Three Forms of Unity* (Winnipeg: Premier Printing, 1999), 85-86.

Mohammed speaks of how many times she fantasized about killing her mother's "husband", who brutally beat and sexually assaulted her from an early age.[19] They lived in a Vancouver basement, while this man lived on the first floor with his favourite wife and children. Feelings of revenge in such extreme situations are fully conceivable, yet even they should be "laid aside", never mind how hard it may be. We know this is not a Muslim struggle. The powerful cravings for revenge can stalk us all.

The life and teaching of Jesus show us the way. He taught his disciples to bless those who curse them, to pray for those who persecute them, to do good to those who use them, and to love their enemies. He also taught them to quickly settle issues with each other as brothers and never to allow grievances to fester. Christ's teaching was, in essence, nothing new, only more radical. In Leviticus, every Israelite was charged by the Lord to talk with his brother if he had an issue with him, or else his heart would become a pit of murder, plunging him into depression (as Cain found out so sadly). Therefore, "you shall love your neighbour as yourself, for I am the Lord" (see Lev. 19:18). The highlight of the New Testament's teaching on overcoming evil is found in Romans 12:17-21:

> Do not repay anyone evil for evil. Be careful to do what is right in the eyes of everyone. If it is possible, as far as it depends on you, live at peace with everyone. Do not take revenge, my dear friends, but leave room for God's wrath, for it is written: "It is mine to avenge; I will repay," says the Lord. On the contrary: "If your enemy is hungry, feed him; if he is thirsty, give him something to drink. In doing this, you will heap burning coals on his head". Do not be overcome by evil but overcome evil with good.

The New Testament is replete with illustrations and examples of good overcoming evil. The most famous story is the *Parable of the Good Samaritan*, where the despised Samaritan (from a Jewish perspective) acted contrary to all expectations, stopping his donkey to pour out his love on a poor Jew who had fallen among robbers. There were many practical instructions of Jesus too, for example, to walk a second mile with the Roman officer,

19 Published by Fee Hearts Free Minds, Victoria, 2019.

who demanded that you carry his burden for only one mile; or to give also your coat to someone who sued you for your shirt, or to turn your other cheek, to the one who had just insulted you. The entire epistle of First Peter, in some way or another, encourages believers to overcome evil with good, following in the footsteps of him who prayed for his enemies from the cross while they were hurling insults at him. So central was this idea that Paul could write to believers in Thessalonica before closing his letter, "Make sure that nobody pays back wrong for wrong, but always strive to do what is good for each other and for everyone else" (I Thess. 5:15).

But what do we find in Islam? It would be easy to find countless reports of Muslims taking revenge on each other for whatever reason, doing so in the name of Allah. The offense could be anything, but the most basic is leaving Islam or supposedly blaspheming it. To the collective Muslim mind, all of that is unforgivable, for it amounts to "spreading corruption in the land", something punishable with death, even by crucifixion.[20] Rejecting Islam felt to the early Muslims like "persecution," and ever since, whoever is "persecuting" Islam may be slain.

But revenge could also be taken for lesser reasons, like for supposed "immodesty," as in not wearing a burka or hijab in public, walking without a male guardian in the street, or dating a young man who is not Muslim. In the worst cases, it may lead to an honour-killing to restore the family name. Yasmine Muhammed's story, which is quite typical, recounts how easy it is for a teenage girl in a Muslim household to incur the wrath of her parents and community for very ordinary "offenses." Yasmine was severely beaten, abused, grounded, threatened with hellfire, and punished, for among other things:[21]

> not reciting the Quran properly from six-years-old,
> listening to any music,
> not getting up to pray in time,
> not wearing her hijab when she should,

20 Surah 5:32-33, see also 2:10-12 and 30:41.

21 Mohammed, *Unveiled*, 6-96.

spelling her name with a "J" instead of a "Y",
daring to accept an invitation to a Christmas party,
having a Christian friend,
not hating the *kufar* (unbelievers) like all Muslims should,[22]
reading *Anne of Green Gables*,
resisting sexual exploitation by the man upstairs,
eating ham,
of course, the very worst, for going to the police to seek help.

All of that was repaid with brute force in a fundamentalist Muslim home. Many radical Muslims today still dream about settling scores of centuries ago. It was well known how Osama bin Laden complained about losing Andalusia to the Spaniards in 1492. Taking revenge flows through the Quran like the Nile through Africa. It is everywhere and impossible to miss.

Let us now turn again to our Australian imam for concrete examples from early Islamic history. The early caliphs did not take any nonsense. They established a culture of revenge impossible to break. One of those early victims was Lady Fatima, the innocent daughter of Muhammed.[23] The murder of Lady Fatima, who was loved by all Muslims, resulted from a political conflict, as she and her husband Ali (Islam's fourth caliph) refused to pledge allegiance to Abu Bakr. Fatima was the closest child of Mohammed and his only daughter by the time of his death. To many Muslims, she ranks among the likes of Mary, the mother of Jesus.

Since Lady Fatima refused to pledge allegiance to caliph Abu Bakr (he had stolen her inheritance from her father), Omar went to her house with some of his men to set it on fire. At the time, Ali was also there, for he refused to pledge allegiance too. Upon her adversaries' arrival, Fatima said: "O Abu Bakr and Omar! Do you want to widow me!? Have you arrived to set my home on fire?" Omar answered: "Oh daughter of Mohammed! I

22 Surah 5:31.

23 Narrated in chapter five of Tahwidi's work, "The Murder of Mohammed's Daughter and Her Unborn Child: The Worst Crime of our Caliphs," *The Tragedy of Islam*, 175-187.

swear by God that we love you, but if your house continues to be a meeting place for conspiracy any longer, I will set fire to it on account of this!"[24]

As Omar and his men approached the house, Fatima closed the door. She believed that they would not enter the house without her permission. Omar set fire to the house and entered it without consent by kicking the door open. He wanted Ali to pledge allegiance to Abu Bakr. The pregnant Fatima stood right behind the door when it burst open, so that a large nail in the back of the door impaled her, causing her to lose the baby. She was brutally beaten and suffered smashed ribs as a result. She died a few months later from the wounds. A truly shocking way to settle accounts!

Another tragic story is the killing of Hussain, the second son of Fatima.[25] Hussain did not participate in Islam's early invasions and conquests since he opposed them. He preached a message of humanity, peace, and justice. Unfortunately, Hussain also failed to pledge allegiance to Yazid, Islam's sixth caliph and the second of the Umayyad Era. So again, we have a situation where an important figure chooses not to go along with the brutal policies of the leaders. How would they deal with him? Hussain's refusal to pledge allegiance was seen as a threat to the Umayyad Dynasty. Thus, even the very descendants of Muhammed himself, who refused to pledge allegiance, had only one of two options: to submit or to die. Imam Hussain was, however, a man of justice. He refused to yield an inch and stated clearly: "I will never give Yazid my hand, like a man who has been humiliated, nor will I flee like a slave… I only desire to enjoin good values and to prevent evil."[26] He also said that death with honour is far better than life in humiliation.

And so, the day of the decision arrived in Karbala, Iraq, when thousands of Yazid's soldiers surrounded Hussain and his seventy-two men. During the dawn of that October morning in 680, the swords of jihad were being sharpened. Since Hussain, his family, and companions had not consumed water for many days in the extreme heat, he walked outside with

24 Tahwidi, *The Tragedy of Islam*, 178-179

25 Narrated in chapter six of Tawhidi's work, "The Great Crime: The Killing of Hussain," 189-205.

26 Ibid., 191.

his six-month-old son, holding the boy up towards Yazid's army, pleading for water. Suddenly an arrow struck the infant so that he died instantly. A former commander of Yazid's army was so heartbroken witnessing this tragedy that he was reluctant to fight. And so, since tension was building among Yazid's soldiers, it was decided to "do battle" at once.[27]

When the "battle" began, a Christian man named Wahab, who sacrificed himself to defend Hussain, became the first casualty. He was crucified like his Saviour six centuries earlier. By the afternoon, all of Hussain's companions had been murdered and beheaded. Only Hussain and his son Ali remained. Hussain suffered severe thirst but bravely stood his ground until his body was transformed into a bed of arrows. He was then beheaded, and his head was placed on a spear for everyone to gaze at.[28] Yazid's army took the head to Egypt to boast about their "victory." A Christian archbishop in Egypt rebuked them for their cruel lunacy, washed the head, and wept over Hussain, saying that Christians would never have treated a grandchild of Jesus likewise. The Holy Shrine of Hussain in Karbala is still today one of the most sacred places in the Muslim world. Here was a man who "opposed violence in the name of Islam, who stood for reform, freedom, and dignity, and for a better tomorrow," writes Imam Tawhidi.[29] Thus the Muslim cleric states, "Hussain inspires me until this day, never to shake the hand of any radical extremist, and to strive towards global peace."[30]

Let it be known this is how the earliest Muslim leaders often responded to the best among them, when they felt threatened by their refusal to support them. There was nothing in their religion to help them "overcome" their feelings of betrayal. Brutal force and eventual bloodshed were the only means at their disposal. These atrocious crimes were only covered with a layer of Arabian sand, waiting to be blown away as soon as some Salafist sheik arrived, looking into the *hadith* for new inspiration.

---

27 In early Islamic history, "massacre" was often called "battle," as "rape" was often called "marriage."

28 Ibid., 198-199.

29 Ibid., 204.

30 Ibid., 205.

But what about Mohammed himself? How did he overcome evil? Muslims claim that Mohammed is a greater example to follow than Jesus, and Islam presents itself as the ultimate alternative to Christianity. Let us then see how Mohammed overcame evil. We know how patiently Jesus endured until he finally openly rebuked the Pharisees; how he prayed for those who spat on him and drove spikes through his tender palms; and how he shed his blood for us all, who were his enemies. So, what did Mohammed do? I will restrict myself to two examples.

A group of Jews made an allegiance with the Meccans and others to attack Mohammed, who raided their caravans and forced all clans and tribes around Medina to accept Islam. Mohammed was a masterful military strategist. He sustained this attack in what is known as the "Battle of the Trench." In its aftermath, Mohammed turned his attention to the remaining Jewish folk in Medina, the Bani Qurayzah, who secretly allied themselves with their Jewish brothers who launched the attack.[31] What was Islam's prophet going to do with them now?

Muslim sources tell us that Mohammed rode out to their forts and called out: "You brothers of apes, has Allah disgraced you and brought his vengeance upon you?"[32] The Jews had no choice. They could convert or face Mohammed's judgment. Martin Lings writes: "They replied that death was preferable and that they would have nothing but the Torah."[33] Mohammed asked one of his lieutenants, Saed, to make the call. The latter replied: "Their soldiers should be beheaded, and their women and children should become slaves." Mohammed was pleased and said: "You have made a ruling that Allah or a king would approve of."[34]

Bear in mind that "soldiers" meant every male that had reached puberty. So, what happened to these last living Jewish men of Medina? Reports vary how many they were, somewhere between six and eight hundred. A long grave was dug on the square of Medina, before the poor Jewish men were

31 For a full account, see Martin Lings, *Muhammed, His Life Based on the Earliest Sources* (Rochester, VT: Inner Traditions, 2006), 222-241.

32 Harry Richardson, *The Story of Muhammed, Islam Unveiled* (2013), 48.

33 Lings, *Muhammed*, 238.

34 Quotation from Sahih al-Bukhari, as quoted in Richardson, *The Story of Mohammed*, 49.

led out to it, their hands tied behind their backs. Their wives and children were made to sit opposite them to behold their end. They were all put to the sword. Mohammed and his teenage wife, Aisha, sat and watched all day into the evening, until "[t]he last to die was beheaded by torchlight."[35]

The spoils were then divided up, with Mohammed taking his usual twenty percent. The women were taken to a nearby town to be sold as sex slaves. There was one exception, though, Mohammed took the prettiest one for his pleasure, after she witnessed the brutal slaying of her husband, uncles, and other male relatives. It is hard to imagine how the first marriage night must have felt for this poor Jewish beauty. This, then, is how Mohammed overcame the "evil" he found in his hometown, a Jewish tribe that did not want him to rule over them. It has to be said, though, that Mohammed later "received revelation" to allow Jews and Christians to live if they were willing to pay the poll tax, and accept their inferior status as *dhimmis* for the rest of their lives.

If that is what happened to an insubordinate tribe, how about an insubordinate individual? Here is one story from the *hadith*. In Arabia poets were highly esteemed. In such a desert land long nights were often spent by the open fire. Few things were as highly prized as a new poem that could make everybody think or laugh. And so, a promising young poetess dared to write a poem against Islam's prophet due to all the brutality she had witnessed. Her tribe was not prepared to resist the new religion, so all she could do to vent her frustration was to compose a poem. We only know her as Marwan's daughter.

Mohammed soon got wind of the poem. He knew the woman posed no threat to him; her tribe said they would not attack the Muslims. On one sad evening, Allah's messenger said: "Who will rid me of Marwan's daughter?" One of his followers, a blind man, heard him say that and rose to kill her. He fulfilled Mohammed's wish in the dark, when the poetess was fast asleep with her infant on her breast and her other children around her in her house.

The following day, when the blind man asked Mohammed about the consequences of his deed, Islam's prophet answered: "Two goats won't butt

35 Lings, *Muhammed*, 240.

their heads together over this." Mohammed then turned to everyone in the mosque and said: "If you wish to see a man who assisted Allah and his prophet, look here," pointing to Omar. Apparently, Islam became powerful that day because many saw the power of Allah in the killing of the poetess.[36] Surah 4:84 says: "So fight for the cause of God.... God may fend off the power (violence) of those who deny the truth, for He is stronger in might and stronger in inflicting punishment."

Consider what would happen to our world if we all followed this example in the slightest way, when confronted with criticism or insubordination. I am no advocate for all Mahatma Gandhi's ideas, but how can I forget what I once read in his autobiography, that when some white youths hurled stones at him upon his arrival in Durban's harbour, he refused to report them to the police. "They did it out of ignorance," said Gandhi, "one day, they would know better!"[37]

Do not be overcome by evil, but overcome evil with good. *This* is the story of the Bible, the message of the gospel, and the mission of Christ. *This* is also why no other movement, religion, or ideology has shaped the world as Christianity did over the last two thousand years. Islam's dilemma is that it is incapable of adequately *defining* evil, and whatever problem you cannot define, you cannot solve. Islam cannot define evil because it has no good concept of man as the *Imago Dei* or of the fall in paradise. Furthermore, it was designed to oppose Jesus as the Son of God and the redeemer of a sinful humanity, from its inception. This makes it obvious why it struggles so much against evil. In Islam, sin is defined religiously, not ethically. It's the unbelievers who are evil. The Quran forbids you from making friends with them or helping them.[38] The gospel teaches the opposite. In the Bible, those who deliberately violate the royal command—which calls us to love God with all our heart and our neighbour as ourselves—commit evil. For love does the neighbour no harm.

---

36 Richardson, *The Story of Mohammed*, 71-73.

37 Gandhi, *An Autobiography*, 195. My paraphrase of his words.

38 See Surah 5:51-57.

But how shall we then overcome evil? The last Czar of imperial Russia, Nicholas II, shows us the way. Nicholas was not a very strong leader, but a devout Christian and family man. The Bolshevik Revolution of 1917, which forced his abdication, was raging fiercely, causing him and his family to be placed under house arrest in Ekaterinburg. On the night of 17 and 18 July, 1918, Nicholas and his family faced the full brunt of Bolshevist brutality, as the White Army was approaching from the east, and the Red Army went into panic mode. Sometime that night, Nicholas, his wife Alexa, their children, and servants were all woken up before being escorted down the stairs to the basement, supposedly for their safety.

Nicholas carried Alexei in his arms, followed by his wife and their four daughters, Olga, Tatiana, Maria, and Anastasia. Then came their physician and the four servants. They were given chairs and asked to sit, supposedly for a family picture. At that moment, a Bolshevik officer, Yakov Yurovski, stepped forward and announced that they were sentenced to death by the Presidium of the Ural Soviet. After a couple of dozen gunshots, they were all dead. Earlier, in the spring of that year, the oldest daughter Olga, 25, had written in her diary,[39]

> "My father asked those who remained loyal to him,
> that they should not avenge him,
> as he has forgiven them all,
> and prayed for them all.
> He asked them to remember that the evil which is now in the world
> will only become stronger.
> But evil will not triumph over evil; only love will."

His words proved true. The Soviets tried their level best to eradicate Christianity, only to see it rise out of the ashes all over Russia when Communism finally collapsed under the weight of its insidious lies. Let all Fascists, Marxists, Islamists, and other bloodthirsty anarchists of the world take note: Evil shall not triumph over evil. Only love will.

---

39 "The Romanovs: The Real History of the Russian Dynasty, Episode 8", by *StarMedia, YouTube.*

CHAPTER 15

ONLY LOVE WILL CONQUER EVIL

The words of Czar Nicholas II, jotted down by his daughter Olga in her journal in 1918, should never leave us: "Evil shall never conquer evil. Only love will."[1] But what does *that* kind of love look like that will conquer all evil? The apostle of love told us long ago, "By this we know love, that he laid down his life for us, and we ought to lay down our lives for the brothers" (I John 3:16 ESV). That love is not any love, but God's righteous love, only fully known in the Son of his love, who then wants to display his love to the world, by the power of the Holy Spirit, though his people. This Son of God's love spoke words so revolutionary that they stun us two millennia later when he said in Matt. 5:43-48:

> "You have heard that it was said, 'Love your neighbour and hate your enemy.' But I tell you, love your enemies and pray for those who persecute you, that you may be children of your Father in heaven. He causes his sun to rise on the evil and the good, and sends rain on the righteous and the unrighteous. If you love those who love you, what reward will you get?

1 See end of previous chapter.

> Are not even the tax collectors doing that? And if you greet only your own people, what are you doing more than others? Do not even pagans do that? Be perfect, therefore, as your heavenly Father is perfect?"

Jesus' point was: What credit is it to us if we love those who love us? He was going against the conventional Jewish wisdom of his day, which said, "love your neighbour and hate your enemy." Jesus was not speaking of personal enemies—someone down the street or in the next town—but of national enemies, political enemies, religious enemies, distant enemies. How do we know that? The conventional wisdom of Jesus' day *would not have allowed* you to hate your fellow Jew, which amounts to a direct violation of the Torah (see Lev. 19). But, to hate your "distant" enemy would not only have been considered a necessity but a virtue, at least according to the Greek philosopher Aristotle.[2] Likewise, a God-fearing Jew would have been ashamed to reveal their hatred for someone in their community, but none would have frowned about hatred for the Romans occupying the land; or for the despicable tax collectors who collaborated with the enemy and defrauded their Jewish brothers. That was just "normal."

What was Jesus then calling for? Was he even realistic? Or did he impose an impossible standard that we may ignore? In their book *Kingdom Ethics, Following Jesus in Contemporary Context*, Glen Stassen and David Gushee show that Jesus' words were never meant to be an impossible ideal. Instead, it served as a revolutionary *transformative initiative* (as in the rest of the Sermon on the Mount). In other words, God's Kingdom comes where his disciples obey his words. By following him and obeying his words, they will experience a strange new power at work in themselves and even in those around them. It will break the vicious cycle of in-group preference, blind retaliation, prejudice and racism, and of all-consuming hateful ideologies, all of which are plunging our world into ever deeper chaos.

These mighty transformational initiatives are found right through the *Sermon on the Mount* as the only way to break out of the vicious cycles of evil. They only become possible once we realize how much God loved

2 Glen Stassen and David Gusshee, *Kingdom Ethics* (Downers Grove, IL: IVP Academic, 2003), 51-52.

us—hell-bound sinners— in the Son of his love. They are not to be argued about but to be obeyed! That is what discipleship means. That is how God's kingdom breaks into this world and how his disciples will begin to look more and more like their heavenly Father, whose rain and sunlight fall on Jews and Romans or on Christians and Muslims alike.

Is it any wonder that these few words of Jesus have converted more Muslims than any other in the Bible? They illustrate the pre-eminence of the gospel and the unicity of Jesus of Nazareth in all of history; why the penniless carpenter from Nazareth, and not the caravan raider from Arabia, towers above all of history as the only One who offers real hope to this world.

But let our dear Muslim friends remember that these words (nowhere to be found in the Quran) were spoken by the very Son of God whom Abd al Malik's Arab marauders loathed so much when they invaded Jerusalem towards the end of the seventh century. It is this "Son of God" that al-Malik deliberately mocked in the magnificent Arabic mosaics crafted in the inner ambulatory of the Dome of the Rock in Jerusalem.[3]

The Dome of the Rock, along with the adjoining Aqsā Mosque, "constituted the first great religious building complex in the history of Islam."[4] The site was deliberately chosen. Jerusalem was never mentioned in the Quran, but it would be right there on the Temple Mount, so precious to both Jews and Christians, where the Arabs would challenge Christianity: on that rock which (according to tradition) Abraham bound his son to be sacrificed, and on which the ark of the covenant later came to rest. Abd al Malik's statement was clear: his new religion was going to outshine and replace whatever went before, for he needed religion to justify his new

3 The fact that some of these inscriptions are not identical to the words of the Quran indicates to scholars today that they predate the final composition of the Quran since the Quran may only be quoted accurately. Tourists can still read today "Praise be to God, who begets no son, and has no partner." Or "People of the book! Commit no excess in your religion: and say nothing of God but the truth. Jesus Christ, the Son of Mary, was indeed an apostle of God… Therefore, believe in God and in his apostles, and do not say 'Three'. Desist, and it will be better for you, for indeed God is one God, exalted above having a son…"

4 Bernard Lewis, *The Middle East*, 68.

emerging empire.[5] And he chose the most sacred spot on the earth to make his point. Abd al Malik was basically saying: "The Son of God does not rule the earth; my new empire does." At the time, this strange new religion was not represented by men known as Muslims but as Hagarenes, Ishmaelites or Saracens.[6]

The consequences of the denial of God's Son would be dire. The austere deity of Islam violently opposed any idea of the incarnation and failed to compel love from mortal hearts. If not for endless threats of hellfire and the sword, very few *voluntarily* bowed before him. Even today, devotion to Allah is driven home through memorizing the Quran, accompanied by many threats. It fails to generate love but only fear, suspicion, envy, and even hatred.

The cross, however, tells us of the love of God's only Son, given over for our transgressions when we were still God's enemies (Rom. 5:6-8). It was God's design that this love would compel us through the everlasting gospel of his grace and by the power of the Holy Spirit, to love our brothers and sisters and even those who might still be enemies. That happens when we embody and exemplify (albeit still imperfectly) God's love for all in our flesh-and-blood existence, as we seek to imitate the example of the Good Samaritan in Jesus' famous parable.

Let us then look at that righteous love, which alone will conquer all evil. We do so by first looking at the flesh-and-blood context in which God wants to exhibit his love today: the church. Then we will look at the gospel that gives birth to the church. Thirdly we look at the obvious theological implication of the gospel: that God is eternally triune. Lastly, we look at the inspired written foundation for everything Christians believe, the New Testament. God's unconquerable righteous love (1) manifested through his people, comes to us (2) through his gospel, which is predicated on (3) the amazing wonder of the Trinity, which on its part is proclaimed by (4)

5 Ibid., 69.

6 That was according to St. John of Damascus, born in 675, see Spencer, *The Critical Quran*. 11.

God's inspired, infallible Word. Christianity will never thrive, let alone survive, without us cherishing these four mighty "ideas".

The Love of Christ in His People

What will happen when our friends and fellow sinners from a Muslim background enter the irresistible orbit of Christ's redeeming love embodied in his church, regardless of how scarred or radicalized they may be? This seldom happened over fourteen centuries, either because the church was forbidden in Muslim lands for so long or because many churches did not live up to their holy calling. So, what will it look like when Muslims come in contact with *the body of Christ* today?

Thankfully we do not have to speculate. A Ph.D. candidate at the Free University of Amsterdam, Scott Gustafson, provides us with a rather astonishing answer. In an article entitled "Moving Toward the Enemy: A Case for Missiological Engagement in Counter/Deradicalization,"[7] Gustafson writes:

> The great migratory people movements of the last few years, especially in the Middle East, have brought the church into more intimate contact with historic enemies and the results are arguably unprecedented. Unexpected stories of worldview change among former extremists and exponential church growth in the Levant are widespread.

His paper looks at what has been happening in Lebanon over the last few years after the Syrian War. The result of this study is nothing short of phenomenal.

What did Gustafson see in Beqaa Valley of Lebanon and beyond? The author focused on deradicalization in his research, particularly among Muslims. He mentions that scholarship has accurately defined the path *toward* radicalization. In most cases, several factors contribute to the radicalization of an individual. But, the *way back* from radicalization poses a

7 Scott Gustafson, "Moving Toward the Enemy: A Case for Missiological Engagement in Counter/Deradicalization" in *Journal for Deradicalization*, Winter 2020/21, Nr. 25, ISSN 2363-9849.

much tougher problem. A solution for radicalization has been hard to find. Sociological studies mostly focus on reducing terrorist behaviour. Though several scholarly proposals for deradicalization have been suggested, positive results have been very few. The whole academic topic of deradicalization still needs to be clarified.

What is extremism? Gustafson answers: "I define extremism… as a worldview that seeks superiority and fulfillment by advocating for the discrimination, persecution or destruction of others who hold different views." Religious conversion is usually viewed only negatively in this whole field of study, namely as a pathway *towards* radicalization, for instance, when inmates convert to radical Islam in state prisons. Little wonder "religion" is rarely viewed as a valid *exit* from extremism. But that, says Gustafson, is exactly what is happening in the Beqaa Valley, to the embarrassment of secular scholars who have little time for Christianity's role in solving the problem of radicalization. His study comprised numerous background conversations, visits, and interviews with Christian clergy and former Muslims from Lebanon, Iraq, Egypt, Jordan, and Syria.

Gustafson says that whereas religion is often reduced to a personal spiritual endeavour in secular circles, those who advocate for an "embodied Christology" suggest that the life and teachings of Jesus ought to function as a concrete (and surprising) alternative to what we can expect in this world. Beautiful things can happen when Christians seek to participate in God's "space-time-matter mission of justice, beauty, and evangelism" writes Gustafson. Such a mission is not simply rooted in a desire for numerical growth, or even conversion but in a willingness to live out an abundant hope and to witness genuine human flourishing. In the context of the Middle East, where Gustafson worked, he saw no church *intentionally* aiming to deradicalize anyone. It happened spontaneously. It was a demonstrable side-effect of church programs and missional activities seeking to proclaim and live out an "embodied Christology." And yet nearly every one of the many churches he worked with had stories to tell of former Al Nusra, Al Qaeda, Isis, or Hezbollah fighters who converted. Research studies have identified three familiar drivers for radicalization: (1) a perceived grievance un-addressed through normal channels, (2) exposure to an extremist narrative or ideology, offering a compelling rationale for what must be done about the perceived grievance, and (3) a social network which creates a sense of belonging.

Amazingly enough, whereas deradicalization programs struggle to meet these three challenges, the church, in fulfilling her missionary calling of an "embodied Christology," addresses all three simultaneously, albeit unintentionally. The church addresses the *practical* needs in its ministry of mercy. It addresses the *ideological* narrative through the gospel message embedded in the Biblical story. And it addresses the *social need for belonging* through the experience of genuine fellowship among believers. While secular experts struggle to address these three areas in the lives of radicalized individuals, the church in the Middle East meets them organically. Let us then look at each of these areas and how the Holy Spirit meets the deepest needs of radicalized Muslims through the ministry of God's people.

The first concerns the whole area of grievances. Amazing things happen when deep hurt and felt needs are met in a practical, compassionate and comprehensive way by the church. Harsh government policies rarely move anyone away from radicalization, and no retaliatory violence has ever served as a permanent decoy from terrorism. Root causes must be addressed. The Christian emphasis on love for the enemy is unique in this regard. The simple ministry of love toward fighters who were marginalized and stigmatized has had enormous effects in the Beqaa Valley. A former Isis fighter from Syria, who moved his family to Lebanon, for example, renounced *jihad* after first experiencing deep disillusionment during the war in his in-group, but then also, the surprising love of Christ in a local fellowship. He is now a brother in the faith delivering aid to Christians whom he formerly considered "infidels".

One church consists of 85 percent former Muslims, many among them former extremists. A Sunni radical who fought with Al Qaeda in Iraq and Syria came to the church after escaping prison. He underwent a complete change and became a teacher in the church. The pastor of that church counted eleven former extremists in his church once fighting for terror organizations.

The second area overlap is that of worldview. The Christian message and community have a unique ability to challenge extreme worldviews.

Lebanon's refugee situation brought many extremists into closer contact with Christians for the first time. Individual deradicalization is often triggered by a traumatic incident in the person's life or in-group, which is then followed by a human intervention by the former "enemy" or "out-group." That leads the radicalized person to question their deep-seated beliefs. In Lebanon, these encounters are frequent, due to the Syrian crisis and the unexpected grace of Christian hospitality toward fleeing refugees. It completely disarms those who have never met a Christian before. Sometimes a radical saw their worldview change through the care of Christians, which may also be accompanied by supernatural phenomena. A female Sunni Kurd said: "We used to say, 'don't get near him, that's a Christian, never, don't get near'. But now really… the love we see in them we have never seen before, ever".[8]

Their stories of deradicalization are often filled with encounters of miraculous protection, healing, and visions. The miraculous has become so commonplace that no one seems surprised at it anymore. All of these factors have caused the churches in Lebanon and Syria to grow numerically and in rich diversity, with new believers coming from a wide variety of backgrounds and origins, another testimony to the truth and beauty of the gospel. The influential South African missiologist David Bosch (1929 – 1992) once remarked that a "talk-alike, think-alike, look-alike" congregation hardly reflects the alternative community Jesus called into being through his death and resurrection. The grace-ability of Christ's people to genuinely reach out across cultures proves to strangers that the body of Jesus represents a new supernatural reality. This greatly helps to lower hurdles. In other words, these folks have not known a God who hears prayer and who loves those who don't love him, and that knowledge radically challenged their existing worldview.

Reflecting on how the church loved her family, one interviewee said to Gustafson: "This is something that brought us closer to the Gospel and made us want to see Jesus." Formerly opposed to Jesus' divinity, they now embrace him as God with us and can't imagine missing his divine presence. Others tell how they came to believe when Christians prayed for

8 Ibid.

their children to get better when they were sick. It is a known fact that Christian prayer for Muslims often leads to positive results, which leaves a deep impression on them. The body of Christ is therefore seen to have a tremendously positive effect on broken people from various backgrounds in a way that contributes towards their personal and collective flourishing, as they embrace an entirely new grand narrative, the apostolic gospel.

The third area of overlap is the loss of community. The discovery of a new family and a new sense of belonging can have a huge effect on Muslims. The church of Jesus is the only community in the world that exists for those outside, said Bonhoeffer somewhere. Gustafson writes, "In breaking bread in the presence of another, hosts and guests alike silently confess a shared fragility, a mutual admission of need, humanity and weakness."[9] The profoundly egalitarian dimension of the shared table is especially poignant in Lebanon's sectarian context. Historically persecuted Christians and refugee Muslims in the Middle East are helping each other to restore dignity and honour to one another as beleaguered compatriots. This is truly amazing. One church studied by Gustafson grew from sixty Lebanese folks to a mix of fifteen-hundred Arab, Kurdish, Druze, and Iraqi attendees, one hundred-and-five of whom were former extremists. A Sunni extremist who came to church intending to kill the pastor and others, was converted and is serving actively in the congregation today. Many churches working among refugees have had similar experiences.

It is clear from these stories from the southern Levant that the Christian practice of integral mission and love toward all can have amazing results. The common elements in the anecdotal reports are worth repeating:

- a past experience of suffering, loss, violence, injustice and reduction of social status,
- an unexpected welcome and hospitality shown by pastors and members of the Christian community,
- the meeting of practical needs with food, household goods, winter supplies, and even education and counseling,

9 Ibid.

- the tangible experience of love, friendship, and a sense of belonging to a new family,
- a growing attraction to the teaching of the truth, the person of Christ, and God's supernatural power.

The church, as the living body of the risen Christ, is the first "idea" and reality that must be grasped and appreciated in this war of ideas. Gustafson's study shows what it means when the church is the "fragrance of life" towards those who are being saved; she becomes a letter written by God, not on clay tablets, but on human hearts (see II Cor. 2:14-3:3). Here we witness before our eyes the amazing "expulsive power of a new affection".[10] Christ's righteous love expels from our hearts the toxic mix of Satanic evil, our own sin, and life's hurt and shame. What these radicalized folks experienced in those Christian fellowships in Lebanon and Syria was long ago proclaimed in Christ's *Parable of the Good Samaritan*:[11]

- They experienced genuine compassion from an unexpected out-group.
- They experienced real, concrete loving acts of deliverance.
- They were welcomed into a new community of truth, justice, and freedom.
- They realized that the Good Samaritan was none other than Jesus whom they despised, and that all their new friends were just as desperately lost as they were.

That brings us to the second big idea, the gospel of God's Son.

10 See Chalmers's quote, chapter 1.

11 See Stassen and Gushee, *Kingdom Ethics*, 334-344.

CHAPTER 16

GOD'S LOVE IN THE GOSPEL OF HIS SON

In responding to the crisis around us in the world and in Islam, Christians should never doubt where the only answer ultimately lies: in the gospel. But what is the gospel? What do we mean when we say that we shall only come to know God's righteous love in the gospel, and that it is the gospel of his one and only Son? I will seek to answer this question carefully, perhaps not so briefly, from an African vantage point, where the faultline between Islam and Christianity is most critically felt. First, we must determine what the gospel is *not* and how it has been tailored to fit our cultures.

A "Westernized" Gospel: Its Origins, Message, and Impact

Not so long ago, a friend of mine told me over the phone: "I am so tired hearing from the pulpit that 'we are all forgiven.' Again and again, all I hear is that we are all God's children, forgiven for everything. Christ is rarely mentioned, God's righteousness is all but forgotten, the cross is seldom preached, nor is the call to repentance ever heard, yet we are all forgiven."[1] I can sympathize with him. This gospel of common clichés neither causes the world to pause nor the church to marvel. The problem in Africa is compounded by what is commonly known as the "prosperity gospel," where self-appointed "prophets" mesmerize their spellbound crowds with fake miracles and fantastic promises, in exchange for the little money they might still have in their pockets.[2] However, behind this "prosperity gospel" lies a "westernized gospel" that was preached and believed for too long.

So let us look for a moment at the westernized gospel that held sway over large parts of Christendom, also in Africa. In doing so, we turn to two seasoned missionaries to the African continent, Karl Grebe and Wilfred Fon.[3] In their concise but profound little work *African Traditional Religion and Christian Counseling*[4] Grebe and Fon make bold claims about the "weakness of the Western Gospel in the African context." The two authors argue that the problem of syncretism, so widespread in African Christianity, was caused in part by the kind of gospel presented to generations of Africans by many well-meaning missionaries from the West. This westernized gospel addressed a void in African Traditional Religion (ATR) while never really exposing its core problem.

The authors claim that this westernized gospel provided in the *felt need* of the African people for direct access to a distant God, and for assurance of a blessed future beyond the grave. However, it failed to address the heart of the matter: the predominant African worldview steeped in the superstitious fear of an unseen realm. Thus, the westernized gospel provided an opportunity for having one's sins forgiven and for "going to heaven," both ideas which were foreign to ATR. All that was supposedly needed was "faith in Jesus" and to "go to church." Concrete repentance was not really in the picture. Africans readily received such a message, as it complemented the traditional beliefs they already held to.

1 Telephone conversation with a friend in Cape Town, 2019.

2 See Michael Maura, Conrad Mbewe, et. al., *Prosperity? Seeking the True Gospel* (Nairobi: Africa Christian Textbooks, 2015).

3 They worked in Cameroon in Bible translation and theological education, respectively.

4 Karl Grebe & Wilfred Fon, *African Traditional Religion and Christian Counseling* (Oasis International Ltd, 2006).

The problem was that it resulted (as one could expect) in a *dual* allegiance. As far as daily life was concerned, especially concerning its many challenges and uncertainties, the African believer was still dependent on those in his community who had access to the unseen powers of the spiritual world, for good or ill. But, as far as his hope for "salvation" was concerned, they believed in Christ and therefore went to church. In summary: "They look to the Christian faith for final salvation, but look to pagan practices for present help."[5] This is a severe indictment of the African church by two seasoned Christian missionaries. And yet the root of the problem (according to Grebe and Fon) lay in the gospel that was so readily believed and proclaimed in the West itself.[6]

What did such a gospel sound like here among us? "Trust in Jesus as your Saviour, and he will forgive all your sins." American scholar Marsha Witten analyzed forty-seven sermons of Presbyterian Church (USA) and Southern Baptist pastors on the *Parable of the Prodigal Son* as part of her Ph.D. research project[7] at Princeton University. She concluded that the bulk of these sermons—though originating from a more liberal-leaning denomination on the one hand, and a more conservative one on the other—basically all did the same thing. They greatly diminished Protestantism's view of God, of sin and the fall, and of the Biblical scope of salvation, and it all happened under the pressures of secularization. The gospel both liberal and conservative preachers proclaim to their hearers, says Witten, comes down to telling them "All is forgiven," the title of her dissertation. It is not uncommon here in North America to spot a billboard beside the highway saying:

5 Ibid., 25.

6 I do not doubt that many missionaries did terrific work in Africa, bringing incredible sacrifices and proclaiming a fully-orbed Biblical gospel to the continent's people. One can only think of a pioneer missionary such as Moravian Hans Peter Hallbeck (1784 -1840), who labored at Genadendal in the old Cape Colony. Hallbeck's life and holistic approach still features as a benchmark of true mission. The same can be said of many other missionaries.

7 Marsha Witten, *All is Forgiven* (Princeton, NJ: Princeton University Press, 1993).

Free trip to heaven: details in the Bible!
Or
Heaven or hell? The choice is yours.

In a gospel tract for children, entitled *God knows my name,*[8] children are told how much God knows us and loves us, and then it concludes:

> God knows all about us and loves us… even when we do bad things. He calls these bad things sin. Everyone who sins must be punished, but God loves us so much that He did a wonderful thing. He sent his own Son Jesus, to be punished in our place! Now we can live with God forever in Heaven if we believe and accept God's gift of Jesus to us.

The tract then offers a short prayer that a child may pray to receive Jesus. This sort of thing doesn't surprise us anymore because we have become so used to it. But is this the gospel of the kingdom that Jesus and his apostles proclaimed? Is this the *grace of God that appeared to all men*, to use Paul's words in Titus 2:11-14? Did the apostles tell everyone: "Believe in Jesus so that you can go to heaven?" with no mention of repentance, or the cost of discipleship, or of forsaking a sinful world and the devil's works, or of living a life to God's glory and in service to mankind, or of a new creation coming?

Grebe and Fon say this is why Africa's Christianity is so shallow and powerless to break the shackles of ATR *and* to resist the false gospel of prosperity prophets, for that matter. What is more, it gave rise to what the authors call "a dual allegiance." And yet, if we are honest, we must admit that this "gospel" has not only resulted in a dual allegiance in Africa, it also did so in the West. For centuries it has been difficult to discern the average Christian from the world, first in lifestyle, but eventually also in faith and worldview, as so many surveys in the U.S. have shown. What follows are a few examples illustrating my point.

A missionary report that the legendary David Brainerd (1718 - 1747) wrote to the Missionary Society of Scotland in 1745, mentioned the

8 *God Knows My Name* (Good News Tracts, Crossway).

primary reason why the North American Indian people resisted the gospel as being: *the lives* of the European Christians. The Indians told Brainerd that "the white people lie, defraud, steal and drink worse than the Indians" and pushed them off "their lands by the sea."[9]

A similar scenario repeated itself in Africa. In 1877 chief Khama (1837 -1923) of the Batswana, living in what is today Botswana, had to tell a bunch of Boers (Dutch-speaking farmers) the following:

> We have no confidence in you & you have neither love nor pity for us. We are Kaffirs which means we are dogs and monkeys to be shot or otherwise ill-treated as you find it convenient. These are not mere idle words, but they are the words of the sorrow of every day. No opportunity is ever lost to make us know & feel how much you despise us because God has chosen to make us black and you white... You call yourselves Christians & I also am a Christian, a member of a Christian church. I do all that lies in my power to lead my people to give up the old & sinful customs, to become wise to serve the living God & his Son Jesus Christ, who I believe died for white & black, who does not see any man to be white or black because He looks only at the heart, who loves & would save us all. [10]

These Boers showed little respect for Khama or the Batswana's land as they trekked north to Angola to get away from British influence and their fellow "liberal" Afrikaners. And yet most, if not all of them, would have subscribed to the *Three Forms of Unity*[11] and have taken communion.

Equally sad are the contents of a letter of the Hottentot chief Hendrik Witbooi (c. 1830 - 1905), written to his counterpart of the Herero people in 1890, about the way the "Christian" Germans sought to take his land in the most underhanded fashion. He rebuked the Herero chief for collaborating with the Germans, comparing such cooperation to that of "Herod and

9 John Thornbury, "David Brainerd, Missionary to the Red Indians of North America" in *Five Pioneer Missionaries* (London: Banner of Truth Trust, 1965), 71-72.

10 Nicol Stassen, *Die Dorsland Trek: 1874 - 1881* (Pretoria: Protea Boekhuis, 2015), 220.

11 The *Three Forms of Unity* are the confessional standards of the Dutch Reformed Churches since the early Seventeenth Century.

Pilate of old, who put their differences aside to get rid of the Lord Jesus."[12] The Germans killed Witbooi at Hornkranz on October 29, 1905. Witbooi's worn-out Bible and other personal artifacts were recently returned to Namibia by the German government after more than a century.

Pitirim Sorokin (1889 – 1968) fled the brutal Bolshevist Revolution in Russia in 1922 to later become a professor of sociology at Harvard University, where he founded the *Harvard Research Center in Creative Altruism*. Having witnessed the extreme barbarity of the Bolshevists with his own eyes, Sorokin sought to devote his life to the motivation of selfless virtue. One of the Harvard Center's research projects was conducted among seventy-three converts in the city of Boston, folks who were "brought to Jesus…" in Sorokin's own words. The project showed that only *one* of these converts "changed his overt behaviour in an altruistic direction after his conversion."[13] The grace of God seemingly brought about very little inter-human grace.

Let us not forget it was this sort of Christianity that gave rise to the open mockery of men like Friedrich Nietzsche (1844 -1900) in Germany and Bertrand Russel (1872 -1970) in Britain or that sparked the sincere Christian protest of Søren Kierkegaard (1813 - 1855) in Denmark. It was a Christianity full of *bourgeois* civility but devoid of the radical ethic of the *Sermon on the Mount* and the exalted Christology of Paul's letters. Millions of professing Christians in the West lived with one foot in the church and another in the world, from cradle to grave, without much concern that any priest or pastor might call them out.

It all led to a deep dismay at the hypocrisy of a seemingly Christian civilization, as Peter Hitchens points out so aptly in his book *The Rage Against God*. He explains how Christmas, the high holy day in the Christian calendar of his native England, failed to deliver year after year. The advent season kept reminding him and his brother of the long train journey they took up north every year around that time, to a dreary cold

---

12 *Rapport over de Naturellen van Zuidwest-Afrika en hun Behandeling door Duitsland* (Cape Town: Cape Times Beperkt, 1918), 15.

13 Pitirim Sorokin, *A Long Journey* (New Haven, CT: College and University Press, 1963), 272.

landscape. It promised much but delivered little. They eventually burned their Bibles in an act of defiance.[14] The regular preaching from most pulpits in Christendom allowed this to continue for too long. At the same time, a minority who dared to sound a clarion call for radical conversion faced an arsenal of theological arguments from their fellow clergy, as to why the baptized masses of Christendom needed no conversion.

Again, it was not the "the grace of God that appeared to all men" of Titus 2 that was preached and believed. It was something else. It should be obvious to all that a westernized gospel poses no threat to Islam and leaves Christians woefully unprepared for the battle of ideas that is upon us. It will be swept away like a house of cards. But where did this other gospel come from? As far as Protestantism is concerned, it was the *unintended* consequence of the Reformation's message of the centrality of justification. No one reading the Genevan Reformer John Calvin would ever arrive at the minimalist gospel outlined above. Still, unfortunately, among the protestant clergy and laity, a notion emerged with time after the Reformation that the gospel is all about "having assurance that I am going to heaven." That assurance, then, is to be found in the doctrine of justification, we were told. And since justification was the message "by which the church stands or falls" (Martin Luther), it basically became everything. It requires a small step shifting one's focus from "my only comfort in life and death"[15] to "my happiness, health and wealth" as God's ultimate goal for my life—complete with reference to Jer. 29:13.

And so, slowly but surely, as we moved away from the rich theology of the Reformation, even conservative and well-meaning believers often came to believe that our individual comfort and flourishing is the crux of the Biblical message. It got even worse. Christianity here in North America took this emphasis further in the *contemporary grace movement*,[16] seeking to answer every single issue or question facing the life of the believer with

14 Peter Hitchens, *The Rage Against God* (Grand Rapids: Zondervan, 2010), 45.

15 See Question 1 of the *Heidelberg Catechism*: "What is your only comfort in life and death?" in *Three Forms of Unity* (Winnipeg: Premier Printing, 1999), 40.

16 See "The Gospel of Permissive Grace" in Erwin Lutzer, *The Church in Babylon* (Chicago: Moody Publishers, 2018), 192-198.

the doctrine of justification. It often equates obedience to Christ's lordship to legalism and typically considers a call to repentance as harsh and unloving. For the *contemporary grace movement,* one's adherence to the doctrine of justification puts every single concern in your Christian life to bed. It should be obvious to all that such a gospel poses *no* real threat to Islam.

The Gospel of God's Son

We will have to rediscover and embrace the real gospel, if we are going to win this war of ideas, and if Christians in Africa hope to be rooted and grounded in the truth. If not, they will only be "tossed back and forth by the waves, and blown here and there by every wind of teaching and by the cunning and craftiness of people" (Ephes. 4:14).

But what is the gospel then? To find an answer, one could go one of several ways. I have chosen to go to arguably the oldest gospel account, *The Gospel According to Mark.* It begins like this: "The beginning of the good news about Jesus the Messiah, the Son of God." A bit further, we read,

> After John was put in prison, Jesus went into Galilee proclaiming the good news of God. "The time has come," he said. "The kingdom of God has come near. Repent and believe the good news." (Mark 1:15)

Why does Jesus say the time has come? Many possible reasons could be given, the most apparent being that Jesus' cousin and predecessor was put in prison by Herod. John the Baptist bore a striking resemblance to the legendary Jewish prophet Elijah, whom Isaiah and Malachi prophesied would appear directly before the coming of the Messiah. The time was ready indeed.

The Gospel: Behold your God!

What then, would Jesus (and Mark) have understood by the good news or the gospel? What was this gospel of the kingdom all about? To figure that out, we have to go to that scroll in the *Tanach*[17] (the Hebrew scriptures) which Jesus probably cherished more than any other because its words

17 The Hebrew Scriptures consisting of the Torah, the Prophets and the Writings (i.e., the Old Testament).

were found so often on his lips. i.e., the scroll of Isaiah. No Hebrew prophet spoke more about the coming Messiah than Isaiah, calling him sometimes the *Ebed Yahweh* (the Servant of the Lord). In Isaiah 40, 52, and 61, we first come across the term "good news," (*basar*) so closely related to this *Ebed Yahweh.*

Isaiah 40 addressed the Jews in exile. The prophet spoke to a people who were not only far removed from their own land and God's house of prayer but who knew that they thoroughly deserved it. God had warned them for centuries what would happen if they continued flirting with other gods, but all to no avail. In 586 BC, *Yahweh* made good on all his many warnings and brought upon them the sword and famine. Those who did not perish in the brutal Babylonian invasion were carried off far away, leaving only the poorest behind in Judea.

That's why the opening words in Isaiah 40 sounded so incredible from their perspective. "Comfort, comfort my people, says your God. Speak tenderly to Jerusalem and proclaim to her that her hard service has been completed, that her sin has been paid for" (Is. 40:1-2). It is in Isaiah 40:9 that we first come across the Hebrew word for "good news".

> You who bring *good news* to Zion, go up on a high mountain. You, who bring *good tidings* to Jerusalem, lift up your voice with a shout, lift it up, do not be afraid; say to the towns of Judah, "Here is your God!"

So, what is it? What is this good news all about? "Say to them: *Behold, your God!"* or "Here is your God!" In other words, "He has not abandoned you. He has not forgotten you. He is coming to you. See, the sovereign Lord comes with power…"

As we read on, we see that he will be like a shepherd, tending his flock with care, gathering his lambs in his arms, and gently leading those who are young. The impenitent though will have to face his righteous wrath. Remember, the Messiah was going to be David's son. David was a shepherd, and a good shepherd was the common image in the ancient Near East of a just and good ruler (see Ezek. 34). By now, David was long gone, and his dynasty lay in ruins, with no signs of it ever recovering. And yet, these exiles in Babylon are told that God has not forgotten them and that he will come to them as the ultimate shepherd. "Behold your God!" they are told. That is excellent news. It is the best news ever to a people who deserved what they got and who thought God had abandoned them.

Let us not forget though, Israel in exile symbolizes and represents all of us, humankind, exiled from Eden long ago due to our rebellion against God. What excellent news for such miserable mortals to hear: "Here is your God! He has not abandoned you." And he is not only coming to you as the ultimate Good Shepherd but as the One who has measured the waters of the sea in the hollow of his hand; who made the very heavens and brings out their starry host every night; the One before whom the nations of the earth are but a drop in a bucket, like dust on the scales.

Reading on in Isaiah, we learn that not only Israel, but the furthest islands will hear about the *Ebed Yahweh* and yearn for his teaching (42:1-9). Why? Because he brings justice and peace to the nations. But then, in chapter 52:7, the prophet shouts again, saying:

> How beautiful on the mountains are the feet of those who bring *good news*, who proclaim peace, who bring *good tidings*, who proclaim salvation, who say to Zion: "Your God reigns!"

Again, we get the same idea. A fallen and deeply broken and suffering people hear from a holy God that he is no longer angry with them, and no more will he punish. But then a shocking thing is told as we read on: The *Ebed Yahweh* (Servant of the Lord) will be despised and rejected by men. He will be one from whom we turn our faces away in disgust, for the Lord will lay on him the iniquity of us all. Though no iniquity was found in his mouth, he will be cut off from the land of the living and have his grave among the wicked. And yet, amazingly, the song goes on to say "After he has suffered, he will see the light of life, and be satisfied" (53:11). We are told that he will even "justify many" and receive "a portion among the great… for he bore the sins of many and made intercession for the transgressors" (53:11-12).

But then, a little later in chapter 61:1, the servant himself speaks:

> The Spirit of the Sovereign Lord is on me, because the Lord has anointed me to proclaim *good news* to the poor, he has sent me to bind up the

> broken-hearted, to proclaim freedom for the captives, and release from darkness for the prisoners.

He says that God called him to proclaim good news to the poor. In St. Luke's Gospel we read how Jesus—full of the Holy Spirit—read and preached from this passage in his hometown synagogue (Luke 4:16-19). Everyone was stunned when he said: "Today these words are fulfilled in your hearing."

So, what is the gospel then? If we look around at the wasteland this miserable world has become; how deeply we all have fallen into sin—due to our flirtation with the evil one—and how far we have been cast into exile from the glorious presence of God; how much we deserve his wrath, and how little hope we have of ever finding our way back to him, then there could scarcely be better news than this: "Here I am. I have not abandoned you." To hear that God has come to us—even though like sheep, we have all gone astray—and that he has taken upon himself the punishment due for us, is simply phenomenal. To see how Jesus in his life and ministry exemplifies the ultimate Good Shepherd, as he is even willing to lay down his life for his sheep (John 10), is the best news ever. Not only has God not abandoned us (as he should have), but he laid our iniquity on the Servant, by whose wounds we were healed. Could there be any better news for this lost world? And does it get any better than when we learn that the crucified carpenter rose victoriously from the dead—as he predicted three times—and is now seated at his God's right hand in glory?

The Gospel: Behold the Man!

Mark tells us that Jesus went into Galilee, preaching the gospel of the kingdom. It happened right after his baptism when he was anointed by his Father (Is. 61:1), when the Holy Spirit came down upon him like a dove, and when a heavenly voice spoke: "You are my Son, whom I love, with you I am well pleased" (Mark 1:11). That Jesus was indeed a son like no other, was proven when he sustained forty days of testing in a barren wasteland on an empty stomach, tempted by Satan. It called forth memories of Adam's fall in the lush Garden of Eden at the dawn of time.

But we must take a step back: Jesus' baptism was his public anointing, just like the ruddy shepherd boy David was once anointed by Samuel long ago in Bethlehem, as the one of God's own choosing. However, when Samuel poured the olive oil out on David's head, Jesse's son was still facing an uphill battle to the throne in Jerusalem. And when God poured out his Spirit on Jesus, Mary's son faced an even greater battle to be crowned king of his people and all the earth.

Saul was still in power, even though David was God's designated king. Saul pursued David with his spear so that David only just escaped several times. Sometimes it looked as if David would never reach the throne, even though he was equipped and designated by God for it. That is the exact pattern that Jesus' life would follow too.[18] God was reminding his Son during his forty days in the Judean wilderness that Satan was still in power, and that the kingdoms of this world belonged to *him*. Jesus' mission would not be easy. After his temptation, we are told that angels came to serve Jesus and that the devil left him alone *until an opportune time*. Satan was not done with him yet.

So how did Jesus eventually take the throne? How would he take Jerusalem back? First of all, he had to show Israel that he was indeed that good shepherd by preaching the gospel to the poor, opening the eyes of the blind, healing the sick and broken-hearted, and by setting the captives free. In all of that, they saw and felt how God's heavenly kingdom broke into their miserable world with power. *Never* had anything like that happened before, and *never* since. And yet all the while, Jesus had his face "set like a flint" on Jerusalem. No one could distract him, not even Simon Peter, for Jesus knew he had to go to the holy city to bring about regime change.

He also knew that to take that city and earn for us a new Jerusalem, he had to give up his own life. It would take a bitter street fight into the very heart of the city to dethrone Satan. And so, Jesus arrived humble on a donkey, armed with Yahweh's infallible promises, surrounded with the praises of children, going straight into the enemy's den, to announce his plan by cleansing the temple, the most daring raid ever.

It was Passover when Jesus and his friends were in Gethsemane and Satan launched his final assault. It almost looked from Satan's perspective as if he was going to win the day, for he had mustered all the dark forces

18 Matthew Bates, *Salvation by Allegiance Alone* (Grand Rapids: Baker, 2017), 47-50.

in the universe against Jesus. One of Jesus' own friends came and betrayed him with a kiss before he was led away like a common criminal through the Kidron Valley back into the city. While interrogated by the High Priest, the Galilean rabbi was rudely disowned by one of his best friends, warming himself by a fire while most of the others had already fled. It was now hand-to-hand combat in the spiritual realm, with the casualties rising all the time. Only one man was left standing, and a few loyal women from Galilee. It was the hour of the power of the prince of darkness.

Jesus was falsely accused, and every single principle of justice was perverted to get him sent to a Roman Cross, the cruelest and most shameful execution ever invented.[19] The fighting was fierce. He was spat upon, beaten with rods, and then draped in a fake royal garment with a crown of thorns pressed into his skull. Then he was sent to the Roman governor's residence in Jerusalem, who longed to see him.

Pilate was in panic mode, for he knew this man was innocent, but he was afraid of the crowd outside. And so, as Pilate asked Jesus a few questions, he was stunned by the Nazarene's answers in the midst of silence. When he brought Jesus out to the balcony, the riff-raff below went utterly crazy. What Pilate then said proclaimed the gospel in an unspeakable way. Pointing to Jesus, he said:

> "Behold, the Man!" or "Here is the Man!"
>
> — John 19:5

Let us pause and marvel: "Behold your God!" has become "Behold the Man!" and that is the gospel. The gospel is our Creator coming to us in his Son. It is him, taking on himself our broken humanity, with its guilt and shame. It is him taking on our brutal invincible dark adversary. It is him paying the unpayable ransom for our release. It is him bursting for us the bonds of death. Behold your God. Behold the Man.

The gospel is not merely about you or me. Nor is it merely about going to heaven. It's about nothing less than reconciling the entire cosmos to God through the blood of the cross, and giving back to us the very meaning of

19 See *Crucifixion* by Martin Hengel (Philadelphia: Fortress Press, 1977).

our lives here on earth, which we have lost in paradise (see Col. 1:21-29). Athanasius told us so beautifully in his little treatise *On the Incarnation* that it is about giving back to us the divine life we have thrown away in the garden, by listening to our adversary's insidious lies.[20] Now, at last, the cosmos can be rescued from Satan's grip and from the curse of sin to be brought into the unity and harmony of a new creation, for Satan, death and sin have been defeated forever.

And so, as Jesus is sent out to Golgotha, "the place of the skull", the mocking is fierce and relentless. The hostility against him knows no bounds. Satan fights with every weapon at his disposal, and Jesus fights, but only with "weapons of righteousness" (II Cor. 6:7). He is now all alone in this brutal fight for Jerusalem, for Judea, for the ends of the earth, and for our very bodies and souls. Even as they drive the nails through his hands, and as he is hoisted up in the air, and hangs there, he is fighting against evil. He prays for his enemies and comforts the poor convict hanging beside him. He tells John to take care of his widowed mother Mary, who is now also bereaved of her son. When he cries out with a loud voice, "My God, my God, why have you forsaken me" the enemy thinks he has conquered, but Satan is mistaken, for soon after, Jesus said: "It is finished… Father into your hands I commit my spirit." His mission was completed. As Jesus breathes his last, and drops his head on his chest—the last man standing in this cosmic street fight of good against evil—blackness covers the earth.

All you hear is the wind howling, earthquakes rumbling, dogs barking and women weeping. Many walk home beating their breasts, saying: "What have we done?" Others hiss and curse. But then a lone Roman centurion—his horse circling before the man on the cross—says it out loud: "Truly this was a righteous man!" God's righteous love has triumphed over all evil. Satan could not even once provoke Jesus to react in kind.

At this moment, a never-ending revolution began.[21] A revolution of the living God using the weak things of this world to confound the strong; of the Almighty using the so-called fools of this world to confound the wise

20 Athanasius, *On the Incarnation*, Published by Parables, 2019.

21 See NT Wright, *The Day the Revolution Began* (New York: HarperOne, 2016), and Tom Holland, *Dominion*, chapter 20.

(see I Cor. 1). It would begin with one-hundred-and-twenty fearful men and women gathering somewhere in hostile Jerusalem for prayer, as their master told them to do. The greatest's revolution the world has ever seen would begin when the Holy Spirit fell on them all. The very Spirit that was poured out on Jesus at the River Jordan was now freely flowing onto his body, the church.

On that first morning after the sabbath, they were shocked when the womenfolk arrived at Jesus' tomb. The tomb was open; his body was gone. No, it wasn't stolen. Neither was it ever found. Rather, he was *seen*, as he appeared to many after his resurrection and before he ascended to his Father. The angel said to the women: "Why do you look for the living among the dead?" (Luke 24:5). Now it made sense why Jesus once said: "I saw Satan fall like lightning from heaven" (Luke 10:18), for in just a little while Jesus will be seated at the right hand of the Ancient of Days, as Daniel prophesied (Dan. 7:13-14). From there he would soon come to judge the living and the dead.

The Gospel and Our Response

The gospel is captured in those two phrases, one from Isaiah, another from Pilate: "Behold your God! Behold the Man!" And now we may also add "Your God reigns!" (Is. 52:7). It is the gospel of God's Son; the gospel of the humble shepherd of God's people who was crowned as king of the universe, and who will finally bring his Father's Kingdom down to earth. When Simon Peter entered a Gentile home for the first time in his life to bring those folks in Caesarea the gospel, he told them the good news about Jesus of Nazareth, and all that had happened in the land of the Jews, before he added (Acts 10:39-43):

> We are witnesses to everything he did in the country of the Jews and Jerusalem. They killed him by hanging him on a cross, but God raised him from the dead on the third day and caused him to be seen. He was not seen by all the people but by witnesses whom God had already chosen—by us who ate and drank with him after he rose from the dead. He commanded us to preach to the people and to testify that he is the one whom God has appointed as judge of the living and the dead. All the prophets testify that everyone who believes in him receives forgiveness of sins through his name.

Peter said: "He commanded us to preach to the people and to testify that he is the one whom God has appointed as judge of the living and the dead." This is truly incredible. I may even now be reconciled with the One who is about to appear as judge of the world, so that I won't have to face him as judge, but as my redeemer and friend. But how does the judge become my friend? By settling with him. By accepting his guilty-verdict on my life. By casting down my weapons of rebellion. By forsaking my sin and flirtation with the devil. By kissing the Son's feet. That is why he said: "The Kingdom of God has come near. Repent and believe the gospel." God came seeking Adam and Eve in the garden, and so he comes looking for you and me in the gospel, wherever we may be hiding.

To *repent* means to "enter through the narrow gate," as Jesus once put it—to leave everything behind that cannot and may not come along through that gate in following Jesus. Every attitude or deed, every thought or idea not worthy of him, every sin and idol, must be left behind and confessed with sorrow to God *and* in sorrow to our fellow human beings (where necessary). It is like going through the scanner at the airport. The only difference is we can't take anything back once we are through.

Faith is the flip side of repentance. No one can repent without the grace of faith. *Faith* means believing everything about Jesus we are told in the gospel *and* embracing him as he is freely offered to condemned sinners for salvation, resting on his work and righteousness alone and on nothing of ourselves. It means swearing lifelong allegiance to him alone, even unto death.[22] When we repent and believe like this, we receive complete forgiveness for all our sins, the gift of the Holy Spirit, and eternal life. While Peter was still speaking, the Holy Spirit fell on those in Caesarea listening to him, for they believed.

22 See Bates, *Salvation by Allegiance*, chapter 2. Bates summarizes the gospel as follows in light of I Cor. 15: Jesus the king (1) pre-existed with the Father, (2) took on human flesh, fulfilling God's promises to David, (3) died for sins in accordance with the Scriptures, (4) was buried, (5) was raised on the third day in accordance with the Scriptures, (6) appeared to many, (7) is seated at the right hand of God as Lord, and (8) will come again as judge.

After his resurrection, Jesus summarized the gospel as follows in Luke 24:46-49 (NKJ):

> "Thus it is written
> and thus it was necessary for the Christ to suffer
> and to rise from the dead on the third day,
> and that repentance
> and remission of sins
> should be preached in His name
> to all nations, beginning at Jerusalem.
> And you are witnesses of these things.
> Behold, I send the Promise of my Father upon you,
> but tarry in the city of Jerusalem until you are endued
> with power from on high."

It is in light of all this that Christians sing with tears of joy:[23]

> *Do you feel the world is broken? We do...*
> *Do you feel the shadows deepen? We do...*
> *But do you know that all the dark won't stop the light*
> *from getting through? We do...*
> *Do you wish that you could see it all made new? We do...*
> *Is all creation groaning? It is...*
> *Is a new creation coming? It is...*
> *Is the glory of the Lord to be the light within our midst? It is...*
> *Is it good that we remind ourselves of this? It is!*

The Gospel's Goal: Christ in Us and We in Him

When we believe and repent by God's free sovereign grace, we become Christians. Yet, the gospel's goal is not primarily to give us access to heaven one day, but to bring fallen sinners on earth back into full harmony with God and each other, and to restore to us our God-given calling on earth. That only happens when our eyes are opened, and we are brought over

23 Andrew Peterson and Ben Shive, "Is He Worthy?" published in *Awake to Praise Choir*, Concert Program (Smithville, On: Carruthers Printing, 2019) 16-17.

from the realm of darkness into the kingdom of God's Son through the forgiveness of our sins (Col. 1:13, Acts 26:18). From that very moment, Christ, who is the hope of glory, remains in us, and we in him. To be "in Christ" (the most common way Paul referred to Christian believers) means to have God's broken image restored in us, so as *to be* and *to become* that child, woman, or man that God intended us to be, by fulfilling our heavenly calling on earth as stewards of his good creation, to the Father's eternal praise. And then, as some old saint once said, "If we have lived well saved by his grace, our dying will take care of itself." Christ is *the hope of glory* in us.

To appreciate what it means to be "in Christ," let us listen to a protestant scholar who, in recent years, discovered the gospel anew. In the preface of his book entitled *One with Christ: An Evangelical Theology of Salvation,*[24] Marcus Peter Johnson admits how his reading of the reformer John Calvin opened his eyes (with shock) to the fact that *salvation* implies much more than what we were so readily made to believe.

> The fact that Calvin's theology exceeded my expectations was delightful and enriching, but that was not what was shocking. What was shocking to me was the way in which Calvin spoke of salvation. This was both familiar and foreign to me at the same time. I expected and found familiar concepts ... However, I was constantly disrupted by Calvin's consistent and ubiquitous refrain about being joined to Jesus Christ. At first, I simply absorbed this element of his theology into my pre-existent understanding, assuming that Calvin's language about union with Christ was simply another, perhaps sentimental, method of expressing that believers are saved by the work of Christ on the cross. But then I realized, in a way that was initially disconcerting, that when Calvin wrote of being united to Christ, he meant that believers are personally joined to the living, incarnate, crucified, resurrected Jesus... My shocking encounter with Calvin revealed to me the beauty, wonder, and mystery of salvation in Christ and along with it, the beauty, wonder, and mystery of the church.

24 Marcus Peter Johnson, *One with Christ* (Wheaton, IL: Crossway, 2013), Preface.

Let us ponder the far-reaching implications that such a view of salvation must have for Africa and us all.

First of all, if the risen and exalted Christ is indeed seated "above all principalities and powers in this world and the next" (Eph. 1 and Col. 1), and if it is true that we are now "seated above all principalities and powers" in him and with him, what does it mean for God's people in Africa? It must mean that we will respond differently to fear-mongering rumours ahead of a political election. It will also mean we will laugh at the latest aberrations spouted by some prosperity prophet in our city. It will mean that we will stand firm when bad things happen to us, refusing to succumb to the traditions of our ancestors, by seeking help from mediums and sorcerers. *And* it will mean we will receive the strength from above to overcome Islamic intimidation, since our lives are now "hidden with Christ in God," in whom we have already conquered all the forces of evil.

Secondly, African believers will no longer live in sin, for if one is joined to Christ, says Paul in I Cor.6, how can he also be joined to a prostitute? If our bodies are now temples of his Spirit, should we not cleanse ourselves from everything that defiles both body and spirit (II Cor. 6:14-7:1)? The Son of God came to set us free. We are now his possession. It is, therefore, unthinkable that one could be a Christian while living in slavery to anything; whether to alcohol, pornography, gaming, gambling, social media, television, food, tobacco, *khat*, narcotics, or whatever. Whoever is in Christ Jesus is a new creation. The old things have passed away; the new has come (II Cor. 5:21). At the very least, a true believer in Africa would engage in a gut-wrenching fight of faith and repentance to conquer sin and to walk with God. But even in that struggle, we are never alone, for Jesus came to "bind the strong man" and to "destroy the works of the devil" so as to be with us always in the Holy Spirit. That tells us how vital prayer is in the Christian life (Luke 11:1-13).

Thirdly, being "in Christ" must have huge implications for our emotional healing regarding forgiveness and reconciliation. The history of Rwanda and South Africa has taught us how precious and real the Christian truth of forgiveness is. In 1994 South Africa had its first democratic elections, and Rwanda its shocking genocide. After those elections, many whites and blacks who were formerly hostile to each other learned to trust and love each other, motivated by the gospel. In Rwanda, Hutus, and Tutsis who came to know Jesus received each other in grace, killing the bitter cravings for revenge.

How could anyone claiming to be in Christ still drink the poison of bitterness, by nursing the grudges of yesterday? That is why Islam has no answer to evil, for it has no cure for our deepest hurt and pain. Every sinner who has been freely forgiven in Jesus, however, is taught by grace to forgive his fellow sinner "from the heart" (Matt. 18:35), opening up a new tomorrow. But what if the guilty *other* refuses to repent and be truly sorry? Then we must pray passionately that God's blessing of conversion may be granted to them too, and do good to them in the meantime. Whatever the case, bitterness, and feelings of revenge are never an option for a Christian.

So, the gospel teaches us to affirm *LIFE*—in every sense of that word—as the gift of Him who *is* life (John 1:4) and who was made man for us and for our salvation. His life was freely given over on the cross for us miserable mortals, who were irrevocably stuck in death due to our sin. But, having been slaves of death and sin, we have now been brought over to the reign of God's beloved Son, through his glorious resurrection, to share in the life, light, and love of the triune God in the Spirit, with all his redeemed in love. Indeed, we have become partakers of *the divine nature*, the ante-Nicene fathers reminded us according to II Peter 1:4. The very life of God himself has been poured into our beings by the Holy Spirit, when we were born of him, and that life is eternally indestructible. That is the timeless message of St. Athanasius' little classic *On the Incarnation*, which every Christian should read through once a year. [25]

25 Athanasius, *On the Incarnation*, Published by Parables, 2019.

CHAPTER 17

NO GOSPEL WITHOUT THE TRIUNE GOD

The gospel implies the Trinity. It makes no sense without it. No one who denies the Trinity ever had a gospel to proclaim. We saw how the Bible tells us that at Jesus' baptism, the Father declared from heaven his love for his one and only Son, and how the Holy Spirit descended upon Jesus as a dove. The Father is not the Son. The Son is not the Holy Spirit. The Holy Spirit is not the Father. The Father is divine and eternal. The Son is divine and eternal. The Holy Spirit is divine and eternal. But there are not three eternal divinities, only One. Three distinct divine persons were involved in Jesus' baptism, yet it was the act of only one awesome God.

The Son of God and the Holy Spirit

As Moreland and Craig point out in their *Philosophical Foundations for a Christian Worldview*, there is no way around this: Jesus referred to himself as the Son of man—which is a divine-human eschatological figure in Daniel 7—*and* as the unique Son of God (compare Matt. 11:27; Mark 13:32, and Luke 20:9-19). They also show how most New Testament critics agree that Jesus' teachings and actions clearly point to an implicit Christology. Jesus did what no Jew would dare or dream of ever doing when he "revised" the divinely Mosaic law in the *Sermon on the Mount.* He even declared himself Lord of the Sabbath. He proclaimed what no one ever did or would, before or after him: that God's reign was breaking in on the earth *through him.* His teaching, miracles, and exorcisms were the unmistakable sign of that. Jesus also said that he was going to restore Israel and that he was going to judge humankind on the last day. He even claimed to have divine authority on earth to forgive sins.

Can anyone reading the gospel accounts avoid the feeling that Jesus consciously acted in God's place, with divine authority, grace, and power? That is why German scholar Horst Georg Pöhlmann could say that Jesus' authority presupposed a unity with God that goes far beyond our unity with God through faith. It implies "a unity of essence." Pöhlmann says this "claim to authority is explicable only from the side of his deity," an authority only God himself can claim. He continues: "With regard to Jesus there are only two possible modes of behavior; either to believe that in him God encounters us or to nail him to the cross as a blasphemer. *Tertium non datur.*"[1]

Muslims like to ask, "But where did Jesus unequivocally say: 'I am God"? It seems like a smart question until one realizes how anachronistic it is. Nothing is clearer in the gospel than that Jesus had a mission to fulfill, which he consciously did according to his Father's plan. He would not be derailed in any way, as Simon Peter found out the hard way. If one thing *would* have derailed his mission for sure—throwing it into utter confusion and chaos, causing him to be stoned in Galilee long before he could reach the cross—then it would have been him going around saying, "Did you know, I am God?"

Jesus once said that "wisdom is justified by her children" (Luke 7:35). In other words, anyone born of wisdom would know that such conduct would be plain stupid. Mature people don't act that way; they know that

---

1 As quoted by JP Moreland and William Lane Craig in *Philosophical Foundations for a Christian Worldview, 2nd Edition* (Downers Grove, IL: IVP Academic, 2017), 576. The Latin phrase means there is no third logical possibility.

the exceptionally gifted should make sure not to show off too much, or they will suffer the consequences. Only narcissists don't understand that.

The simple common-sense explanation for the so-called "messianic secret" (the "don't tell others"- passages in the synoptic gospels) is obvious: As early as in Mark 2—when news about Jesus spread like wildfire, and as large crowds were gathering from everywhere—Jesus' own family thought he was "out of his mind." The Jewish elites, in their envy, even alleged the prince of demons possessed him. This alone makes Jesus' reticence for a commotion and unnecessary controversy obvious. He would let his teaching, example, and works do the talking for three years, until the High Priest asked him point blank: "Are you the Messiah, the Son of the Blessed One?" (Mark 14:61). To this, Jesus answered affirmatively, and he was sentenced to death for it. And yet long before that, when Simon Peter confessed, "You are the Messiah, the Son of the living God" (Matt. 16:16), Jesus not only did *not* rebuke him; he commended Peter for saying it, while also warning his disciples not to say it out loud yet. Moreover, in St. John's Gospel we read that the Jews wanted to kill Jesus, not only because he was "breaking the Sabbath", but because "he was even calling God his own Father, making himself equal with God" (John 5:18).

The New Testament furthermore consistently refers to Jesus as "Lord" (*kyrios*), a term reserved for Yahweh. God's role as creator and sustainer of the universe is ascribed to Jesus in Col. 1:15-20, Heb. 1:1-4, and John 1:1-3. Sometimes the New Testament even literally refers to Jesus as God (*ho theos*), as can be seen in John 1:1,18; 20:28; Rom. 9:5; Titus 2:13; Heb. 1:8-12; I John 5:20. That Jesus Christ was truly man and truly God in one person, is the foundation of all Christian belief. It is written on every page of the New Testament. It is the wonder of the incarnation, and the only hope for a lost humanity, that each one of us—body, soul and spirit—were precious enough for God to "empty himself", and to come down, becoming obedient to death, even the death on a cross, so that we, so utterly lost in our sin, may share in the divine life and love of God.

But "truly God and truly man" is something that skeptics would brush aside as nonsense, since their brains can't fathom something so wonderful and profound. A Dutch physicist rightly pointed out that the same skeptics, when it comes to physics, can embrace a parallel and equally profound statement as absolutely true, namely that "an electron is at the same time a particle and a wave." It shook none other than Albert Einstein to his core when it was first discovered.[2]

The Holy Spirit is also identified as God in Acts 5:3-4 or as the Spirit of God in Matt. 12:28 and I Cor. 6:11. He is conceived as distinct from the Father and the Son. The Holy Spirit is never seen as an impersonal force but as a personal reality who teaches and intercedes for believers, who possesses a mind, who can be grieved and be lied to, and who is ranked as an equal partner with the Father and the Son.[3] No, Jesus did not prophecy the coming of Mohammed in John 16:7 (as Muslim imams tell their people) when he said: "But very truly I tell you, it is for your good that I am going away. Unless I go away, the Advocate will not come to you; but if I go, I will send him to you." He prophesied the coming of the Holy Spirit, for the next verse tells us what the Spirit will do: He will convict the world of who Jesus really is and how Satan utterly failed (cf. John 16:8-11). Yes, he will convince each of us with power that we are not ready to face Judgment Day without this Jesus. He will also guide the church in all the truth that Jesus spoke about while he was with us. The Spirit will not come with new revelations contradicting all that Jesus taught and did, but only continue the Lord's ministry. The Advocate will not obscure the Son and demote him to be just another prophet, as Islam does. Above all, the Spirit will teach the church to walk in love, for love is the fulfillment of the law (Rom. 13:8-12 and Gal. 5:13-26). He will set us free from the fear of death, from slavery to sin, and from endless manmade taboos, to live in the freedom of God's children (Gal. 5:1-26). That is not what Islam brings us.

To quote Moreland and Craig again: "In short, the New Testament church was sure that only one God exists. But they also believed that the Father, Son, and Holy Spirit, while personally distinct, all deserve to be called God." The challenge of the post-apostolic church was how to make sense of this. How could the Father, Son, and Holy Spirit each be God

---

2 Anthony van den Beukel, *The Physicists and God* (North Andover, MA: Genesis Publishing, 1995), 127.

3 Moreland and Craig, *Philosophical Foundations*, 577.

without there being either three Gods or only one person?[4] The fact that the north-African church father Tertullian first coined the term *trinity*, or that the early church councils formulated creeds confessing and defending the Trinity, does not mean that the idea was a novelty. It simply means that the early church grappled with how to succinctly formulate that which they not only received from the apostles, but Whom by faith they already worshiped and loved as God Most High.

The Doctrine of The Trinity Under the Assault of Rationalism

So how important is the doctrine of the Trinity to Christianity? It is the very heart of our faith. Dutch pastor-theologian Berend Wentsel, whose seven-volume work on Christian doctrine totals five thousand pages, introduced volume three with these words: "The Triune God: Heart of the Christian Faith and Confession."[5] Someone who has written five thousand pages on something must be qualified to know what its *heart* is. Likewise, Donald Fairburn, in his book *Life in the Trinity*[6] proves abundantly that the Trinity was the very heart of the Christian faith in the early church, before and after the Council of Nicaea in 323 AD. All of this means that when Islam assaults the doctrine of the Trinity, it aims not at some aspect of our Christian faith but at mortally wounding its very heart. That, incidentally, is what any skilled warrior would do when going for the kill.

But what about the church? How strong and healthy is her heart still? If the Trinity was the very lifeblood of early Christianity, according to Fairburn and others, how is it going with the *body* of Christ today? Is her heart still in good shape? When reading most of the church fathers, for instance, Irenaeus, Tertullian, Athanasius, Chrysostom, the three Cappadocians, or Augustine, one can feel how profoundly trinitarian their thinking was. That is why they struggled much less than us to keep life and doctrine together: to preserve unity among believers, to approach worship with deep reverence and joy, to expect the miraculous to occur, or how to show compassion to an unbelieving world and even to their enemies. The

4 Ibid., 577.

5 Berend Wentsel, *God en Mens Versoend* (Kampen: Kok, 1987), 299.

6 See Donald Fairburn, *Life in the Trinity* (Downers Grove: IL: IVP Academic, IL, 2009).

Trinity was critical. Faith in a Triune God saturated their beings, worship, communion, view of reality, walk and hope for the future. Herman Bavinck once wrote: "It is only as we contemplate this Trinity that we know who and what God is" and that he can only be approached with holy reverence and childlike awe, like Moses did at the burning bush, when he feared greatly and covered his face. When we know God as Triune, we want to pour our hearts out in worship and love to him.[7] That is what inspired Christian worship for ages, as can be heard in the timeless choral singing of the *Psalms of David* by the King's College of Cambridge, when they conclude each Psalm with: "Glory be to the Father, and the Son and the Holy Spirit, forever, amen."[8]

Sadly, Protestant Christianity in particular has lost this emphasis over the last couple of centuries. That is why we have also struggled to connect faith with life,[9] truth with love, creation with worship, the objective with the subjective, and the natural with the supernatural. The unity of our world was split apart.[10] We seldom realize that this split was the direct consequence of the rise of *pure reason* ever since the days of René Descartes (1596 – 1650), the French mathematician who concluded so proudly: "I think therefore I am" (*cogito ergo sum*). Ever since those days, Western man began to experience severe issues with a doctrine that says God could be one and three simultaneously. It sounded like an absurdity, a logical impossibility. As lady reason ascended to the throne not only in France but eventually in all of Europe, life in the church and the world gradually broke apart, becoming ever more fragmented, cold and tough, with hubris feeding unbridled rationalism.

Sadly, not only were philosophers mesmerized by rationalism's charm, the church was soon also seduced by her beauty. If we can't reason it out, or prove it empirically, then it must go. It never dawned on us, though, that by taking such an approach, we have already denied that we are tiny, sinful

7 See Herman Bavinck, *Our Reasonable Faith*, (Grand Rapids: Baker, 1977), 143-145.

8 Choir of King's College, Cambridge, conducted by Sir David Wilcocks and Sir Philip Hedger, *The Psalms of David* – CD recording (EMI Classics, 2003).

9 See also Fairburn, *Life in the Trinity*, 3-6

10 See Van den Beukel, *The Physicists and God.*

mortals in the presence of an awesome, infinite and holy God. The very insistence on such an approach betrays the deep-seated folly and hubris of our hearts. And though not all discarded the doctrine of the Trinity entirely, many just stuck it away in the attic, fearing embarrassment.

Descartes had a younger contemporary, the brilliant French mathematician Blaise Pascal (1623 – 1662). Pascal looked at the same world through entirely different eyes, for he knew that *the heart has its reasons, that reason knows nothing about.* Pascal was at loggerheads with the rampant rationalism of his day. His God was not the god of Descartes, Leibniz, and Spinoza, the dominant rationalist European philosophers of that time, but the God of the Bible. Pascal underwent a personal encounter with God that led to his conversion in 1654, causing him to pen his ecstatic confession down on a piece of paper, sewn into his garment, and found after his death. The shriveled note read:[11]

> Fire
> God of Abraham, God of Isaac, God of Jacob.
> Not of the philosophers and the scholars.
> Certainty. Certainty. Feeling. Joy. Peace.
> God of Jesus Christ. My God and your God.
> Your God will be my God.
> The world and everything are forgotten, except God.
> He can only be found in the gospel. Jesus Christ.
> I forsook him. I fled from him. I denied him. I crucified him.
> That I would never be separate from him!

Pascal saw the same world through entirely different eyes. He had met with Jesus. He knew the Father intimately and personally, for the Holy Spirit had taken the veil from his eyes. It all makes us think of Jesus' words in Luke 11:34:

---

11 Translated from Dutch, G van den Brink, *Orientatie in de filosofie* (Zoetermeer: Boekenzentrum, 2000), 178-179.

> Your eye is the lamp of your body. When your eyes are healthy, your whole body is also full of light. But when they are unhealthy, your body is also full of darkness.

There is a veil covering our eyes and hearts; a veil that keeps us from seeing. Only when *we turn to the Lord* is that veil taken away (II Cor. 3:16).[12] If the gospel is still veiled, wrote Paul, then it is veiled from those who are perishing, whose vision has been blinded by the god of this world, to keep them from seeing the light of the glory of Christ, who is the image of God (II Cor. 4:3-4). But when the veil is ripped away, our vision of *everything* changes from a dull black and white to the most splendid colours. Such was the experience of countless coming to faith, including Prof. Rosalind Picard of the Massachusetts Institute of Technology, who, writing for *Christianity Today* about her conversion said:[13]

> After praying, "Jesus Christ, I ask you to be Lord of my life," my world changed dramatically, as if a flat, black-and-white existence suddenly turned full-color and three-dimensional. But I lost nothing of my urge to seek new knowledge. In fact, I felt emboldened to ask even tougher questions about how the world works. I felt joy and freedom— but also a heightened sense of responsibility and challenge".

That is what made the difference between René Descartes and Blaise Pascal. And that illustrates perfectly why a Triune God is the very heart of Christianity. The Holy Spirit reveals the Son. The Son declares the Father. The Father pours out the Spirit of his Son on his people. How sad then, when we neglect the doctrine of the Trinity, leaving us badly exposed to Islam's message and its close ally, liberal Christianity, all over the earth. That is perfectly illustrated in the words of Harry Kuitert (1924 - 2017), a

---

12 For a brilliant exposition of II Cor. 3 and 4, see Scott J Hafemann, *Paul Moses and the History of Israel* (Peabody, MA: Hendrickson, 1995)

13 Rosalind Picard "A MIT Professor Meets the Author of All Knowledge," *Christianity Today*, March 15, 2019.

liberal Reformed theologian in the Netherlands, who was, for all practical purposes, an unbeliever when he wrote:[14]

> the traditional view of God as triune is ... incomprehensible and unimaginable. People have to study theology for years 'to be able to understand the ins and outs of the matter'. Of course, we might worship the Trinity without understanding what (it is), as the Eastern Church does... However, we Westerners want *doctrine*, and doctrines are intended to offer some degree of understanding. That, however, is something the idea of "one substance and three persons" falls short of. Moreover, both Muslims and Jews can only see the doctrine as a sign that Christianity worships three Gods rather than one. All in all, the doctrine is an occasion for fundamental misunderstandings about the Christian faith.

The Bible's testimony and the wonderful operations of Father, Son and Spirit in our hearts convince us that God is Triune. That is what Kuitert lacked: faith. And that led him to cave in to Islam, as seen in his words above. Remember, the Quran considers faith in a Triune God as an unforgivable sin, *shirk*. As we have seen, Islam was designed to oppose Christianity and erase it from humanity's collective memory. That meant that the truth of the Trinity would always be in the crosshairs of their assault. No Trinity means no Son. No Son means no gospel. No gospel means no Christianity. No Christianity means no salvation. No salvation means no hope. Thus, if we view the battle between Islam and Christianity as a game of chess, giving up the Trinity is like sacrificing our king. It is game over.

Only let us remember that the Triune God is not *a doctrine*. It is not even a cardinal Christian truth in the first place. Instead, the Triune God is our very life, for wherever we see and sense the beautiful harmony between unity and diversity in creation, we are reminded of him. His self-revelation in creation and Scripture is our life and being, for he fills our entire

14 Gijsbert van den Brink and Stephan van Erp, "Ignoring God Triune? The Doctrine of the Trinity in Dutch Theology" in *International Journal for Systematic Theology, Vol. 11. Number 1*, January 2009.

universe and makes it so beautiful and meaningful. There is not the slightest disharmony but only a symphony of unity in his cosmos of diversity.[15]

To yield but an inch on Christ's sonship, or the Spirit's divinity, is to give everything away. It is to sell the family farm, with horse, buggy, and everything. Only those not knowing what they are doing can do such a thing. They have never been on the farm; they never sat in the shade of its trees, never worked its fields, never wiped its sweat from their brows walking home.

So, when Surah 4:169 says, "Say not three, God, Jesus, Mary," we respond:

> Absolutely, we *must* say 'three' but then: Father, Son, and Holy Spirit. We must say it for God's matchless glory's sake, for our souls' sake, and out of love for our Muslim friends, even if that means we commit *shirk*, deserving death by the sword. For nothing will be able to separate us from God's love in Christ, not even the sword. The Holy Spirit assures us of that.

The beautiful thing is, none of the worship of God Triune is ever coerced, for there is no compulsion in Christianity. The Father draws, the Son redeems by his blood, and the Holy Spirit grants new life. And yet not three gods but One, who lives and reigns forever and ever, amen.

Furthermore, no Messianic Jew in early Christianity ever had any qualms about worshiping the Father *and* the Son. The late Larry Hurtado from Edinburgh University has shown convincingly how the earliest Christians (who were all Jews) made Jesus the recipient of their worship, without compromising their deep monotheist convictions. Of this there is abundant evidence in the New Testament, e.g., where the former Pharisee Paul refers to the church as "those who in every place call on the name of our Lord Jesus Christ" (I Cor. 1:2).[16] For any first-century Jew, to "call on the name" is to worship!

What was all promised and contained in the old covenant was now fully revealed in the new. God's revelation opened up like a rose in the desert for our pleasure to enjoy, to his eternal glory. We who love God see the marvelous operations of Father, Son, and Holy Spirit on every page of the Bible, in the sunlight filtering through the leaves of the trees, and in our own lives, says the

---

15 See Augustine's amazing confession, "What do I love when I love God?" in Nick Needham, *2000 Years of Christ Power* (London: Christian Focus, 2016), 288-289.

16 Larry Hurtado, *Honoring the Son* (Bellingham, WA: Lexham Press), 56.

Belgic Confession in Article 9.[17] We must be careful with analogies, yet when the sun breaks over the horizon, and its rays burst into our homes, and we feel the warm sensation on our bodies, we are reminded of the amazing operations of the Father, and the Son, and the Holy Spirit. May the grace of our Lord Jesus Christ, and the love of God, and the fellowship of the Holy Spirit, remain with everyone reading these pages. Amen.

---

17 "The Belgic Confession" in *The Three Forms on Unity* (Premier Printing: Winnipeg, 1994), 12.

CHAPTER 18

THE TRIUNE GOD HAS SPOKEN

The gospel of God's love was delivered to us by the apostles of Jesus and a few other key witnesses. Their reliable unanimous witness is contained in the documents of the New Testament. The New Testament on its part, claims to be the fulfillment of what God has promised from the beginning through his servants in the Old Testament (the Hebrew Scriptures).

Everything Christians believe is based on God's Word, the Holy Scriptures, contained in the sixty-six books of the Old and the New Testament. The Christian Bible has sustained a barrage of higher-critical artillery over the best part of three centuries. All these attacks proved only to be a blessing in disguise, for the documents of the New Testament, in particular, emerged from it all the more trustworthy, precious, and relevant, as God's inspired, infallible and authoritative Word. In many ways, Christians today reap the enormous benefits of the excellent scholarly work in many fields that weathered these storms. It established Scripture's historical claims and reliability in ways that earlier generations did not yet benefit from.

Contemporary Muslims, though, typically launch their attack on our *reliance* on the Bible as God's inspired and infallible word, often using the outdated arguments of liberal Christian critical scholars. Muslims *have* to attack the Bible since Islam won't be able to stand if the Bible is true. The message of the Bible and the Quran simply cannot exist side by side. One or the other must go, since the core message of either book is diametrically opposed to the other on almost every key doctrine, despite some very superficial similarities.

The Bible and the Quran

Have you ever spoken to a Muslim about Christ, or have you ever listened to a Muslim imam talk about Christianity? You would have noticed something immediately: They all begin by saying, "The Bible has been corrupted." There is a reason for that. Ayub A. Hamid, in his booklet *A Book Unlike any Other*," says:

> [The Quran is] the only complete, all-inclusive and preserved version of God's revelations. With its revelation the God [sic] has rendered the old books (like the Torah, Psalms and the Gospels) totally obsolete. Whatever good and truth is contained in those books, is fully covered in the Quran. No-one therefore has any need whatsoever to refer to the old books.[1]

Now, this just makes sense. Suppose you claim that you have the final revelation from God, which you received almost six centuries *after* the last Bible books were written, and which radically differs from the Bible, then you *must* claim that your book is the ultimate one, and that the others should be ignored. Contemporary Muslims do not state things so diplomatically, though. They say it point blank, "the Bible has been corrupted," more particularly the New Testament. They never offer any details of how, when, or where it could have happened. They state it axiomatically. Of course, if they want to win you over to the message of the Quran, they must insist that the Bible has been corrupted. No rational being can believe in both messages.

The funny thing is that the Quran says nothing of the kind. It nowhere claims that either the *Torah* or the *Injil* (gospel) has been corrupted. Many

1 Ayub Hamid, *A Book Unlike Any Other* (Ontario: Bayaan Communications, 2006), 3.

times, it claims that the Jews were corrupt and that they either misinterpreted the *Torah* or did not live according to it, but nowhere does the Quran say that the *Torah* has been corrupted.[2]

Bear in mind that there were lots of Jews and Christians living in Arabia during Mohammed's lifetime. Arabia was part of Byzantium, which was formally Christian. Mohammed really hoped that they would believe his message without much resistance. Yet one thing would have clearly derailed his plans: if he claimed *their* holy books were forgeries. That would only have alienated the Jews and Christians from him. That is exactly why the Quran says much to the contrary.

What's more, Mohammed would have had to back any such claims of corruption up with solid "proof", something he could not do, since he was not lettered, according to Muslim scholars. The *hadith*, dating from centuries after Mohammed's life, neither claims that the Bible was corrupted, except for perhaps one vague and ambiguous saying. If anything, the Quranic statements about the Christian Scriptures leave serious questions about the authority of the very Quran itself. In Surah 10:94, Allah says to Mohammed:

> If you are in any doubt concerning what We have sent down to you, then question [ask] those who have read the Book before you: the Truth has come to you from your Lord, so do not be one of the doubters— do not be one who rejects God's signs, for then you would become one of the losers.

"Question those who have read the Book before you" no doubt refers to the Christians and their Bible. Surah 29:46 goes further to say, addressing Muslim believers:

> Believers, argue only in the best way with the People of the Book, [but contend not at all] with such of them as are unjust. Say, "We believe in what has been revealed to us, and what has been revealed to you; our God and your God are one; and to Him we submit."

2 It is even unclear what the Quran means by Jews not living according to the *Torah*. Were they Jews living in Mohammed's day, or in Old Testament Israel?

Note, the Quran claims "our God and your God are one," and what was revealed to both of groups is true. There was no other way the early Muslims would have been able to rationally persuade Jews and Christians to join them, but by claiming they were serving the same God. Surah 3:3-4 goes so far as to say:

> He sent down the Torah and the Gospel in the past as guidance for mankind; He has also sent down the Standard by which to discern the true from the false. Surely those who deny God's signs will suffer severe punishment. God is mighty and capable of retribution.

All of this not only shows that the Quran nowhere teaches that the Bible has been corrupted; to the very contrary, it only commends it again and again. Thus, Islam did what most Christian cults have done for centuries: It does not renounce the inspiration and authority of the Bible, for that will be counter-productive. It adds new revelation to draw the ignorant and gullible away from the pure gospel into the arms of a new heretical movement. That is always the strategy (see I John 2).

Let us never forget there was one thing that Jews and Christians heartily agreed on by the end of the first century: the *Tanach* (the Old Testament) was the Word of God. There were zero claims by anyone that it had been corrupted. Jews and Christians even agreed that the apocryphal books, though valuable and interesting, should not be part of the *Tanach*.

So, when was the Old Testament supposedly corrupted then? Mohammed never claimed it was, so it must have happened *after* his life. Thus, if the *modern* standard-Muslim-narrative is true, then the *Tanach* must have been corrupted somewhere since the mid-seventh century after Mohammed's death. But no evidence exists for such a claim either. If anything, the Dead Sea scrolls, discovered since 1947, debunked any such myths. These scrolls proved, for instance, that the Isaiah-prophecy which the church is reading today, is the same one that Jesus read in his hometown synagogue.

And when was the New Testament supposedly corrupted? Remember, we concur that the modern-day standard-Muslim-narrative makes perfect sense: If you want to recruit followers from among Christians or sell your Muslim faith to a broader public, then you must claim that the New

Testament was corrupted. But not even their prophet Mohammed dared to make such a claim.

So how do they "prove" it? They do so, quoting from overtly liberal and critical Christian sources of the last century or two, something I have experienced personally on several occasions. Now, this is truly amazing on two counts. So-called Christian writings are being used to attack Christianity. What does that say of these so-called Christian scholars? It is not that we have any problems with honest critical scholarship. The Bible can stand up to any honest, unbiased research, and Muslims should be willing to subject their book to it as well. However, the resources Muslims like to quote against Christianity are anything but honest unbiased sources. These books are often written from hostile philosophical presuppositions, seeking to destroy the foundations of Christianity. What is more, the same authors would usually not dare to say a single word against the Quran in fear of the consequences. Thereby these so-called Christian scholars unwittingly affirm the enormous difference between the messages of the Bible and the Quran. The one will let you criticize it; the other won't.

But it is also amazing on another count. Muslims criticize the "People of the Book" using the tools provided by liberal critical scholarship from the West. Why is this so strange? One of the central tenets of the Muslim faith is its elaborate teaching about Satan and the *jinn*.[3] Satan is seen as the source of all evil in this world. According to Muslim scholars, Satan promotes atheism, agnosticism, *and* rationalist inquiry. That is why Islam must supposedly fight secular Western values and its corrupt education. The name Boko Haram (a West African terrorist group most Muslims would despise) means something like "Western education (i.e., books) is forbidden."[4]

Unfortunately, they are not far from wrong. Western secular education has deteriorated so much over recent decades that no one wants to subject

3 See Sookhdeo, *Understanding Islamic Theology*, 112-142.

4 That is why poor schoolgirls are often abducted and killed in Nigeria and Cameroon. Boko Haram, an organization known for its barbarity and cowardice, fights against innocent school girls with machine guns and machetes because Western secular education is from the devil.

any child to it anymore.[5] But how can my peace-loving Muslim friends explain the following: Not even your own prophet Mohammed attacked the New Testament, which predates modern Western secularism by at least eighteen centuries. And yet your scholars and imams are using the very tools of the devil— extremely critical secular scholarship—to attack the holy book? "You can't have your cake and eat it too," we say here in the West. That means: you can't enjoy the benefit of two mutually exclusive alternatives at the same time. If you hate atheist, secular critique, how dare you use it against Christians and subject their holy gospel to it? We are not supposed to collaborate with the devil, are we? And if you affirm atheist secular critique, then please submit your Quran to it as well.

The Manuscripts of the New Testament

Let us now look into some major claims against the New Testament. Muslims who don't know their history think that the Quran was received almost instantaneously in its final form as we have it today, and that there exists only one version of the Quran, which is, of course, not true. And so, they love to ask us Christians: "Why are there so many manuscripts of the New Testament?"[6]

What is a manuscript? It's a copy, or a part of a copy, of the original New Testament documents. Why then, are there so many of these ancient manuscripts? Isn't that a sign that many people had a hand in the final outcome? If there were so many manuscripts, i.e., ancient copies of the original, from the first few centuries, wouldn't that increase the likelihood of a corrupted text?

To the very contrary. The fact that there are so many manuscripts (far more than of any other book of late antiquity) is because this book was so much cherished and read all over the eastern Mediterranean basin and beyond. A Gospel-Scroll was so highly prized that it was sometimes

5 That is not to say that the education these girls in Nigeria were receiving was bad, far from it. Africa is fortunately "behind" the West in some respects.

6 I am gratefully using "The Reliability of the New Testament – Introduction," *Inspiring Philosophy, YouTube.*

requested as payment to cross the Mediterranean.[7] The New Testament would soon become an all-time best-seller. And so that is why we have 5,800+ Greek manuscripts of the New Testament, 10,000 in Latin, 4,000 in Slavic, 2,000 in Armenian, and hundreds of others. The second most popular book of antiquity in terms of preserved manuscripts was Homer's *Iliad*, with only 1757 manuscripts, followed by Suetonius, with 900 manuscripts. The more manuscripts we have of an ancient book, the better the chances are of determining the integrity of its original text.[8]

But maybe we are not out of the woods yet. Our Muslim friend might say: "But these manuscripts contain 400 000 variants (i.e., different readings)." That sounds pretty bad, does it not? Not at all, if you consider that a variant means instances where words were not exactly the same as in other copies. Consider that 5800 Greek manuscripts of the New Testament comprise some 2.6 million pages of copied text. Do we have an idea today how these texts were copied? Yes, by hand! First on scrolls made of animal skin and later onto papyrus, from which a book (or *codex*) was made. Every document had to be copied or translated by frail human hands, often by candlelight, under the strictest conditions.

So, let us divide 2.6 million pages of manuscripts with 400 000 variants. What do we get? Only one variant in every 6.5 pages. But what are these variants like? 75% contain spelling errors, 15% contain synonyms, 9% consist of very late changes (which do not affect the text), and less than 1% involve the meaning of the text. None of them affect any essential Christian belief or doctrine at all. None. Even the fiercest contemporary New Testament critics will admit this. Only forty lines of the New Testament text remain unresolved. That is 0.5% of the whole. Consider that in the light of the fact that roughly one fifth (or 20%) of the Quran is considered unintelligible, even according to Muslim scholars. And that Homer's *Iliad*, with far fewer manuscripts, can only claim a 95% accuracy. Furthermore, most serious Christians know which parts of the New Testament are contested since our

7 Jerome "Life of Hilarion" in *Early Christian Lives*, translated and edited by Carolinne White (Penguin Books: London), 109.

8 See Tim Challies & Josh Byers, *Guide to the Bible* (Grand Rapids: Zondervan Reflective, 2019), 19-33.

Bibles tell us that: the long ending of Mark, the story of the woman caught in adultery in John 8, and a few other verses here and there. So, was there possible textual corruption? Maybe. How much of the New Testament was affected? Half a percent! Not too bad for a book written by several authors two thousand years ago.

Against This Book, Nothing Can Be Said

All Christians will heartily agree with Article 4 of the Belgic Confession, which says: "We believe that the Holy Scriptures consist of two parts, namely, the Old and the New Testament, which are canonical, *against which nothing can be alleged*" because they are from God.[9]

That "against this book nothing can be alleged" means this book alone is the foundation of our faith. Christians are convinced of this because of the witness of the Holy Spirit in their hearts, not because any human being or church authority told us that, even though the Bible carries within itself the evidence of its divine inspiration. Countless former atheists and Bible skeptics (like Dr. Rosalind Picard of the MIT mentioned before) can testify to this. The Bible itself turned them downside up!

But what is the most famous atheistic argument against Christianity today? "You are only a Christian because you were born in America (or wherever) and were raised in a Christian home. Had you been born to a Hindu family in India or a Muslim family in Jordan, you would have been a Hindu or a Muslim, respectively." Nonsense, says the Belgic Confession. Yes, it is true of millions, even billions, that they simply believe what they are being told. It is most of all true of atheists themselves. But as the stories of countless former Muslims, New Agers, or secular atheists, testify, they

9 While discussing the canon of Scripture falls beyond the scope of our study, I dare not neglect to mention the invaluable work by possibly the world's greatest living scholar on the topic, Prof. Lee Martin McDonald, as well as a recent book, *Canon Revisited*, by Michael J. Kruger (Wheaton, IL: Crossway, 2012). Let us avail ourselves of the best scholarship on the origins and authority of the New Testament canon. The enemy knows that if we falter here, our fall is guaranteed, which is why so many attacks in recent years have been launched at the canon of the New Testament. In *Canon Revisited*, the curious Christian will learn that *none* of these attacks have anything to stand on: indeed, nothing can be alleged against these twenty-seven books of the New Testament.

were convinced by the Word. Though they had a violent bent against the Christian Bible, when God began to move in mysterious ways, he removed the veil from their eyes. Many were convinced of the truth of the Bible, even while trying to refute the good old book.

This does not mean a Christian cannot encounter serious doubts about the Bible. We are in the midst of a cosmic struggle of epic proportions. The adversary still comes with the same old question "Did God really say?" That was the question the serpent asked Eve in the garden in Genesis 3.[10] When we deny God's truth and created reality today, we are flirting with the same insidious lies of the old serpent, the devil.

How shall I ever forget going through a life-and-death struggle for my own faith, when a simple question, as from nowhere, entered my mind at an unguarded moment, confronting me for the first time: "Is your life and salvation merely based on a book? Just a book? What is left of it when the book is gone?" The devil knows when to fancy his chances, for it happened when I was exhausted by a long senseless quarrel among Christians, and after a long flight across the ocean. When I then briefly glanced through a book hateful of the gospel, written by a liberal Christian theologian, an arrow as from nowhere pierced my armour. From that moment—for six grueling months—I battled existential doubt every waking moment of the day. It was brutal, as I hovered over the dark abyss of unbelief every moment of the day.

After many days, God took me back to Africa in his good providence. One sublime morning in 2006, as I sat on the sandy beach of Lake Malawi near Nkhata Bay, with the sun breaking across the water, the battle was finally won. I opened the Gospel of John, tired of my long spiritual struggle and determined to hear God's voice again. And I did. I saw him again who came from the Father, full of grace and truth, and suddenly the heaven opened wide above me. Satan's rockets that assaulted me so relentlessly for

---

10 People quibble about whether this event ever happened. I have no qualms believing it did, but a far more serious question is whether it is existentially true, says Dr. Jordan Peterson somewhere. That means it is true for you and me, no matter who we are, or where we come from. The fundamental cause of chaos in our lives is when we start to ask: "Did God really say?"

months, causing so much mental agony, were stopped by a divine missile shield on that sublime April morning, as I felt the power of his WORD. The Lord spoke to me again with great power, through the grand symphony of nature and Scripture, as I read, "In the beginning was the Word and the Word was with God, and the Word was God..." It was as if Jesus came walking on the water to me. After meditating for a long while on John's prologue, Satan was gone. I got up and limped back to my chalet, like Jacob of old stumbling out of the Jabbok, with the sun rising upon me. It was all over; I knew that my Redeemer lived and that "against this book, nothing can be said!" I also knew better than ever what Anselm of Canterbury (ca. 1033 – 1109) meant long ago when he said, "unless I believe, I shall not understand."[11]

For months afterward I had to avoid any material criticizing Christianity, like a recovered alcoholic avoiding even the smell of alcohol. Today, I am stronger than ever, only due to his love and faithfulness. During those months of darkness, I searched for every possible clue whether the Biblical narrative and the gospel in particular, could be fake. I scanned every ideology and worldview presented as an alternative to Christianity. I considered every argument of Biblical critics against the Bible I could think of. I compared the founders of other religions with Jesus. I wanted to know why this book is divinely inspired and not simply manufactured, for I was battling the demonic suggestion *that it is only all in a book.* I was no longer content with mere cliches and dogmas. I was searching for deep and lasting existential certainty just like Pascal.[12] And thank God, I found it again. He placed my feet on a rock higher and stronger than I ever knew—like that famous Pulpit Rock in Norway—from where I could look out over the entire world in confidence. I know so well today why Pascal scribbled those few lines on a piece of paper, found sewn into his garment: the risen Son of God is real, absolutely real, and he speaks to us through his marvelous creation and incredible Word, through the Holy Spirit.

The reason I told my story here is so that no one would ever feel ashamed when experiencing doubt, but also to emphasize how much

---

11 *Anselm of Canterbury* (Oxford: Oxford University Press, 2008) 87.

12 See his poem "Fire" in chapter 18.

we must protect *our minds* from the lethal attacks of the evil one. We are involved in a brutal spiritual conflict, where there is no place for sissies, and no room for the sloppy, the naive, and the faint-hearted. Our minds are the citadel of faith and the devil's primary target. The calling to be strong and full of courage is found throughout God's Word. Therefore, let us be diligent every day to put on the whole armour of God, for we are not fighting against mere humans but against very dark and sinister forces in the air, seeking to ruin the church and the entire world (Ephes. 6:3-10). Him we must resist, says Paul, standing firm in the faith, until Christ will crush Satan under our feet and we will receive the crown of life.

CHAPTER 19

BLESSED ARE THOSE WHO OVERCOME

What shall we say of all this? Suppose the world may experience a "clash of civilizations" on many fronts during this century, as some have predicted, then the ultimate one will no doubt be between the House of Islam and the Body of Christ. The war in Ukraine, which almost seems like a brutal stand-off between the "woke" liberal globalist West in decline, and the socially-conservative traditionalist "Rest" on the rise, is no doubt the major conventional frontline at this moment. Its outcome, by the way, might have far bigger consequences for humanity than any war of the last century. The more permanent spiritual frontline though, is fast developing in Sub-Saharan Africa. It might yet prove to be the epi-center of a global stand-off between light and darkness in the twenty-first century, with casualties rising on all sides, both physically and spiritually. This is simply true from a mere demographic perspective. While the Caucasian population in the West is dying, and the growth of some other major people groups in the world is stagnant, Africa's population is growing faster than any other. It is estimated that up to 40 percent of all Christians will live in Africa by 2050, with Africa's population reaching around two billion. Meanwhile Islamic *dawa* is firing on all cylinders to capture the whole continent. That means whoever loves the church of Jesus Christ will have to keep a close eye on the African continent over the coming decades.

We are convinced that only Biblical Christianity can ultimately stop political Islam, not with arms like worldly powers have, but with superior *ideas* and with that amazing faith that overcomes the world. Secular humanism has shown itself to be increasingly impotent in inspiring integrity and valour and offering any real meaning to life, with most other systems and religions not doing much better.[1]

Any idea or ideology can only be defeated by a superior one. Islamism, as we have seen, is an immensely powerful ideology. So powerful, in fact, that none other than Bertrand Russel, Carl Jung, and Karl Barth, all European academic heavyweights of the twentieth century, have pointed to the obvious comparison between totalitarian systems like Bolshevism and Naziism on the one hand, and political Islam or Islamism on the other. Carl Jung wrote in the late 1930s in Europe:[2]

> We do not know whether Hitler is going to found a new Islam… He is already on the way; he is like Mohammed. The emotion in Germany is Islamic, warlike and Islamic. They are all drunk with a wild man.

The optical alliance between Islamism and totalitarianism is not incidental. There is an affinity on an even deeper level that we may not miss. Many observers have been intrigued by the seemingly strange bond between political Islam and the radical left (and sometimes also the far-right) in the new post-Cold War and post-Christian West. Someone like Yasmine Mohammed has shown convincingly in her book how Western liberals empower radical Islam in a country like Canada.[3] But what explains this attraction?

---

1 This is why an Italian Chief Defense of Staff, General Camporini, once asked in his keynote address at a NATO conference: "For what do our soldiers fight? We have no ideology.", see Sookhdeo, "The Role of Religion", 40.

2 Stephen Ulph, "Islamism and Totalitarianism: The Challenge of Comparison," in Fighting the Ideological War (McLean, VA: Isaac Publishing, 2012), 46.

3 Yasmine Mohammed, *Unveiled: How Western Liberals Empower Radical Islam.*

At its deepest level, both movements have little respect for the human being as the *Imago Dei*. Both also profoundly despise the Man on the Cross as the ultimate image of weakness and contempt. They would have nothing to do with a helpless Nazarene dying in God-forsaken dereliction to redeem a lost humanity.

It is in this regard that we must take a closer look at Friedrich Nietzsche. His hatred for the Man on the Cross was so intense that ordinary Germans did not want to greet him on the street. It may even have driven him to insanity. Nietzsche, however, was the spiritual antecedent of National Socialism in Germany. His push for *einer umwertung aller werte* ("the reevaluation of all values"), and his brutal arrogance and obsession with the will to power, led him to mock Jesus and the "movement he founded" as the epitome of ultimate "decadence." The Messianic movement was the revolution of the resentful weak, said Nietzsche, which must be crushed at all costs. Christianity infected Germans with a weak *bourgeois* herd mentality, which is one reason why Nietzsche had so little time for his fellow Germans, as can all be seen from his last book *Why I am so Wise*, (written in 1888).[4] Amazingly, the same Nietzsche has become one of the most popular thinkers studied by philosophy students in the West, along with someone promoting the worst perversions imaginable, Michel Foucault.[5]

A young Egyptian student of history, Hussein Aboubakr Mansour, opened my eyes to the Nazi roots of Modern Arab Antisemitism.[6] He shows how nineteenth-century German Idealism had such a fascination for Islam and mystical Sufism in particular. There was an admiration for Muslim power and great sympathy for the idea that Western civilization was inferior to Islam. The infatuation later proved to be mutual. Mansour claims, among other things, that the first modern Arab philosopher, and intellectual aid of Egyptian president Nasser, Abdulrahman

---

4 Finally published as *Ecce Homo* two decades later, see Friedrich Nietzsche, *Ecce Homo* (London: Arcturus Publishing, 2019). See also his work *Beyond Good and Evil*, first published in 1886.

5 See Chris Horrocks and Zoran Jevtic, *Introducing Foucault – A Graphic Guide* (London: Icon Books, 2013).

6 "The Nazi Roots of Arab Antisemitism," February 4, 2022, *EMET — Endowment for Middle East Truth*, on emetonline.org.

Badawi (1917-2002), was a great admirer of Adolf Hitler. Moreover, the very influential Arab thinker, Fayez Sayegh (1922-1980), connected the Arab and secular left. Sayegh, who was ardently antisemitic and fluent in German, headed a Nazi-inspired Pan-Syrian movement. The Arab left later turned to Islamism, according to Mansour.[7] What tied the two movements in Germany and the Middle East together is that they both admired Nietzsche's critique of the Man on the Cross and the movement he founded.

There is another striking similarity between radical secular revolutionary movements and political Islam. When pushed to the brink, both opt for extreme violence, i.e., Nietzsche's *will to power*. When the Bolshevik Red Army feared being overthrown by the rising White Army in Russia, they resorted to their only means of holding on to power: unrestrained terror. An eyewitness and Russian intellectual of the time, Pitirim Sorokin, tells us what happened:

> In Arkhangelsk the most horrible purge was going on. The Bolshevist Commissar Kedroff was executing people by the hundreds and thousands. Victims were being shot, drowned, or murdered with unnamable mutilations. Feeling the ground under their feet insecure, the Bolsheviki tried to strengthen their position *by unrestrained terror*.[8]

"Unrestrained terror" was their only means to hold on to power. Let that sink in. Sorokin said their gruesome deity demanded everything: "Revolution is God, and God cannot be questioned." People were being mowed down like animals, intellectuals and peasants alike. Almost anyone, who, in the slightest degree might be seen as a possible counter-revolutionary or an informant, got killed.[9] "In forty-seven provinces of Soviet Russia," wrote

---

7 See "The Roots of Arab Nazi Alliance: The Secret History of the Middle East (2010)", *The Film Archives: YouTube*.

8 Sorokin, *A Long Journey*, 150.

9 The despair was unimaginable. A beautiful young woman threw herself down from the fifth-story balcony of Sorokin's apartment. She died two hours later. A notable Russian philosopher, Professor Kyostoff, hanged himself. A geologist, Professor Inostrantzeff, took cyanide. Another, Professor Rosenblatt, also ended his own life. All just in Sorokin's circle of acquaintances. So many died, or took their own lives, that the living were pleading with

Sorokin, "the population has diminished by eleven million." Yet the same Sorokin, who was not a believer, amazingly wrote about those who steadfastly resisted, that they typically replied to the Bolshevists in these words: "Man shall not live by bread alone" and "Thou shalt worship the Lord thy God, and Him only shalt thou serve".[10] Two quotes from the Bible and from Jesus' lips.

The Bolshevist ideology was atheist. But does it make any difference if your ideology is theist? Does ultimate brutality then become less reprehensible? Remember Sahih al-Bukhari's famous *hadith* (commenting on Surah 3:151) that Islam shall be made "victorious through terror."[11] What motivated the mass decapitation of Jews in Medina, but to strike terror in the hearts of the infidels? The more brutal, the greater the fear. That is the idea inspiring Islamist terror groups, and what lies behind militant *jihad*. Both the Bolshevists and the Muslims resorted to ultimate terror, not only on combatants but on all who refused to bend the knee to their cause. To use Nietzsche's language, all *Untermenschen* (the herdlike masses) must bow to, or perish before, the *Übermensch* (the super-human).

Who can stand up to such terror? When a dear brother recently posted a video of the gruesome beheading of a Nigerian Christian on an isolated road in Kaduna State (Nigeria) on social-media, another one responded with Romans 14:8: "If we live, we live for the Lord; and if we die, we die for the Lord. So, whether we live or die, we belong to the Lord." The reason is simple, yet profound: "For Christ's love compels us, [and] we are convinced that one died for all, therefore all died. And he died for all, that those who live should no longer live for themselves but for him who died for them and was raised again" (II Cor. 5:14-15). Notice, all who belong to Jesus have died. They died to their sin, to the world, and to Satan's monstrous threats. When they die the next time, they sleep in the arms of Jesus. That's why they are not afraid to die and why they can now live and die for him,

---

each other not to commit suicide. When you left your home, you were never sure you would return. See Sorokin, 180.

10 Ibid., 183.

11 Durie, *The Third Choice*, 115.

for whether we live or die, we are the Lord's. The sword may perhaps sever our heads, but it will never sever us from God's love in Christ our Lord.

This is the decisive Christian *idea* that will conquer political Islam. He who loved us died, rose, and lives forever, and we live in him, through him, and for him, forever. What's more, none of those who hate us are beyond his love either. That is what Jesus told a broken American Christian, Dan Baumann, who was detained at the Iranian border and sentenced to death in 1997. Sometime during the nine-week brutal torture that he experienced in an Iranian prison cell, and after trying to commit suicide, Dan asked God, "What do you think of this man?"—the one guard who hated and beaten him the most? God's answer was clear: he loved this sinner too. And so, the next day Dan asked this cruel man, "Sir, if I am going to see you the rest of my life, every day, why don't we just become friends?" "No, that is impossible," the guard responded angrily. Not fazed in any way, Dan then said, "Sir you can start by telling me your name." So, he stuck out his hand, and added, "Let's be friends." The Iranian guard stood there frozen. After a few minutes, he started shaking, until Dan saw his hand moving slowly toward his own. The cruel guard grabbed his prisoner's hand as tears rolled down his face. For minutes he held Dan's hand, weeping. "My name is Razak" he replied, "and I would love to be your friend." The next day, Dan heard three of the guards speaking to each other, saying: "These are Christians. They have a reason to live." Dan soon after appeared in court. When asked what he was doing in Iran, God gave him the audacity to tell the plain truth. Filled with the Holy Spirit Dan said: "I am here to spread the Good News of Jesus Christ..." He was released soon after.[12]

There were, of course, many other powerful ideas discussed in the pages before, but the truth of the gospel, and the love of our God for even our worst enemies, are the decisive ones. And so, for us to rise to the challenge, we need to listen once more to that wise old Chinese saying:

> If you know the enemy and yourself,
> you need not fear the result of a hundred battles.
> If you know yourself but not the enemy,

---

12 "Imprisoned in Iran Part 2 – CBN.com" on *The 700 Club – YouTube.*

for every victory gained, you will suffer defeat.
If you know neither the enemy nor yourself,
you will succumb in every battle.

It all comes down to this: Islamism claims that Mohammed is the new Moses, that *sharia* is the new *Torah*, and the entire world the Promised Land, to be cleansed from all infidels.[13] It claims Mohammed is the fulfillment of Yahweh's promise to Moses to raise up in Israel "a prophet like me from among you" (Deut. 18:15), to whom every Israelite *had* to listen. It also claims that Mohammed is the Advocate Jesus promised to send to his disciples after he would physically leave them (John 16:7). If these claims were true, then the church would have to close its doors and burn its Bibles.

The truth is quite different though. Jesus—who came six centuries before Mohammed—was the new Moses. He was *that* prophet to come (see John 6:14 and Acts 3:17-26), for he was not only a Jew (i.e., "one from among them") which an Arab could never be, but he towered above Moses in character, word and deed. In him God gave us the true bread from heaven and living water gushing forth in the desert. Yet when crowds flocked to hear and see him, Jesus said to them: "If anyone comes to me and does not hate his father and mother, wife and children, brothers and sisters—yes even his own life—such a person cannot be my disciple." (Luke 14:26). For a moment it may sound like *jihad*, but as Richard Hays points out,[14] Jesus' words play on Moses' blessing to Levi in Deut. 33:8-9, as Moses was thinking back to the darkest chapter in Israel's early history, when three thousand were killed by Levi's sons after the debacle with the golden calf (see Ex. 32 and 33).

Jesus' radical call to discipleship goes the exact opposite way of Mohammed's *jihad*, for he continues in Luke 14:27, "And whoever does not carry their cross and follow me, cannot be my disciple." For the sake of Israel's Messiah and God's kingdom, we must be willing *to be cut off even*

---

13 For an excellent treatment of the difference between the Bible's "holy wars" and *jihad*, see Paul Copan "Aren't the Bible's 'Holy Wars' just like Islamic Jihad?", in *When God Goes to Starbucks* (Grand Rapids: BakerBooks, 2008).

14 Richard, B Hays, *Echoes of Scripture in the Gospels* (Waco, TX: Baylor University Press, 2016), 210.

from our dearest of kin. "By alluding to this grim episode [in Ex. 32], Jesus challenges the crowd of would-be followers to reckon with the radical implications of joining his movement," says Hays.[15] "Hating" one's own, has nothing to do with a lack of love, with blind zeal leading to cruelty, but with being willing to surrender *all attachments*, yes even your own life, [family,] and possessions, for the sake of the kingdom." It is the very opposite of drawing swords. When a disciple drew his sword in Gethsemane to fight back, Jesus said: "No more of this!" (Luke 22:51 ESV).

I am writing these closing paragraphs, having just returned from a six-week trip to Africa.[16] Everything I wrote before was confirmed to my eyes and ears. Islam is on the march. They have a plan. Mosques are being built like crazy. African shops are taken over by Muslims at an alarming rate. *Dawa* billboards spring up where they were never seen before. The sight of hijabs and niqabs have become ever so common. The *adhan* sounds louder and louder. I read of British tourists killed by Isis jihadis and fed to crocodiles in KwaZulu Natal,[17] and was told that the city of Johannesburg got its first Islamist mayor. On the plane to Ethiopia, I am told how jihadis wreak havoc in northern Benin. Upon arrival back home I see reports of over thirty Congolese Christians beheaded west of Lake Kivu, and of two dozen Christians slain in northern Mozambique. Meanwhile, Islam is looking forward to the FIFA World Cup in Qatar as a godsend for *dawa*, sending their very best apologists to the tournament.

But it was the other side of the story that really touched me. I saw hundreds of former Muslims worshipping Jesus in East Africa, despite the persecution they are facing. They are coming to the Saviour all the time, drinking in every word, and breaking out in spontaneous praise to the Lamb. I witnessed the joyful fearlessness of many gospel couriers, honoured to be used by the Lord, regardless of the grave risks involved. I saw church leaders in Malawi desperate to be better informed about *dawa* and

15 Ibid.

16 In September 2022.

17 Spencer, Robert. "Islamic State Jihadis murdered British Tourists and fed them to crocodiles" on *jihadwatch.org* Oct. 5, 2022.

what they can do to resist it in Africa. I heard an old friend humbly telling me in a coffee-shop that he's eager to suffer for Christ, and spent days with a missionary tirelessly and joyfully proclaiming the gospel, saving even witchdoctors from the bondage they are in. I saw Christians everywhere laying aside petty differences to stand together proclaiming and defending the truth. I picked up a newly released book in Pretoria and read:

> "My name is Mariam Ibraheem, and I am a Christian from the Islamic nation of Sudan. After fleeing the country of my birth several years ago, I finally decided to sit down and share my testimony. I am not ashamed of the name of Jesus Christ. I have been arrested, tried, whipped, kicked, beaten, mocked, spit on, imprisoned, sentenced to death by hanging, and forced to live as a refugee for refusing to deny the name of Jesus Christ. Yet, His is the only name that gives eternal life, and it is only by the grace of his holy name that I am alive to recount my experiences".[18]

And then I see a brave woman on *YouTube*—sister Rose—rising to confront Dr. Zakir Naik during the World Cup Tournament in Qatar, telling him before a packed audience: "Jesus is my Saviour and my Lord." She stands there firm and courageous, even when Naik intimidates her with Islam's shallow arguments that Jesus is not God. I weep and know: we shall overcome! The Spirit who dwells in us is mightier still, and Jesus did not die in vain. He reigns and is coming soon. We have to realize once and for all though, that our Father did not call us to be nice. For heaven's sake, he called us to be holy and faithful, courageous and strong, to take up our cross and to follow Jesus, proclaiming and defending the truth of the gospel together in love.

This means that it is time to draw the line. Let us in the West stop yielding ground, in the name of God! Let us fight for that freedom for which Christ has made us free. Let us proudly bear the cross around our necks, and boldly say our prayers also in the restaurant. Let us ask the shopkeeper why we must all eat *halal*, and eat our pork also when our Muslim friends appear. Let us ask them those questions nobody dares to, with love and

---

18 Mariam Ibraheem, *Shackled: One Woman's Dramatic Triumph Over Persecution, Gender Abuse, and a Death Sentence* (New Kensington, PA: Whitaker House, 2022), 12.

respect.[19] Let us confess the Son of God, who died for our sins, and rose again in glory. Let us defend the Trinity *and* the New Testament canon with joy. Let us memorize those Quranic verses attacking our faith,[20] and read our *printed* Bibles on the airplane or wherever we go. Let us defend the Christian mission of our schools, and share the amazing impact of Christianity on the history of the world, far and wide.[21] Let us make the sign of the cross wherever we want, and ring our chapel bells *also* close to the mosque. Let us chant our Christian songs and share our faith *even* in the mall, and let us take the separation between church and state with a big grain of salt, for the *Great Day of the Lord* is coming! In other words, let us stop being wimps… for we shall overcome the dragon by the blood of the lamb, by the word of our testimony and by not loving our lives unto death (Rev. 12:11), or as David once said, not with sword or javelin, but in the name of the Lord Almighty (I Sam. 17:45). Let us remember Stephen, who received a standing ovation from the risen Lord in glory, when he died as the first martyr of the church (Acts 7:55). For, there will be no place for the cowardly in the New Jerusalem (Rev. 21:8). They will only hear: "Whom have you so dreaded and feared, that you have not been true to me?" (Is. 57:11).

Thus, in order to rise to the greatest challenge facing the church and the world in this century, let us be resolute…

1. *To read our Bibles like never before,* as the Bible *wants* to be read: book by book, chapter by chapter, verse by verse, as God's very Word to us. Whoever loves God wants to hear *his* voice (Ex. 19:4 ESV) above the cacophony of voices in the world today. Meditating

19 An excellent resource is: *Questions to Ask your Muslim Friends: A Closer Look at Islamic Beliefs and Texts* by Beth Peltola and Tim Dieppe (London: Wilberforce Publications, 2022).

20 For instance, Surah 4:171, 5:73, and 5:116 denying the Trinity; Surah 19:35 denying Jesus as the Son of God; and Surah 4:157-158 denying that Jesus died on the cross. Study also these entire chapters for context.

21 So many excellent books have been written on this theme in recent decades. See the titles by Holland, Hurtado, Mangalwadi, Stark, Schmidt, and Scrivener in the bibliography.

on Scripture "day and night" (Ps. 1) will not only cause us to experience the power of silence again, but will transform our lives from the inside out, filling us with courage, hope and joy. Let us throw our stupid phones aside, and read *Scripture* as the early church did, focusing on the fourfold Gospel, then on Acts and the apostolic writings, with the entire Old Testament as its vital background and redemptive framework.

2. *To observe much better habits of prayer*, both privately and corporately with God's people. Prayerlessness is practical atheism stemming from our inherited secular-materialist worldview of the Enlightenment. God wants to be reminded of his everlasting promises by the watchmen on Jerusalem's walls (Is. 62:6-7). He wants to hear our voices and smell the aroma of our supplications, for *he is able* to do far more than we can pray or think. He will give good things, especially the Holy Spirit, to all who earnestly beseech him in Jesus' name (Luke 11:5-13). Let us pray the *Lord's Prayer* daily before God's throne, closing with the ancient *kyrie eleison*, "Jesus, Son of David, have mercy... on me a sinner, on us your people, and on our entire human race, and saturate us with your holy presence."

3. *To return to the example of the Early Church* by passionately promoting the apostolic *kerugma* (cf. Acts 10:34-43 and I Cor. 15:1-11) and by joyfully obeying the *Sermon on the Mount*, as well as all the other commands of our Lord and his apostles. Let us remind ourselves daily, as they did, that all of life is a choice between life and death, or light and darkness, of that narrow path that leads to glory and the broad way leading to destruction. Let us hold on to the *Apostolic* and *Nicene Creeds* summarizing the earliest *kerugma*, and let us feed on the body and blood of our Lord in holy communion, eagerly anticipating the marriage supper of the Lamb.

4. *To confess our faith without wavering.* Let us seek to do so spontaneously, winsomely, and sincerely, relying not on ourselves but on the Holy Spirit speaking through us. Let us seek to live out the *Great Commission,* taking the Good News to all nations—for the "fields

are white unto harvest." Let us do so mindful of how much damage hypocrisy has done to the church, walking wisely before a watching world (Col. 4:5-6). Let us pray for that gift of joyful fearlessness, as the very sign that "we have been with Jesus" (Acts 4:13), in the glad anticipation that the trumpet will soon sound when Jesus shall appear like lightning flashing across the dark sky.

5. *To follow Christ more closely than ever*, by denying ourselves and by daily taking up our cross. Let us shun all narcissism and selfishness by our humble, selfless service, forgetting ourselves, thinking more of the needs of others than our own. Let us live like those who heard our Master's call in the gospel, considering a life of humble devotion to Jesus as the only one worth living, instead of wasting it by living for comfort, pleasure, and ease (Gal. 2:20). Let us be zealous in doing good to all, especially to the household of God, considering that giving even just a cup of water to the least of his disciples, is like giving it to Jesus (Matt. 25:31-46).

6. *To pursue Christian virtue and godliness in this age*, as Christ's apostle taught us in Gal. 5:13-26. Let us pursue love in an age of loneliness, joy in an age of despair, peace in an age of turmoil, patience in an age of anger, kindness in an age of rudeness and indifference, goodness in an age of malice, faithfulness in an age of betrayal, gentleness in an age of arrogance, and self-control in an age of rampant addiction and rage. Let each of us remind ourselves that the *Ten Commandments* were given to protect my neighbour from me and my sin, and that love does the neighbour no harm. Let us resolve to make the parables of the *Prodigal Son* and the *Good Samaritan* the templates of Divine grace and love in our lives.

7. *To love all God's people* as those born of the Spirit, loved by the Father and redeemed by Christ (John 17 and I John 4:16-5:5). Let us passionately love the church—universal *and* local; the church-triumphant in glory, *and* the one down here, locked in battle with darkness still. Let us cherish the sound preaching of God's Word, the loving fellowship of his saints, and the holy office of those

watching over us. Let us strive to keep the unity of the Spirit in the bond of peace, warning those in love who threaten to tear Christ's body apart through sectarianism and a useless wrangling about words. Let us celebrate the beauty of the one, holy, catholic, and apostolic church with all the saints in love (Ephes. 3:14-21), until the morning star rises in our hearts.

8. *To love all people,* for the Son of God became man to offer up his life for the world; yes "he put on a body (Athanasius once wrote) so that in the body he might find death, and blot it out." For as death and corruption came through one man and spread to all, so the resurrection and eternal life came through one Man for all. For there is but one God and one Mediator between God and humankind—the man Christ Jesus—who died for us and rose again, desiring that none should perish. If he then so loved all humankind, how shall we, redeemed by that love, not follow in his footsteps and love them too?

9. *Not to fear persecution for righteousness sake,* for if we want to save our lives, we will lose them, but if we willingly lose them for Jesus' sake, we shall save them (John 12:24-25). Let us appreciate anew how much in the Bible was written for the church suffering under the cross, cherishing those passages in the Psalms, the Gospel, and the Epistles calling us to patiently bear our cross for the Lord and for his elect's sake. Let us remember those who are in prison as if we are there with them (Heb. 13:3) and shun all fear as the devil's deadly snare (Is. 51:12-13), for no-one can separate us from Christ's love.

10. *To love and respect all Muslims,* never mind their thoughts about *dawa* or their feelings about *sharia.* Let us approach them with genuine love and respect, as fellow mortals made in the image of God. Let us be eager to invite them over, to do them good, to bless them and to pray for them, never withholding the gospel of God's

Son from them while we have the opportunity to share it.[22] Let us never seek revenge against those who did us harm, knowing that evil shall never conquer evil (as Czar Nicholas said) but only love will (Matt. 5:38-48, Rom. 12:17-21).

11. *To study the great ideas of Christianity and Islam,*[23] never underestimating what is at stake in the cosmic battle between light and darkness. Let us strive to be well aware of what the church believes concerning the gospel, the deity of Christ, the Trinity, and the formation of the Biblical canon. Let us try not to be ignorant of the main teachings of the Quran, the *hadith,* and the origins of Islam. And may God help us never to sell out our children's freedom to worship his Son in the Spirit, for the little comfort and ease we crave for ourselves.

12. *To raise awareness about dawa.* Let us study the age-old Islamist quest for world domination, bringing it to God in prayer. Let us remind the liberal academia of the West that it is *their* unfounded romantic portrayal of the Islamic golden age which emboldens radical Islamists today. Let us also remind them that the Islamic world has never renounced its colonization of vast parts of the earth through conquest, nor its brutal slave trade of so many centuries.[24] Let us stop enabling radical Islam, while betraying those countless peace-loving Muslims who have fled to our shores from the harsh rule of *sharia.* Let us remain sober and vigilant, passionately

22 An excellent resource is: *Questions to Ask your Muslim Friends: A Closer Look at Islamic Beliefs and Texts* by Beth Peltola and Tim Dieppe (London: Wilberforce Publications, 2022). Another more dated resource is *Anyone Anywhere Any Time: Leading Muslims to Christ Now*, by Mike Shipman (Monument, CO: WIGtake Resources, 2013).

23 Two easy-to-read resources for the African context are published by the Barnabas Fund, *Engage: Christian Responses to Islam* and *Unveiled: A Christian Study Guide to Islam.*

24 The reason, for instance, that there is no black community in Arabia today, is due to the fact that African slave boys, shackled and shipped to Arabia for centuries, were all castrated, causing millions of them to die on the way, while African girls had to serve as sex-slaves in Arabian harems. See Azuma, *The Legacy of Arab-Islam in Africa.*

defending *reverence for truth* and *reverence for life* as absolutely paramount for the survival of a free and civilized society.

13. *To witness boldly against oppression and injustice,* both in our own communities and in the world. Let us do so as the Lord would have us, without favouring any person, gender, nation, race, culture, class or creed (James 2:1-13). Let us follow in the footsteps of the Hebrew prophets and Jesus of Nazareth, doing justly, loving mercy, and walking humbly with our God (Micah 6:8), knowing that peace shall never prevail where injustice or oppression are tolerated, and that silence in the face of evil (when we can still speak) basically equals complicity. Let us freely admit where Christians or Christianity have seriously failed in the past, while refusing to sell out our God-given inheritance *out of a misplaced sense of guilt.*

14. *To pursue courage and wisdom in politics,* seeking to witness to the truth as Jesus did before Herod and Pilate, and his apostles before the Sanhedrin (Acts 4:23-31). Let us refuse to use the so-called "separation between church and state" or our fear for controversy, as an excuse for cowardice. Let us remember that the world will consider us useless and irrelevant if we keep on hiding in a corner. Let us be wise as serpents, and harmless as doves, and never seek influence through worldly power, wealth, or fame, but only to be salt to the earth and light to the world, to the glory of our heavenly Father (Matt. 5:13-16).

15. *To long for our Lord's appearance* (I Thess. 4:13-18). Let us remind ourselves daily of the high calling by which we have been called, fulfilling our vows and duties out of reverence for Christ, never mind what office, location, or stage of life we may find ourselves in. Let us always be ready to render account for what we have done in the body (Luke 12:35-40), so that we may look with confidence to his appearance to judge the world, *and* to make all things brilliantly new again. Maranatha, Come, Lord Jesus!

Let us be watchful, firm in the faith, courageous and strong. And let all that we do, be done in love. (I Cor. 16:13-14).

EPILOGUE

A deeply moving German hymn *Dank sei Dir, Herr*—sung by the famous Dutch contralto Aafje Heynis (1924-2015)—featuring equally moving newsreel footage of jubilant liberated Dutch citizens in 1945, was posted on *YouTube* by Jack Gibbons. These Dutch people were thanking Canadian soldiers who liberated Amsterdam and their country from the ghastly tyranny of the Nazis (which lasted a mere four years). Singing "Thanks Be to Thee" in the deepest reverence is the *only* fitting posture at such a solemn occasion. That is what Psalm 107 teaches us. But sadly, that is what we have long lost and forgotten in the West. We don't know how to say "thank you" in joyful reverence anymore. And that is exactly why we are in such big trouble and mortal danger now, as we struggle in the throes of eternal discontent, rage, complacency and anxiety. Our great wisdom, wealth and worldliness have all but killed us. Meanwhile we read somewhere in the archives of the Muslim Brotherhood of America what their clearly stated goals were since the 1990s:

> The process of settlement is a "Civilizational-Jihadist Process" with all the word means. The Ikhwan (Arabic for Muslim Brotherhood) must understand that their work in America is a kind of grand jihad in eliminating and destroying the Western civilization from within and "sabotaging" its miserable house by their hands and the hands of the believers [Muslims] so that it is eliminated and God's religion is made victorious over all other religions.[1]

1 *From the Archives of the Muslim Brotherhood in America – An Explanatory Memorandum on the General Strategic Goal for the Group in North America* (Washington

Moreover, a decade after 9/11 the brave Jewish woman Bat Ye'or wrote the following in the conclusion to her book on Europe and the "coming universal caliphate":

> While writing this study I was reminded of a question that greatly troubled me twenty-five years ago when researching *Les Chrétientés d'Orient entre jihad et dhimmitude* (1991). How did Christian peoples and states, some with powerful armies and the richest cultures of their times, collapse when faced with the onslaught of jihad and dhimmitude from the seventh to the fifteenth centuries? Now I no longer ask myself the question. The breakdown process that I used to study and documented in old chronicles I have seen taking place in today's Europe. When I examined the past, I saw it repeated in the present, under my very eyes.[2]

God Almighty, have mercy, and deliver us from evil. Begin doing so by filling us with gratitude again—genuine humble gratitude—for the gift of your beloved Son, but also for your countless other gifts, above all the gift of worshipping you in freedom. That will make us bold as lions. Thank you for the multitudes of brothers and sisters from Cairo to Cape Town, who show us the way in their humble gratitude, and how they are willing to pay the ultimate price for your gift of salvation. Why are they so joyful and fearless oh Lord? Because gratitude and anxiety cannot possibly occupy the same heart! We beg you dear Father, will you be pleased to watch over Yeshua's bride in Africa. Use her to wake us all up, just as you have used us once to bring her to you, out of her long dark night. We ask this of you, not doubting your promise that Yeshua will soon come to finally crush Satan under our feet. Glory be to the Father, and to the Son, and to the Holy Spirit, amen.

DC: The Center for Security Policy, 2013), 6.

2 Bat Ye'or, *Europe, Globalization and the Coming Universal Caliphate* (Madison, WI: Fairleigh Dickenson University Press, 2011), 183.

The author, with his Xhosa interpreter and friend, in the Eastern Cape, South Africa.

CHRISTO HEIBERG (M.TH. KAMPEN) has been a follower of Jesus the Messiah, and a living member of his redeemed community, since 1982. He was born and raised on the African Savannah, as the descendant of three nineteenth century German missionaries to Southern Africa. Christo and his family emigrated to Canada by the turn of the century, where he has been a pastor in two churches. He has also been speaking and teaching in several African countries over the past two decades. Christo is married to Margherita and they have been blessed with four children. He writes regularly at www.soberminds.ca

SELECTED RESOURCES

Al-Sheha, Abdurrahman. 2005. *Mohammed the Messenger of Allah*. Riyadh: Islam Propagation Office.

"An Explanatory Memorandum" from the Muslim Brotherhood in America. 2013. Washington, DC: The Center for Security Policy.

Asserate, Asfa-Wossen. 2018. *African Exodus Migration and the Future of Europe*. London: House Publishing.

Athanasius, 2019. *On the Incarnation – Pathways to the Past*, Published by Parables.

Azuma, John Alembillah. 2001. *The Legacy of Arab-Islam in Africa: A Quest for Inter-religious Dialogue*. Oneworld Publications.

Bailey, Ronald & Marian Tupy. 2021. *Ten Global Trends Every Smart Person Should Know*. Washington DC: Cato Institute.

Banaz, A Love Story. YouTube, https://www.youtube.com/watch?v=VepuyvhHYdM

Barnabas Fund. 2012. *Engage - Christian Response to Islam*. United Kingdom: Barnabas Fund.

Barnabas Fund. 2015. *Unveiled - A Christian Study Guide to Islam*. United Kingdom: Barnabas Fund.

Bates, Matthew. 2017. *Salvation by Allegiance Alone*. Grand Rapids: Baker.

Bavinck, Herman. 1977. *Our Reasonable Faith*. Grand Rapids: Baker.

Bonhoeffer, Dietrich. 1975. *The Cost of Discipleship*. London: SCM Press.

Booyens, Harry. 2014. *Amabhulu - Birth and Death of the Second America*. Vancouver: Cliffwood Fogge.

Bosma, Martin. 2015. *Minderheid in Eigen Land*. Amsterdam: Bibliothecha Africana.

Byfield, Ted. (ed). 2005. *The Christians - A Pinch of Incense, A.D. 70 to 250*. Christian History Project.

Catherwood, Christopher. 2003. *Christians, Muslims and Islamic Rage - What is Going on and Why it Happened*. Grand Rapids: Zondervan.

Challies, Tim & Josh Byers. 2019. *Guide to the Bible – A Visual Theology*. Grand Rapids: Zondervan Reflective.

Cook, Faith. 1989. *Grace in Winter - Rutherford in Verse*. Edinburgh: Banner of Truth Trust.

Copan, Paul. 2008. *When God Goes to Starbucks – A Guide to Everyday Apologetics*. Grand Rapids: BakerBooks.

D'Ambrosio, Marcellino. 2014. *When the Church Was Young - Voices of the Early Fathers*. Cincinnati, OH: Franciscan Media.

Davies, Brian & G.R. Evans (eds). 2008. *Anselm of Canterbury: The Major Works*. Oxford University Press.

Dieppe, Tim & Beth Peltola. 2022. *Questions to Ask Your Muslim Friends - A Closer Look at Islamic Beliefs and Texts*. London: Wilberforce Publications.

Dostoevsky, Fyodor. 2003 (1880). *The Brothers Karamazov* (translated by Andrew R. MacAndrew). New York: Bantam Classic.

Dreyfus, Robert. 2005. *Devils Game: How the United States Helped Unleash Fundamentalist Islam*. New York: Owl Books.

Durie, Mark. 2010. *The Third Choice - Islam, Dhimmitude and Freedom*. Deror Books.

Fairburn, Donald. 2009. *Life in the Trinity*. Downers Grove: IVP Academic.

Gandhi, Mahatma. K. 1993. *Gandhi – An Autobiography*. Boston: Beacon Press.

Gatestone Institute website, https://www.gatestoneinstitute.org/

Gibson, Dan. 2016. *The Sacred City*. Documentary *Youtube*. https://www.youtube.com/watch?v=jtIyeREGCYI

Global Terrorism Index 2020 - Measuring the Impact of Terrorism. Institute for Economics and Peace. Sydney. Download, GTI2020Terrorism.pdf

Grebe, Karl & Wilfred Fon. 2006. *African Traditional Religion and Christian Counseling*. Oasis International Ltd.

Groenewald, A. & E. Mnyandu. 2016. *Thuli Madonsela on Leadership*. E-book. Candid Media Group.

Gustafson, Scott. "Moving Toward the Enemy: A Case for Missiological Engagement in Counter/Deradicalization" in *Journal for Deradicalization*, Winter 2020/21, Nr. 25, ISSN 2363-9849.

Hafemann, Scott. J. 1995. *Paul, Moses and the History of Israel*. Peabody, MA: Hendrickson.

Hanegraaff, Hank. 2015. *Muslim - What You Need to Know About the World's Fastest Growing Religion*. Nashville: Thomas Nelson.

Hamid, A. 2006. *A Book Unlike Any Other*. Ontario: Bayaan Communications.

Hammond, Peter. 2010. *Slavery, Terrorism and Islam*. Cape Town: Xulon Press.

Hays, Richard, B. 2016. *Echoes of Scripture in the Gospels*. Waco, TX: Baylor University Press.

Hengel, Martin. 1977. *Crucifixion*. Philadelphia: Fortress Press.

Heschel, Abraham. J. 2001. *The Prophets*. New York: HarperPerennial.

Hirsi Ali, Ayaan. 2007. *Infidel*. New York: Free Press.

Hirsi Ali, Ayaan. 2015. *Heretic - Why Islam Needs a Reformation Now*. New York: HarperCollins.

Hirsi Ali, Ayaan. 2021. *Prey - Immigration, Islam and the Erosion of Women's Rights*. New York: HarperCollins.

Hirsi Ali, Ayaan. "Paulina Neuding on Crime in Sweden" on *The Ayaan Hirsi Ali Podcast* - 036, https://ayaanhirsiali.com/podcasts/paulina-neuding.

Hirsi Ali, Ayaan. "Yasmine Muhammed on Divorcing a Terrorist" on *Ayaan Hirsi Ali Podcast- 027*, https://ayaanhirsiali.com/podcasts/yasmine-mohammed.

Hitchens, Peter. 2010. *The Rage Against God*. Grand Rapids: Zondervan.

Holland, Tom. 2019. *Dominion - How the Christian Revolution Remade the World*. New York: Basic Books.

Holland, Tom. 2012. *Islam, the Untold Story*. Documentary on *Youtube*. https://www.youtube.com/watch?v=zzKk0L6H1ms

Horrocks Chris & Zoran Jevtic, 2013. *Introducing Foucault – A Graphic Guide*. London: Icon Books.

Huntington, Simon. P. 2011. *The Clash of Civilizations and the Remaking of World Order*. New York: Simon and Schuster.

Hurtado, Larry. 2016. *Destroyer of the gods – Early Christian Distinctives in the Roman World*. Waco, TX: Baylor University Press.

Hurtado, Larry. 2018. *Honoring the Son - Jesus in Earliest Christian Devotional Practice*. Bellingham: WA: LexhamPress.

Ibraheem, Mariam. 2022. *Shackled - One Woman's Dramatic Triumph Over Persecution, Gender Abuse, and a Death Sentence*. New Kensington, PA: Whitaker House.

Ibrahim, I.H. *A Brief Illustrated Guide to Understanding Islam* (Second Edition).

Isbouts, Jean-Pierre. 2014. *The Story of Christianity*. Washington DC: National Geographic.

Jeffrey, Anthea. 2019. *Peoples War - New Light on the Struggle for South Africa*. Jeppestown, RSA: Jonathan Ball.

Jenkins, Philip. 2008. *The Lost History of Christianity - The Thousand Year Golden Age of the Church in the Middle East, Africa and Asia and How it Died*. New York: Harper One.

Jihad Watch and The Left Column, https://www.jihadwatch.org

Jik, 1946. *Kyk Hoe Slinger Hulle*. Stellenbosch: Christen-Studentevereniging van Suid-Afrika.

Johnson, Marcus. P. 2013. *One with Christ - An Evangelical Theology of Salvation*. Wheaton, IL: Crossway.

Johnstone, Patrick. 2011. *The Future of the Global Church - History, Trends and Possibilities*. Downers Grove, IL: IVP.

Kant, Immanuel. 1952. "The Science of Right" in Volume 42 of *Great Books of the Western World*. Chicago: Encyclopedia Britannica.

Khan, Maulana. W. (translator). 2009. *The Quran*. India: Thomas Press.

Kilmeade Brian & Don Yaeger. 2015. *Thomas Jefferson and the Tripoli Pirates - The Forgotten War That Changed American History*. New York: Sentinel.

Korkie, Yolande. 2016. *558 Days… A True Story*. Vereeniging, RSA: Christian Art Publishers.

Kruger, Michael. 2012. *Canon Revisited - Establishing the Origins and Authority of the New Testament Books*. Wheaton, IL: Crossway.

Levy, David. 2011. *Gray Matter - A Neurosurgeon Discovers the Power of Prayer One Patient at a Time*. Carol Stream, IL: Tyndale House.

Lewis, Bernard. 2002. *The Middle East - 2000 Years of History from the Rise of Christianity to the Present Day*. London: Phoenix Press.

Lewis, Bernard. 2002. *What Went Wrong? - Western Impact and Middle Eastern Response*. New York: Oxford University Press.

Lewis, Bernard. 2004. *The Crisis of Islam - Holy War and Unholy Terror*. New York: Random House.

Lewis, C.S. 2002. "Mere Christianity" in *The Complete CS Lewis Signature Classics*. New York: HarperSanFrancisco.

Lings, Martin. 2006. *Muhammed, His Life Based on the Earliest Sources*. Rochester, VT: Inner Traditions.

Lutzer, Erwin. W. 2013. *The Cross in the Shadow of the Crescent*. Eugene, OR: Harvest House Publishers.

Lutzer, Erwin. W. 2018. *The Church in Babylon*. Chicago: Moody Publishers.

Mangalwadi, Vishal. 2011. *The Book That Made Your World - How the Bible Created the Soul of Western Civilization*. Nashville: Thomas Nelson.

Manji, Irshad. 2005. *The Trouble with Islam Today*. Toronto: Vintage Canada.

Mansour, Hussein. A. 2020. *Minority of One: The Unchaining of an Arab Mind*. Self-published in the US.

Maura, Michael, Conrad Mbewe, et.al. 2015. *Prosperity? Seeking the True Gospel*. Nairobi: Africa Christian Textbooks.

Mendietta, E. & J. Vanantwerpen, (eds). 2011. *The Power of Religion in the Public Square*. West Sussex: Columbia University Press.

Mohammed, Yasmine. 2019. *Unveiled - How Western Liberals Empower Radical Islam*. Victoria, BC: Free Hearts Free Minds.

Moore, Johnny & Abraham Cooper, 2020. *The Next Jihad - Stop the Christian Genocide in Africa*. Nashville, TN: Thomas Nelson.

Moreland, J.P. & William Lane Craig, 2017. *Philosophical Foundations for a Christian Worldview, 2nd Edition*. Downers Grove, IL: IVP Academic.

Murray, Douglas. 2017. *The Strange Death of Europe - Immigration, Identity, Islam*. London: Bloomsbury Publishing.

Murray, Iain. H. 2006. *A Scottish Christian Heritage*. Edinburgh: Banner of Truth.

Needham, Nick. 2016. *2000 Years of Christ's Power* (Vol. 1). London: Christian Focus.

Nietzsche, Friedrich. 2019. *Ecce Homo*. London: Arcturus Publishing.

Onize Ohikere, 27 June 2020. "Brutal and Brazen" *World Magazine*, 74-79.

Peterson, Jordan. P. 2018. *12 Rules for Life: An Antidote to Chaos*. Toronto: Random House Canada.

Qureshi, Nabeel. 2016. *Answering Jihad - A Better Way Forward*. Grand Rapids: Zondervan.

Rapport over de Naturellen van Zuidwest-Afrika en hun Behandeling door Duitsland. Cape Town: Cape Times Beperkt, 1918.

Reilly, Robert. R. 2015. "Information Operations: Success and Failures" in Bekele, A & P. Sookhdeo (eds.) *Meeting the Ideological Challenge of Islamism*. McLean, VA: Isaac Publishing.

Reilly, Robert. R. 2017. *The Closing of the Muslim Mind - How Intellectual Suicide Created the Modern Islamist Crisis.* Wilmington, DE: ISI Books.

Richardson, Harry. 2013. *The Story of Muhammed - Islam Unveiled.* Self-published in the US.

Schaeffer, Francis. A. 1990. *How Should We Then Live: The Rise and Decline of Western Thought and Culture.* Westchester, IL: Crossway.

Schmidt, Alvin. J. 2004. *The Great Divide - The Failure of Islam and the Triumph of the West.* Boston: Regina Orthodox Press.

Schweitzer, Albert. 2009. *Out of My Life and Thought.* Baltimore: Johns Hopkins University Press.

Scrivener, Glen. 2022. *The Air We Breathe – How We All Came to Believe in Freedom, Kindness, Progress and Equality.* The Good Book Company.

Scruton, Roger. 2002. *The West and the Rest - Globalization and Terrorist Threat.* Delaware: ISI Books.

Shariat, Hormoz. 2020. *Iran's Great Awakening.* Melissa: Iran Alive Ministries.

Sheikh, Bilquis and Richard Schneider. 1979. *I Dared to Call Him Father.* Kingsway.

Shipman, Mike. 2013. *Anyone Anywhere Any Time - Leading Muslims to Christ Now.* Monument, CO: WIGtake Resources.

Solomon, Robert C. 2000. "No Excuses: Existentialism and the Meaning of Life" in *The Great Courses: Philosophy and Intellectual History.* Chantilly, VA: The Teaching Company.

Sookhdeo, Patrick. 2009. *Understanding Islamist Terrorism - The Islamic Doctrine of War.* McLean, VA: Isaac Publishing.

Sookhdeo, Patrick. 2013. *Understanding Islamic Theology.* McLean, VA: Isaac Publishing.

Sookhdeo, Patrick. 2014. *Dawa: The Islamic Strategy for Reshaping the Modern World.* McLean, VA: Isaac Publishing.

Sookhdeo, Patrick. 2015. "The Role of Religion in the Battlespace" in Bekele A. & P. Sookhdeo (eds.) *Meeting the Ideological Challenge of Islamism.* McLean, VA: Isaac Publishing.

Sookhdeo, Patrick. 2019. *Hated Without Reason - The Remarkable Story of Christian Persecution Over the Centuries.* McLean, VA: Isaac Publishing.

Sookhdeo, Patrick. & Stephen Ulph (eds). 2014. *Reforming Islam - Progressive Voices from the Arab Muslim World.* McLean, VA: Almuslih Publications.

Sorokin, Pitirim. 1963. *A Long Journey - An Autobiography of Pitirim Sorokin.* New Haven, CT: College and University Press.
Spencer, Caitlin. 2017. *Please Let me Go - The Horrific Story of a Girl's Life in the Hands of Sex-Traffickers.* London: John Blake
Spencer, Robert. 2011. *Muslim Persecution of Christians.* Sherman Oaks: David Horowitz Freedom Center.
Spencer, Robert. 2021. *The Critical Quran - Explained from Key Islamic Commentaries and Contemporary Historical Research.* New York: Bombardier Books.
Stack, Megan. K. 2010. *Every Man in This Village is a Liar - An Education in War.* New York: Anchor Books.
Stark, Rodney. A. 1996. *The Rise of Christianity.* New York: HarperOne.
Stark, Rodney. A. 2010. *God's Battalions - The Case for the Crusades.* New York: HarperOne.
Stark, Rodney. A. 2011. *The Triumph of Christianity.* New York: HarperOne.
Stassen, Nicol. 2015. *Die Dorsland Trek: 1874 – 1881.* Pretoria: Protea Boekhuis.
Stassen Glen. H. and David. P. Gushee, *Kingdom Ethics - Following Jesus in Contemporary Context.* Downers Grove, IL: IVP.
Stiff, Peter. 2000. *Cry Zimbabwe - Independence Twenty Years On.* Alberton, RSA: Galago Books.
Tawhidi, Mohammed. 2018. *The Tragedy of Islam - Admissions of a Muslim Imam.* Adelaide: Reason Books.
Tertullian, *Apologia.* Chapter 50. *New Advent.* https://www.newadvent.org/fathers/0301.htm.
Tertullian, *De Corona*, Chapter 1. *New Advent.* https://www.newadvent.org/fathers/0304.htm.
The Book of Common Prayer and Administration of the Sacraments and Other Rites and Ceremonies of the Church. 2016. New York: Church Publishing Incorporated.
The Religion of Peace website, www.thereligionofpeace.com
Thornbury, John. 1965. "David Brainerd, Missionary to the Red Indians of North America" in *Five Pioneer Missionaries.* London: Banner of Truth Trust.
The Three Forms of Unity. Winnipeg: Premier Printing. 1999.
Todenhöfer, Jürgen. 2014. *My Journey into the Heart of Terror - Ten Days in the Islamic State.* Vancouver: Greystone Books.

Turley, Steve. R. 2019. *The Return of Christendom - Demography, Politics and the Coming of the Christian Majority.* Turley Talks.
Ulph, Stephen. 2012, "Islam and Totalitarianism - The Challenge of Comparison" in Gorka, K.C & P. Sookhdeo (eds.). *Fighting the Ideological War.* McLean, VA: Isaac Publishing.
Van den Beukel, Antony. 1995. *The Physicists and God - The New Priests of Religion?* North Andover, MA: Genesis Publishing.
Van den Brink, G. 2000. *Orientatie in de Filosofie.* Zoetermeer: Boekenzentrum.
Waller, J. Michael. 2015. "The Muslim Brotherhood: Doctrine, Strategy, Operations and Vulnerabilities" in Bekele, A. & P. Sookhdeo (eds.) *Meeting the Ideological Challenge of Islamism.* McLean, VA: Isaac Publishing.
Ward, Terrence. 2018. *The Wahhabi Code - How the Saudi's Spread Extremism Globally.* New York: Arcade Publishing.
Wells, David. 2008. *The Courage to be Protestant.* Grand Rapids: Eerdmans.
Wentsel, B. 1987. *God en Mens Versoend - Dogmatiek Deel 3a.* Kampen: Kok.
Wessels, Hannes. 2015. *A Handful of Hard Men - The SAS and the Battle for Rhodesia.* Philadelphia: Casemate.
Witten, Marsha. 1993. *All is Forgiven - The Secular Message in American Protestantism.* Princeton, NJ: Princeton University Press.
Wright, N.T. 2016. *The Day the Revolution Began - Considering the Meaning of Jesus's Crucifixion.* New York: HarperOne.
You Deserve to Know About Islam. No date. Islamic Society of Niagara Peninsula.
Ye'or, Bat. 2001, *Islam and Dhimmitude - Where Civilizations Collide.* Madison, WI: Fairleigh Dickenson University Press.
Ye'or, Bat, 2011, *Europe, Globalization, and the Coming Universal Caliphate.* Madison, WI: Fairleigh Dickenson University Press.
Youssef, Michael. 2015. *Jesus, Jihad and Peace.* Franklin: Worthy Publishing.

GLOSSARY

'Allahu akbar'	'Allah is greater'
adhan	the call to prayer
ANC	African National Congress
ATR	African Traditional Religion
ayah	a verse of the Quran
aslim taslam	"accept Islam and you will be saved / spared". Ultimatum given to the infidel nations and cities during the spread of Islam
BLM	The movement Black Lives Matter
CAIR	Counsel on American Islamic Relations
CDHRI	Cairo Declaration of Human Rights in Islam
caliph	the Sunni title for the supreme ruler of the Muslim community
da'ee	Islamic missionary, those involved in *dawa*
dawa	literally: call or invitation. Spreading Islam by calling people to submit to Allah
dar al-Islam	house of Islam
dar al-harb	house of war
dar al-salaam	house of peace
dhimmi	(plural, 'dhimmis') protected person or people in Muslim lands, secondary citizen, subject to the conditions of a *dhimma* pact
dhimmitude	the cowed and submissive behaviour of dhimmis in Muslim lands
DRC	Democratic Republic of the Congo
DRC	Dutch Reformed Church of South Africa
Ebed Yahweh	Hebrew for 'servant of the Lord', especially in Isaiah
fatwa	an authoritative statement on a point of Islamic law
fitna	a trial that undermines a Muslim's faith

FGM	female genital mutilation
hakimiyya	Allah's sole sovereignty and rule over human society in all things, as Lord and legislator
hadith	recorded traditions, first spoken and later written, of things Mohammed (or his companions) is believed to have said or done
halal	something which Muslims are free to eat, do or have, i.e., food or property
haram	acts which are prohibited and punishable according to sharia
hajj	pilgrimage to Mecca, at least once a lifetime. One of the five pillars of Islam
hijab	literally 'partition' or 'curtain', hence modesty. Often used to mean the woman's headscarf covering her neck and hair. To be distinguished from the *niqab* which covers everything except her eyes
hijra	migration. Mohammed's flight from Mecca to Medina in 622 (the start of the Islamic calendar)
hisba	duty of Muslim individuals and states to "command good and forbid evil", i.e., to ensure *sharia* is implemented in all society.
hoooris	the female companions, supposedly perpetual virgins, of the saved in Paradise, whose main function is to provide sexual favours
IIIT	International Institute for Islamic Thought
Isa	Quranic name for Jesus
ISIS / ISIL	Islamic State of Iraq and Syria / Islamic State of Iraq and the Levant
ijtihad	the process of logical deduction and reasoning on basis of the Quran or the *hadith*, by which *sharia* was formulated
Imago Dei	Latin for the image of God (in man).
imam	Shia term for the supreme ruler of the Muslim community. Sunnis use the same term for the prayer leader at a local mosque
injil	the gospel

Islamism	the view of Islam as a comprehensive political ideology that aims to establish Islamic states under *sharia* where possible. Political Islam
jahiliyyah	the time of ignorance in pre-Islamic Arabia
jahili	those ignorant of Islam
jihad	holy war or struggle. Literally 'striving'. Could mean a spiritual struggle for moral purity; the effort to correct wrong and support right in society; or military war against non-Muslims in the effort to spread Islam
jinn	the *jinn* are the inhabitants of the immaterial world; they are usually regarded as evil spirits
jizya	a poll-tax levied on non-Muslims (*dhimmi*) within an Islamic state signifying their subjugation
kafir	(plural *kufar*) infidel or unbeliever, usually an offensive term
kerugma	Greek for the essential gospel truths preached by the apostles
kosher	that which is allowed by Jewish law, usually with respect to food
kufar	unbelievers
madrasa	Islamic religious school
mishpat	Hebrew word for 'justice'
mujahadin	soldiers engaged in holy war, *jihad,* well-known in Afghanistan
mullah	religious leaders in countries from Iran eastwards, equivalent to imams in Arab countries
MWL	Muslim World League
NATO	North Atlantic Treaty Organization
OIC	Organization for Islamic Cooperation
People of the Book	Those who have their own revealed scriptures. It is applied to Jews, Christians, Sabeans and sometimes Zoroastrians
Quran	series of revelations that Mohammed believed God gave him through the angel Gabriel in Arabia, from 610 to 632
rasoul	messenger, apostle
regula fidei	Latin for the infallible rule of faith, i.e., the Bible.

Sabeans	followers of John the Baptist, considered in the Quran to have a revealed religion
Salaf	Mohammed and his immediate successors
Salafis	those who want to return to the ways of the salaf
salat	prayer five times a day for Sunnis, three times a day for Shi'a
shahada	testimony, reciting the Islamic creed. Also a legal testimony in court
sheik	literally an 'old man' or 'elder', or an elected village chief
Shia	a branch of Islam, which separated from Sunni Islam in the first century over a dispute about the succession of the caliphate
Silvesternacht	New Year's Eve in Germany
sira	biography of Mohammed, usually referring to the authoritative early accounts by Ibn Ishaq, al-Tabari and others
sharia	Islamic law, literally "the path to the water"
shirk	the unpardonable sin in Islam of associating anything with Allah. Christians commit this sin by believing Jesus is God's Son.
sufis	followers of mystical Islam
sunna	literally "trodden path". The actions and words of Muhammed as recorded in the *hadith*
Sunni	a branch of Islam which separated from Shia Islam in the first century over a dispute about succession of the caliphate
sura	a chapter of the Quran
taharrush gamea	"the rape game", originating in North Africa, targeting 'immodest' women
takfir	the act of declaring another Muslim to be not a genuine believer, but an infidel.
tafsir	commentary on the Quran
talaq	means literally "undoing the knot", whereby marriage is declared dissolute. A Muslim can send his wife away by saying 'talaq' three times
Tanach	Hebrew scriptures, i.e., the law, prophets and the writings.

taqiyya	lawful deception intended to protect a Muslim from persecution, used in broader sense to deceive the infidels or outsiders
tawhid	unity or oneness. Basic doctrine of Islam, based on the absolute oneness of Allah
tzedakah	Hebrew word for 'righteousness'
umma	the worldwide community of the Muslim faithful
UNDHR	United Nations Declaration of Human Rights
Wahhabi Islam	strict puritanical form of Sunni Islam, founded in the 18th century, predominant in Saudi Arabia
wali	a male guardian for Muslim women in public
zakat	one of the pillars of Islam. A tax on wealth benefitting the Muslim poor
ZANU	Zimbabwe African National Union
ZIPRA	Zimbabwe People's Revolutionary Army

Printed in Canada